To Mimi and Frank
from Jac

IN THE SHADOW OF THE ACROPOLIS

POPULAR AND PRIVATE ART IN 4TH CENTURY ATHENS

by John J. Herrmann, Jr.

A loan exhibition from
the Department of Classical Art,
Museum of Fine Arts, Boston

Brockton Art Museum/Fuller Memorial
Brockton, Massachusetts

September 1984–August 1987

Library of Congress Catalog Card Number: 84-72032
ISBN 0-934358-13-3

This exhibition and publication are supported in part with funds from the National Endowment for the Arts, a federal agency; the Massachusetts Council for the Arts and Humanities, a state agency; and the Museum of Fine Arts, Boston. The objects are on loan from the Museum of Fine Arts, Boston.

Printed by Mercantile Press, Worcester, Massachusetts
Designed by Andrea Haraldsson
Photos and illustrations courtesy of the
Museum of Fine Arts, Boston.

inside cover, front: Choregic Monument of Lysicrates, present state. Drawing by H. Bauer. From AthMitt 92 *(1977) Beilage 8.*

inside cover, back: Choregic Monument of Lysicrates, reconstruction. Drawing by H. Bauer. From AthMitt 92 *(1977) Beilage 9.*

Cat. 2.

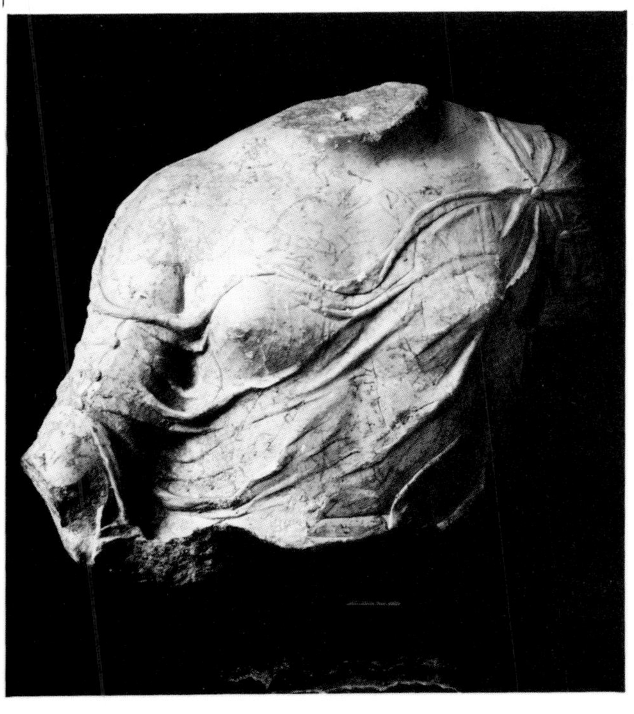

Note

All objects in the catalogue are taken to be Athenian of the fourth century B.C. unless specified to the contrary. "Athenian" and "Attic" are used as essentially interchangeable terms when referring to the authorship of works of art. The geographic and political relationships of the two entities are discussed briefly in the introduction. All dates are assumed to be B.C. unless specified to the contrary.

Table of Contents

Foreword

The Brockton Art Museum/Fuller Memorial is pleased to present *In the Shadow of the Acropolis: Popular Art of 4th Century Athens*, an exhibition depicting the people's art of a rich and important ancient culture. This is the eighth in a series of loan exhibitions from the Museum of Fine Arts, Boston, which holds one of the most renowned art collections in the world. Since its inception in 1971, this exemplary loan program has brought to Brockton art and artifacts from diverse world cultures—from colonial America, medieval Europe, the Orient and the ancient world. We are indeed grateful to Dr. Jan Fontein and the Trustees of the Museum of Fine Arts for their lasting commitment to this endeavor which has so greatly enriched our programs.

In the Shadow of the Acropolis brings to light the art of a vibrant and changing Athens. The exhibition's title bears a double meaning, at once literal and metaphoric. In the literal sense, the physical culture of 4th century Athens lay at the base of the Acropolis, quite truly in its shadow. The metaphorical sense is more complex. The magnificent structures atop the Acropolis have come to symbolize the high culture of the Golden Age of 5th century Greece, obscuring in their grandeur many of the later achievements of the Late Classical and Hellenistic periods. It is these later achievements which form the basis of our exhibition.

Kimon Frair, the poet/translator of Kazantzakis's *Odyssey: A Modern Sequel*, once remarked that the story of the Medusa is an allegory of how the artist must take life, which moves and changes, and hold it on his shield. To look at Nature directly can turn the viewer to stone, but an artist's approach allows many viewers to see the ideals of a lost time without the dangers which confronted Perseus. Through the polished shield of this exhibition it is hoped the viewer will delight in the life of the people of ancient Athens, in their ideals of beauty and their way of seeing the world, appreciating with a new perspective their achievements and their impact on the world today.

A cooperative exhibition of this nature requires the help of many people. Funds for the program were awarded by the National Endowment for the Arts, a federal agency; and by the Massachusetts Council on the Arts and Humanities, a state agency. We are very grateful for their contributions. In addition, local support from the generous Greek community, both businesses and individuals, was outstanding. I wish also to thank the Bank of Greece, the Greek Embassy and the Greek Consulate of Boston for their assistance and encouragement. Special recognition must be given to the "Committee for the Greek Exhibition," headed by Barbara J. Berger, which served as a primary liaison with Greek people throughout the Boston area.

At the Museum of Fine Arts, we must express our sincere appreciation to Dr. Cornelius Vermeule, Curator of Classical Art, for his support of the project. Very special tribute is due Dr. John J. Herrmann, Jr., Assistant Curator of Classical Art, who gave so generously of his time and talent to effectively prepare the exhibition and outstanding catalogue. Dr. Herrmann was ably assisted in this task by Mary Comstock, Associate Curator. Together their knowledge and high standards of scholarship are reflected in every detail of this project.

I wish also to thank the home team. For the Brockton Art Museum, Curator Elizabeth Haff served as coordinator of the project, with the assistance of Jacalyn Cahill and Joanne McQuaid. Interpretive programs and materials were prepared by Linda Woolford, and the exhibit was installed by James Swan. Assistant Director James Keneklis, Jr. provided support throughout the project. The catalogue was designed by Andrea Haraldsson. Each member of the Brockton staff assisted with the project. They are a hardworking and professional group, and I thank them all very much for their help.

Joseph E. Kagle, Jr.
Director
Brockton Art Museum/Fuller Memorial

Author's Preface

One of the joys of employment in the archaeological department of a rich, old museum is the opportunity it offers to explore a fuller texture of ancient life and civilization. The main galleries offer space enough only to present a relatively few masterpieces effectively, but a more nuanced picture of the creativity of a given historical moment can be pieced together making use of the full holdings of the museum. A loan exhibition at a younger institution like the Brockton Art Museum offers a truly satisfying chance to reconstruct and to display one of these moments in depth. When it incidentally offers the opportunity to present a new perspective on as timely a theme as the Age of Alexander, the project is doubly enticing.

My gratitude for the chance to give shape to this entertaining excavation in an office extends to a variety of people: first of all to Jan Fontein, who suggested that I organize an exhibition for display in the Brockton Art Museum. The Brockton Museum has been to the greatest degree supportive and sympathetic. I owe special thanks to its former director, Marilyn Hoffman, and to its curator, Elizabeth Haff, who selected fourth century Athens from a number of possible themes and who expertly and enthusiastically performed an enormous variety of organizational, editorial and curatorial tasks. Heartfelt thanks also go to the National Endowment for the Arts and to its director, Francis Hodsoll, whose support made the project possible.

An exploration of one's own department always inspires a reverence for the curatorial staffs past and present, who have preserved, classified, recorded and studied the objects in their care, great and small. The organized accumulation of opinions and bibliography makes it possible to undertake wide-ranging projects that go beyond the limits of any individual scholar's possible area of expertise. I am under the greatest obligation to Mary Comstock, who has long directed this systematic recording in the Department of Classical Art and who devoted so much of her patient skill to this project. The selection of the objects and the bibliography, the continuity of the catalogue and its accuracy are all deeply indebted to her efforts. My son David also performed numerous tasks, including map-making and reference-checking on behalf of the catalogue. Florence Wolsky assisted in a multitude of ways. A special debt of thanks goes to my wife Ariel and to Cornelius and Emily Vermeule, who patiently endured many preliminary formulations of hypotheses that were developed or downplayed on the basis of their prudent and experienced reactions. Dyfri Williams gave me the benefit of his advice and assistance on a visit to the fourth century collections of the British Museum.

As in most exhibitions, the condition of the objects was greatly improved by the expert attentions of the Research Laboratory of the Museum of Fine Arts under the direction of Lambertus van Zelst. Jean-Louis Lachevre, Margaret Levecque, Barbara Mangum and Merville Nichols all splendidly revived, consolidated and mounted the works to be displayed. They also discovered that many proposed inclusions were essentially pastiches of the last century, whose ancient elements could not always be rendered displayable. What did pass their examination, however, can be viewed with both confidence and pleasure.

The Registrar's Office, particularly Suzanne Koppelman, has performed indispensable services. The catalogue has been enormously improved by the expert attentions of the Department of Photographic Services. Under severe time constraints, Janice Sorkow scheduled much difficult work that was carried out especially by Alan Newman, John Woolf and Joseph Logue.

John Herrmann
Assistant Curator
Department of Classical Art
Museum of Fine Arts, Boston

fig 1. Map of Attica and surrounding regions of central Greece and the Peloponnesos

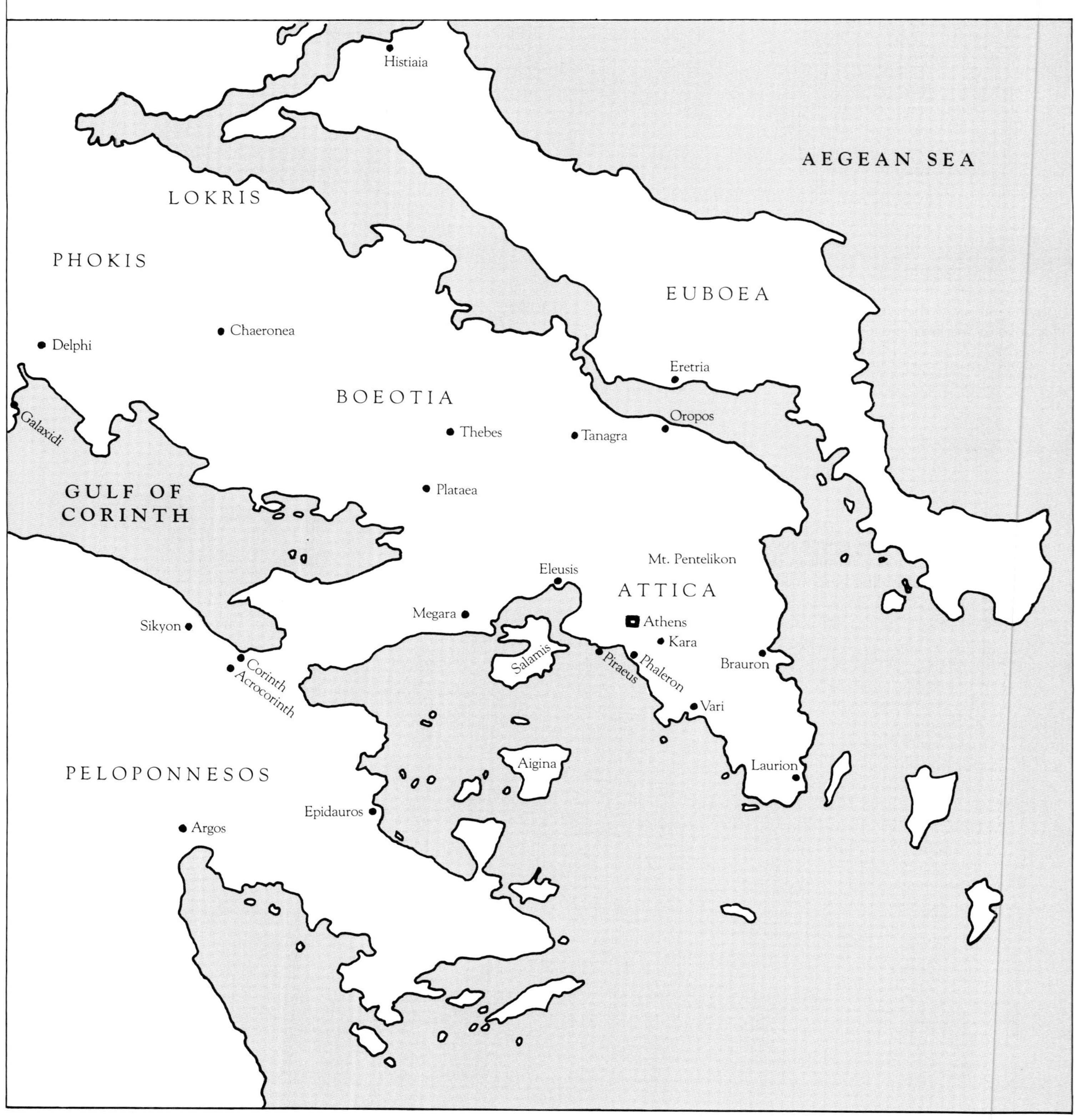

In the Shadow of the Acropolis: Popular and Private Art in Fourth Century Athens

Greek culture traversed what is generally perceived to be its golden age during the Classical period, which extended over the greater part of the fifth and the fourth centuries. The two halves of the period are not, however, always conceded complete critical equality. The earlier phase generally arouses more unmitigated and less complicated praise. On the deepest level, this might be due in part to a certain instinctive preference for what one could characterize as the ascending rather than the descending part of the arc. There are, of course, real differences, and the contrast between the centuries is particularly sharp at Athens. Athens in the fifth century B.C. reached a pinnacle of achievement in both artistic and political matters that it never again attained during Antiquity. Yet in the fourth century, Athens continued to open new artistic horizons in works of great beauty and subtlety.

The Athenian situation can to a degree be suggested emblematically by the monuments on and around the Acropolis. As the ruins present themselves today, the sacred structures in their glorious isolation and visibility on top of the hill all date from the second half of the fifth century and excite almost universal acclaim. Indeed, the Parthenon, the Erechtheion, the Temple of Athena Nike and the Propylaea are individually and as a group uniquely powerful and harmonious. At the foot of the Acropolis screened by trees and jousting with modern Athens lies a group of structures built or rebuilt in the fourth century: the sanctuary of the healing hero Asklepios, the Theatre of Dionysos and a few surrounding theatrical trophies. Their situation is far less dramatic and their structures are less grandly ideal. Yet these monuments have a relevance and beauty that is in no way secondary. While the temple architecture above was in a sense the end of a development, the theatre complex represents a vital beginning for long ages to come. All are works of public utility in a way that is patently in tune with the modern spirit. The Theatre is, of course, the ancestor of countless places of entertainment of all periods. The small Choregic Monument of Lysicrates, lying a short distance from the Theatre itself, is an architectural jewel in its own right. Its imaginatively developed corinthian colonnades present a then-new approach to design that was to be even more fruitful for later phases of Antiquity than were the irrepeatable doric temples on the hill above.

This exhibition explores some of the handicrafts of the fourth century. These crafts present some of the same subtlety and complexity of major public monuments, and many have been subject to the same invidious comparisons with works of the preceding century. In the game of comparisons, it might be noted that some fourth century crafts (like terracotta sculpture) have been recognized as rising to a greater level of achievement. All, however, represent vivid insights into the texture of everyday life at an almost uniquely fascinating historic moment.

fig 2. Columns of the Choregic Monument of Lysicrates. Drawing by H. Bauer. From AthMitt *92 (1977) fig. 3 b.*

Geography and Economy: Athens and Attica

Athens was in a sense created by favorable geography. The city centered itself on a highly defensible hill, the Acropolis, located on a moderately fertile plain at a distance from the seacoast. The interval, on the one hand, granted convenient access to navigation while on the other it insulated the inhabitants from a surprise attack from the sea. From this strategic position, Athens gained control of the nearby towns, particularly Eleusis and Piraeus, and the entire peninsula of Attica. The unification of Athens and Attica had been completed in prehistoric times, and, for centuries, the (free) inhabitants of Attica had held Athenian citizenship

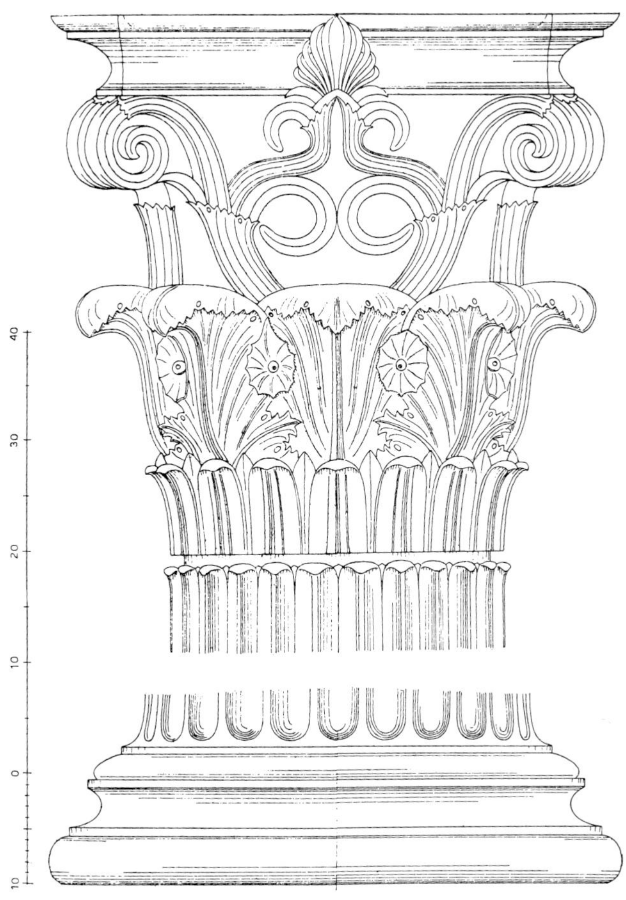

and would take refuge within the walls of Athens in times of siege. Offshore islands like Salamis had also been absorbed and had formed a fortress of last resort during the Persian Wars of the early fifth century, when even the Acropolis itself could not be held. The city-state of Megara lay on the borders of Attica at the north end of the Isthmus of Corinth and generally was subordinate to Athens.

In historic times, Athens and the other towns of Attica had looked outward to the sea for wealth, but in the remoter past, the basis of life had inevitably been the land itself. In the mythological account of events past remembering, the agriculture of Attica had gained a degree of specialization; the goddess Athena had given Athens the gift of the olive. Triptolemos, one of the founding heroes of Eleusis, had learned to cultivate grain and had spread the useful knowledge to mankind. In artistic matters, these ancestral myths had more currency than did contemporary economic realities.

Athens's territorial expansion by land had been blocked by a series of powerful nearby city-states, in particular Thebes in Boeotia and Corinth, but her maritime activities had far outstripped all her competitors. It was primarily her success in projecting her commercial and military interests by sea that made Athens the dominant power in the Aegean for most of the fifth century. In the second half of the century, her maritime empire and seaborne commerce created the extraordinary wealth that paid for the marble monuments on the Acropolis. Athens had prospered and grown on the strength of her maritime activities to the point that the agriculture of Attica was no longer sufficient to feed the population, and trade with distant regions was essential for survival. Athens's principal military rivals during the period 450-350 B.C., Thebes and Sparta, were essentially conservative, landbound powers, and in spite of incessant, murderous struggles, their interests had a curiously complementary rather than overlapping character.

Political History The choice of one century as a subject of attention can seem arbitrary, particularly when the period is reckoned according to modern, not ancient chronological systems. Yet the fourth century before the birth of Christ is bordered by crises of considerable historical significance. In 404 B.C. the Peloponnesian War came to a close with a crushing and decisive defeat for Athens at the hands of Sparta and her allies. In 294 B.C., Athens was taken by Demetrius Poliorcetes ("the Besieger") after a long blockade, and the city's prosperity was shattered more profoundly than it had been 110 years previously. The two low points might be symbolized by the stripping of the gold from the statue of Athena Parthenos for an emergency issue of coinage: for the first time in 406 and the second in 296/5 B.C. Politically and militarily, the intervening period was dominated by Sparta, Thebes and Macedonia, but Athens managed to flourish and even experienced a second golden age despite her more modest role on the international stage.

In constitutional terms, the century saw the survival of democracy in spite of adverse conditions and in spite of periods of externally-imposed oligarchic rule. After the Spartan victory in 404, the government and social system of Athens were brutally transformed. A systematic colonial relationship in the modern manner was not, however, established. Sparta had allied herself with oligarchic parties throughout the Greek world, and she placed the local oligarchic faction in power as the surest method of establishing a durable control in Athens. The local oligarchs were inspired more by the Socratic idea of the philosopher-ruler than by the Spartan constitution, but they deformed their sources of inspiration harshly and unsuccessfully; within the following year the tyranny had been overthrown and democracy reestablished.

Athens resumed her autonomous political course, but with much greater caution. Rather than attempting to reestablish an imperial system by force in the islands of the Aegean, she joined in a variety of more equal alliances with the weak and shifting coalitions with the strong. By 394 she was allied with Corinth and met a new defeat in the "Corinthian War," which was not, however, of devastating proportions. Her rapidly rebuilt fleet, in fact, won a major battle at Cnidos during the war. In the unscrupulous manner of the Greek city-states, no occasion seems to have been missed to stab the currently strongest state in the back. First Sparta then Thebes had their power undercut by curious assemblages of adversaries. This relentless opportunism did not abate even when the dominant power was engaged in the most universally acclaimed pan-Hellenic enterprise: an expedition against the Persian Empire in the effort to liberate the Greeks of Asia Minor from foreign control. By astute use of economic and military aid, the Persian king and his satraps were, in effect, the arbiters of Greek foreign affairs for much of the century.

The second half of the century was undeniably and irreversibly the phase of Macedonian ascendancy. Athens led the struggle against Macedonian expansion, but time and again, the Macedonian kings and their generals defeated the unstable Greek coalitions, which punctually rose up to test the Macedonians after each change of ruler or after every swing in the balance of power. The northerners exhibited a considerable restraint and far-sightedness in their handling of the Greeks. Local autonomy was retained within the framework of overall control. Aristocracy, more congenial to Macedonian traditions, was favored, but the democracy was left intact at Athens. In a sense, democracy came to be fostered by the Macedonians as an excellent form of local government. Overt Macedonian control began at the battle of Chaeronea in 338 B.C., when Thebes and Athens were decisively defeated by Philip of Macedon. At that time Alexander the Great paid his only visit to Athens, bringing the ashes of the fallen Athenian warriors. Philip's magnanimous policy did not prevent Thebes and Athens from recombining against Alexander three years later. This time, Thebes was destroyed, but Athens spared once again. Greek unity was fostered by both Macedonian kings, and Greek aggressiveness was focussed on the Persian expedition, which had been abortively undertaken on previous occasions.

Alexander's conquest of the Persian Empire marks the watershed between the Classical and the Hellenistic periods. A truly drastic change in Athens's status came about, however, only after Alexander's death in 323 B.C. At that time, a struggle for power began between various Macedonian soldiers of fortune (who eventually would declare themselves kings). Under these less-secure figures, Athens was controlled and disarmed to a degree not previously seen. The city's administration, however, still remained in local hands. Kassander, the Macedonian regent in the Balkans, installed Demetrius of Phaleron as leader of an oligarchy (or, at any rate, a democracy with a very limited franchise). Demetrius was a trained philosopher, and he attempted in more durable fashion to establish a rational rule of an elite during the years 322 to 307 B.C. Demetrius, though a rather hedonistic individual himself, introduced many austere economic policies that were intended to maintain Athenian prosperity; they included a variety of sumptuary laws, of great importance for artistic matters, and a drastic reduction of the Athenian fleet, of great importance in military terms.

At the end of the century, Antigonos, one of Alexander's generals, and his son Demetrius "the Besieger" succeeded in gaining ascendancy in the power struggles in the East. Demetrius campaigned in Greece, where he took control of Athens peacefully in 307 B.C. The Besieger was eager to gain all the political as well as military support he could, and he instituted the policy of reestablishing local democracies. He was greeted as a liberator—and much more—at Athens; he was hailed as a god and duly took up residence in the Parthenon. In this climate of incongruous adulation, the Besieger made Athens a principal base of operations for several years. In 306 B.C., Ptolemy I, Alexander's general who had made himself king of Egypt, intruded into Greece and established an enclave at Corinth, but the great victory of Antigonos and Demetrius off Salamis in Cyprus in that same year compelled Ptolemy to withdraw.

In 301 B.C., Demetrius and Antigonos were defeated by a coalition of Alexander's ex-generals (including Kassander and Lysimachus of Thrace) at Ipsus in Phrygia (Asia Minor). Athens took advantage of the situation to attempt to withdraw completely from the world stage. As an aspect of Athens's neutrality, universal military training for citizens was abolished. Neutrality was maintained successfully for several years until internal and external upheavals shook the city's prosperity and autonomy to their foundations. In 295 B.C., Lachares, the commander of the mercenaries, seized power and established a tyranny. In the same year, Demetrius returned to reassert his control in the prolonged and crippling siege that ended with the fall of the city in 294 B.C.

Bibliography: N. G. L. Hammond, *A History of Greece to 322 B.C.* (Oxford 1959); W. S. Ferguson, *Hellenistic Athens* (London 1911, reprinted Chicago 1974); T. L. Shear, Jr., *Hesperia, Supplement* 17 (1978)

Cultural History Athens was not simply one among many political powers and artistic centers of the fourth century. She remained the undisputed intellectual leader of the time. The historian Xenophon undertook great themes in a vivid narrative style. Playwrights continued to create at a memorable level. Euripides, working until the end of the fifth century, was the last of the great writers of tragedy, but comedy flourished. Aristophanes (considered to be the only surviving example of "Old Comedy") had a career that stretched from the fifth into the early fourth century. A large number of comic writers whose plays have not survived but are classified as "Middle Comedy" seem to have been active through the greater part of the fourth century. On the evidence of works of visual art (like terracotta statuettes) that seem to be based on them, their plays, like those of Aristophanes, were evidently quite imaginative and bawdy. At the end of the century, comedy was made less garish and less fantastic by Menander. His works, which are considered the first examples of "New Comedy," turn around love stories. Insuperable class barriers between the lovers are resolved by clever slaves and by the rediscovery of more acceptable but long-hidden parentage. The plot themes of his works, which survive in fragmentary Greek form and in Latin translations by Terence, were taken up by writers of romantic comedy in Roman times and in the Renaissance (among them, Shakespeare). From our point of view, the works of both Aristophanes and Menander/Terence are not only entertaining but also extremely revealing about the society of Classical and early Hellenistic Athens.

In the fourth century, Athens was also the center of philosophy during one of its greatest ages. Socrates had been executed by the Athenians in 399 B.C., but a succession of major figures flourished in the city during the following decades. To get a sense of the achievements of the time, it may be enough merely to cite the names of Plato, Aristotle, Theophrastos and Epicuros. To Zeno, one might append that he was the founder of Stoicism. Throughout this period, philosophy was not only a theoretical study investigating the nature of knowledge, but it also presented richly developed programs for living. Personal conduct and the conduct of government were major concerns, and many philosophers from the Athenian schools advised Greek rulers or became politicians and even rulers themselves. The failures of philosophically-based political programs and methods led to moments when various philosophical schools were criticised and even restricted by the Athenian assembly.

Greek Art: Styles and Phases in the Fourth Century

The art of the years 404 to 296 B.C. is, on the one hand, a continuum; Greek art was at its apogee and developed essentially untroubled by outside intrusions. Patronage and commissions were not lacking, even if they often came from foreigners. Greek artists were undoubtedly confident of their leadership and absorbed outside ideas only when these ideas served their own artistic objectives. While the creative process was continuous, progressive and (loosely understood) logical across the century, it can be broken into three principal phases, which only partly coincide with historical periodization. The first phase is the "Rich Style," a moment of great dynamism and extreme elegance typified best by the late monuments on the Acropolis: the Temple of Athena Nike and the Erechtheion. It spans roughly the years 420 to 380 B.C. The art of the greater part of the century, about 380-320 B.C., is considered the Late Classical Style, a generous and relaxed phase by previous standards. Athens was rich in famous artists at this time; Kephisodotos, Praxiteles and Euphranor were major protagonists. Leochares and Bryaxis were Athenians who worked on the most celebrated monument of the century, the Mausoleum of Halicarnassos. Timotheos stems from the Athenian School although he was active primarily in the Peloponnesos and at the Mausoleum. Among major non-Athenian artists of the time, one might cite Skopas from the island of Paros and Lysippos, the favorite sculptor of Alexander.

A sharper break with earlier traditions is represented by the Hellenistic Style. Dissonance, complexity, extreme frivolity and extreme sweetness are some of its hallmarks. The Early Hellenistic phase is dated around 320 to 230 B.C. The sons of Praxiteles were some of the notable Athenian artists of the time, creating portraits of Menander and of some of Alexander's generals.

Rather than discussing these different artistic epochs any further in the abstract, they will be considered in relation to the objects in the exhibition.

Bibliography: Schefold, *Göttersage*, p. 15f. for a slightly more extensive capsule version of the scheme.

Patronage and Prosperity in Fourth Century Athens

Artistic production had a rather different course at Athens than in other centers. Early in the century, Athens's loss was to some extent her neighbor's gain. Impoverishment in the years around the end of the Peloponnesian War led to a diaspora of artists. The playwright Euripides moved to the court of Macedonia in the latter years of the century, and sculptors like the shadowy figure Strongylion transferred themselves to less distant localities in search of commissions.[1]

For centuries, the local market and local patronage had only represented one source of employment for the Athens-based artist. The potters and vase painters of the city had filled the tombs and presumably the tables of half the Mediterranean with their products ever since the sixth century. Exportation of vases continued in the fourth century. The numbers may, however, have declined. The markets, moreover, shifted from west to east. Local production largely displaced Athenian wares in the once-lucrative Italian market, while greater quantities of ambitious Attic products reached distant markets in the east, especially the northern coast of the Black Sea and North Africa.

In the reestablished prosperity of fourth century Athens, private individuals apparently formed the principal patrons for sculptors working in Attica. As portrayed on votive and especially funerary sculpture in marble, these patrons seem to be the reticent representatives of a stratified yet almost middle-class society. Prosperous families appear again and again, often accompanied by servants with whom they exchange affectionate glances. It is an art of citizens in a slave-owning society, but there is clearly a conscious effort to maintain decent human relationships between the rigorously defined classes. Public sculptural commissions of the time, like the statue of Democracy[2] or the monument to the Eponymous Heroes (the mythical founders of the different "tribes" of Attica),[3] present the picture of an extensive and powerful citizenry from a different point of view, that of overt celebrative allegory.

The many poor tombs excavated in the cemeteries of Athens, on the other hand, give an insight into the modest level of much of the population.[4] However, the situation is complicated by the general reluctance of Athenians of all classes to leave valuable objects in tombs. Artistic attention was focused on the visible, sculpted memorial in marble.[5]

The Macedonian "conquest" did not have the negative effects on artistic production that might have been expected. Under the benign and distant hegemony of Philip and Alexander the Great, Athenian prosperity increased strikingly. In the third quarter of the century, the politician Lykurgos managed the city's affairs so astutely that a major building campaign could be undertaken. An enormous number of structures for defense, for public utility and for public entertainment, including the Theatre of Dionysos and the Panathenaic Stadium, were built or rebuilt. In this period, private patronage also reached its apogee. The choregic monuments around the Theatre

1. *EAA*, 7, p. 518f.
2. O. Palagia, *Hesperia* 51 (1982) p. 99ff.
3. Travlos, p. 210
4. See especially the excavations of the Kerameikos: U. Knigge and B. Schlörb-Vierneisel, *AthMitt* 81 (1966) p. 112ff.
5. D. Kurtz and J. Boardman, *Greek Burial Customs* (Ithaca, N. Y. 1971) p. 100ff.

were created and funerary monuments were produced in impressive scale and numbers.

A radical and in a sense puritanical reaction took place in the Early Hellenistic period (the second phase of Macedonian control). Under Demetrius of Phaleron, laws forbidding extravagant funerary monuments were enacted. The limit was defined as the amount of work that could be performed by ten men in three days.[6] This measure, probably enacted in 317 B.C., effectively put an end to the figured gravestones that had been so characteristic of the century. Perhaps only coincidentally, another typically Athenian art form disappeared at about the same time: red-figure vase painting. While no measure to suppress vase painting is known, the craft's demise may have been hastened by the feeling that, like the sculpting of gravestones, it was an old, inappropriate and overblown practice.[7]

Athenian Art of this Exhibition: The Selection
The works assembled here offer a special perspective on Athens in the fourth century. In a few cases, they are the fruit of scientific excavation in the 19th century (coming from campaigns in Naukratis in the Nile Delta and Assos on the Aegean coast of Asia Minor). Most, however, were acquired from the art market or received as donations primarily as esthetically pleasing works of art. The acquisition of very large collections *en bloc* circa 1900 and on several more recent occasions, however, brought to the Museum many puzzling objects which might not have been purchased individually. These objects make it possible to present certain aspects of Antiquity normally ignored in the galleries of an art museum: in particular, the practical life and the material culture of ancient Athens. The objects in question are essentially instruments for living: lead weights, seal impressions, bronze coins, and plain pottery. Commercial systems, popular communication and distinctive local materials come into focus in ways not usually possible. In most cases, these almost purely functional objects display the same high standards of design manifest in purely artistic fields like sculpture or vase painting.

The exhibition intends to give a reasonably extensive picture of the kinds of objects used or produced in fourth century Athens, and the pieces selected relate to this locus in different ways. Some are certainly made in Athens; there is almost no doubt any longer about the attribution to Athenian artists of red-figure vases or grave reliefs in Pentelic marble. Other objects might never have been attributable to Athens if there had not been reports in the Museum records to the effect that they came from this source. A provenance from the Athenian art market (rather than from Athens itself) has, however, limited value; it means little more than that the object did not come from Turkey or Italy, but, in many cases, even this general signpost is of very great help in identifying the workshop of origin. In addition to works of certain Athenian origin, others have been included that only have a conjectural relationship with Athens. Attributions of bronzes to Athens, for example, are very uncertain. Many objects have been selected because they parallel objects uncovered in Athenian excavations. A few copies dating from Roman Imperial times of freestanding sculptures thought to be by fourth century Attic artists have been added to give an idea of the famous masterpieces of the fourth century.

The foreign presence at Athens has also been recognized. Many objects found in Athens come from other cities. Coins are a principal source of evidence. Whether excavated in the commercial center, the Agora, or discovered at random in hoards throughout Attica, notable quantities of foreign money appear. Other objects that are demonstrably of non-Attic origin are harder to come by, but it is, in any case, clear that oil bottles of alabaster were imported from Egypt. The international travel and trade reflected in these finds suggests that, in spite of the preeminence of Athens in the world of culture, true works of art could also have been imported. Crafts like bronzeworking had famous centers near Athens, and it seems reasonable to conjecture that the prestigious products of Corinth or Euboea would have made some inroads in Attica. Corinthian bronzeworking has, consequently, been represented in the exhibition.

The Social Level: Official or Private Art The major public monuments of fourth century Athens are represented only in the most sketchy way in the exhibition. "Roman copies" give some idea of the statuary dedicated in Attic sanctuaries or in public places like the Agora.[8] It must be kept in mind, however, that these copies were usually made for purposes totally unlike their original destinations. Marble copies of Roman times decorated places of recreation like country houses, baths or theatres. Bronze statuettes were placed in niches or cupboard-like household shrines (lararia) that had no close parallel in the Classical period. The cultural gap led the sculptors of Roman times to summarize, adapt, embellish or simply to fantasize on the inspiration offered by Greek works. The resulting statues and statuettes are often unreliable evidence about the period they are purported to reproduce.

Public art is represented primarily by coins. They display images that were central for the society at large. Lead weights and lead tokens for public events offer another curious viewpoint on the official approach to visual problems.

6. Kurtz and Boardman, *op. cit.*, p. 122
7. On the relationship of these two events, see K. Schefold in J. Bibauw (editor), *Hommages à Marcel Renard*, 3 (Brussels 1969) p. 511ff.; J. R. Green in A. Cambitoglou (editor), *Studies in Honor of Arthur Dale Trendall* (Sydney 1979) p. 81ff.
8. On the places to which copyists had access, see Ridgway, *Copies*, p. 65ff.

The great majority of the works in the exhibition are connected with the strictly private realm. Above all, they stem from graves found both in Attica and around the Mediterranean wherever Athenian wares could be sold. Funerary art represents a distinct and in many respects limited point of view. In Attica, the furnishings of tombs were restricted generally to the simplest toilet articles for the care of the body. The objects in the grave may particularly reflect the equipment, especially bottles of perfumed oil, used in the final preparations for the burial. At times, these minimal gifts were supplemented by clay drinking vessels and the pitchers associated with a favorite spring festival, Anthesteria. Outside of Attica, of course, tombs were fitted out much more richly with drinking sets (often Attic vases) and other kinds of equipment. In Attica, as noted above, elaborate attentions were concentrated above all on the visible marble memorial.

Votive reliefs are a more public kind of art; they are objects dedicated in sanctuaries in thanks for a perceived act of divine favor. On the other hand, these are still private dedications, often made by very humble individuals. Statuettes of terracotta were frequently dedicated in sanctuaries as well as placed in tombs.

Form and Content I: Subject Matter The figures of funerary art strike one as presenting a variety of different, often contrasting moods. The basic scene is a simple and entirely ordinary gesture: a farewell handshake or a final touch of the jewel box. The effect is to commemorate the dignity and well-being of the deceased in life. At the same time there can be mourning figures, human or mythological (Sirens), either carved on the monument or else buried in the grave. They, of course, reflect the basic human reaction to death. Most surprising, however, are the comic statuettes placed in the tomb: amusing dancers, actors in obscene costumes, or grotesques. On the one hand, they are linked to a religious theme; they are connected with the divine saviour Dionysos, god of the theatre and, hence, entertainment in general. On the other hand, the simple, unprogrammatic human feeling found in other aspects of Attic funerary art suggests that such figures also may have been buried out of a sense that the dead will need a little laughter in the long night of the tomb.

The complex interrelationship between Dionysos, entertainment and funerary art manifests itself in a multitude of forms. Pitchers (choes) are frequently found in Attic graves of the earlier part of the century. Since wine was the drink most characteristic of this shape, the connection with Dionysos is obvious. Pitchers may show Dionysos himself, but they may also be linked to him in other ways. Paintings on these vases depict events like chariot races or revelry connected with the spring festival of Anthesteria, which was sacred especially to Dionysos. Babies holding pitchers often appear on these jugs, reflecting the custom of giving Dionysiac gifts to the young on this occasion.

The character of funerary art seems to change in the Early Hellenistic period, when terracotta statuettes of children occasionally appear in Attic graves. Some are dressed in festive costumes; one, for example, wears a tiara (no. 81). Perhaps such figures evoke a child's introduction or dedication to the cult of a divinity. The girl with the tiara carries a hand drum, the instrument of the retinue of Dionysos, evidently the cult in question. Other terracotta statuettes of girls, however, might be representations of nymphs (local geographical divinities); many have been found in a sanctuary to a nymph on the south slope of the Acropolis.[9]

Not all works of art from graves were made for funerary purposes. Many must simply have been objects useful in life that accompanied their owner to his final resting place. Some of these objects, particularly seal rings, show the most disparate possible subjects: animals, birds, insects, tripods, beautiful heads, or anything that could be turned into a handsome emblem. Others echo themes from mythology, like the winged horse Pegasos.

The grand themes of epic appear only rarely. One relief vase (no. 36) shows the tragic and horrendous fall of Troy, a subject that was also represented in major temple sculpture of the time, for example, in the Temple of Asklepios at Epidauros.

On rare occasions, contemporary military events are reflected in mythological terms. A coin of Histiaia on the island of Euboea (no. 112) is such a case. The nymph of the city is seated on the stern of a galley as an emblem of a victory gained (with Athenian support) over the Macedonians in 341/340 B.C. The armed Aphrodite on an oil bottle (no. 22) seems to be another instance. In front of Aphrodite, a Nike sacrifices a bull while a warrior, perhaps Ares, offers a shield, presumably captured in battle. The scene probably alludes to the Athenian naval victory at Cnidos in 394 B.C. since Aphrodite was the patron goddess of that city. Compositionally, the painting on the lekythos echoes the reliefs with Victories and Athena on the parapet of the Temple of Athena Nike on the Acropolis. The direct source of inspiration, however, may well have been the sculptures of the lost Temple of Aphrodite at Piraeus, built as a thank-offering for the victory of Cnidos.

The great Olympian gods appear frequently on the official art of coinage and hold the principal cults of the city-states before the public. Popular examples are Athena and her owl, and Apollo of Megara and his tripod. Coins

9. *BCH* 82 (1958) p. 657ff., figs. 7, 10

also celebrate the primeval heroes of many localities and their deeds, including Ajax of Salamis; Triptolemos of Eleusis, who bore the secret of crop-growing to mankind; and Bellerophon, who tamed Pegasos on the mountain overlooking Corinth. In the Early Hellenistic period, portraits of the great Macedonian rulers, shown as divinized heroes, make their first appearance in numismatic history.

Aphrodite is the favorite of the traditional gods on other objects. The embodiment of love and beauty has a special appropriateness on bottles of perfumed oil. Dionysos has a comparable suitability for drinking vessels.

The choice of divinities and the choice of mythological episode, however, take on a very individual flavor in the fourth century. Private art displays more interest in personal protectors than in the great civic cults. Healing heroes, usually demigods or gods who arrived late on Olympos, assume a much larger role. Asklepios, the god of healing, is the principal one, but Herakles in his aspect as the averter of evil (Alexikakos) was the focus of a cult with strongly curative aspects.

Gods who suffered and died before being elevated to Olympos are a subject of intense interest and must have been regarded as especially close to suffering mortals. Dionysos, the persecuted orphan, and Herakles are the most evident subjects of this attention. The image of both had been very different in the preceding centuries; both were bearded and powerfully mature figures. The infantile or juvenile Dionysos, more persecuted, more affectionate, more paradoxical in his powers, is the favorite of fourth century Athens. Herakles, too, is shown beardless. His exploits with ferocious and improbable monsters are no longer particularly popular. He is normally shown in repose with his companions, drinking, or introduced among the gods. All versions present his apotheosis.

The love of the gods for mortals remains a popular theme. Aphrodite and the Trojan Prince Anchises exchange sultry glances (no. 16). Leda is surprised by Zeus as a swan (no. 62). A frequent figure is Ariadne, the mortal woman saved by Dionysos and made his bride on Olympos. It is a century of warmly-affectionate divinities, who may on occasion turn their attention to humans. Behind this changed focus seems to lurk a fervent and widespread hope for immortality granted through divine grace and earned by heroic effort or personal beauty.

The longing for communion with the gods by no means restricts itself to the realms of magic, medicine or salvation. The elevation and purification of the spirit was also a focus of enlightened attention. Philosophers like Socrates, Plato and Xenophon discussed love in a highly spiritual sense. The intellectual fascination with love is translated into the popularity of Eros in fourth century art.

These intimations of immortality color the choice of subjects so strongly that the portrayal of everyday reality recedes. Athletic scenes, the life of the exercise field (palaestra) or the racecourse, become rare, and when they do appear, they are filled with allegorical overtones. Wreaths of victory are solemnly bestowed by waiting girls or by flying Nikes.

Foreigners and foreign themes intrude humorously into Attic art. Distant markets, travellers and resident foreigners must all have worked on the imagination of Athenian artists. In spite of considerable contacts with the most disparate regions of the Mediterranean, foreigners are treated in terms of the cheerful legends of the past. All people living to the east of the Aegean could be represented wearing "Persian" costume: a cap with earflaps and a pointed top that falls forward (the "Phrygian" cap), trousers and a jacket with long sleeves. Elaborately patterned fabrics were an important ingredient in the effect. Dancers performing the "Persian" or squatting dance (oklasma), inhabitants of the Ural mountains (Arimasps) or the Trojan prince Anchises could all be shown in this fashion.

An addition of the fourth century to this conventionalized gallery of foreign types may be the nude fat ladies that are the subject of several grotesque terracottas (nos. 73, 74). They could have been inspired by the obese, indecent and silly Mossynoecians, whom travellers claimed to have encountered on the southeast coast of the Black Sea. The importance of trade with south Russia seems to have led to a revival of legends connected with the Black Sea region. In addition to the Mossynoecians, the adventures of the Argonauts may have been revived (no. 15). The Arimasps and griffins enjoyed their greatest popularity at this time.

More authentic reflections of Asiatic art did penetrate Attica to a limited degree. One might include changes in the subject-matter of jewelry of the Early Hellenistic period in this category. The gazelle and various eastern monsters migrated from Achaemenid Persian art into the repertory of Greek goldworkers. The most impressive testimony of foreign influence, however, is presented by the votive relief to the sun and moon (no. 7). Astral or celestial divinities were, of course, more important in the ancient Near East than in Greece. This relief makes the source of inspiration quite clear since it represents the moon god of western Asia Minor, Men, with his emblematic animal, the rooster. Like the various other monuments of the cult of Men in Attica, this relief must have been commissioned by resident foreigners.

Form and Content II: Stylistic Issues The variety of media in fourth century Athens, whether exploited by Athenian workshops or available as importation, is at first glance bewildering. The entire spectrum of Greek arts and crafts is to some degree at issue. Each of these different media has its own and in many respects unique history. Vase painting and terracotta sculpture, for example, present developments that move in almost diametrically opposed directions. Red-figure painting comes to an end in the latter years of the century, just when terracotta sculpture greatly expands in popularity and steps into the mainstream of sculptural development. Yet, as products of the same culture, they all to some degree participate in the larger stylistic movements of the time.

Elongation of form, for example, is characteristic of the art of the fourth century. Lysippos was said to have made his statues more slender and with relatively small heads.[10] The figures on marble grave reliefs show this tendency in various ways; the figures on the lekythos are, indeed, quite slender. A comparable tendency can be observed in the treatment of the figures on engraved rings and gems. This approach to proportion permeated even non-figurative media; it is notorious that the shapes of vases became increasingly tall and slender during the fourth century.

Such common features can easily be overemphasized. The proportions of the human figure evidently formed a subject of intense interest during the century. Within the same general framework that favored greater elongation (of one sort or another), strongly contrasted approaches to the design of figurative and non-figurative art alike emerged. One of the principal polarities of the century seems to have involved the question of refinement versus substance. Refinement, understood quite broadly, was a major element in the Rich Style. Minutely detailed rippling drapery, as in the female torso, presents this aspect of the style most attractively. For vase painters of the Rich Style, this impulse produced excessively slender, adolescent figures, even when heroes or athletes were portrayed, as in fragments by the Painter of the Athens Wedding, the fragments with the chariot race, or the victory lekythos (nos. 17, 22, 23). A very analogous kind of "excess" appeared in the shapes of vases. A new shape of the fourth century, the fragile, curvilinear cup-kantharos displayed a remarkable delicacy. The insistence on refinement of shape led one fourth century commentator to question rhetorically whether he was to drink the wine or the wine cup.[11]

Many Rich Style artists, however, developed a much simpler and intentionally solid approach. Two contrasting directions had been manifest throughout the late fifth century (typified by the Meidias Painter and the Dinos Painter), but from about 400 B.C. on, the simple tendency became much more emphatic. The loss of the Peloponnesian War may have engendered a desire for more reassuringly substantial forms. Whatever the underlying motivation, the simple style of the Suessula Painter foreshadows the comfortably bulky figures of the circle of the Pronomos Painter. In sculpture, an increased fullness and rotondity parallels the phenomenon in vase painting. There is a new sense of the softness of human flesh that covers the armature of bone and muscle, which had been so sharply defined in the fifth century. The head of the youth (no. 3) and, in much more modest terms, the stele with the woman and Siren (no. 5) present the masses of the human anatomy in softer terms. The figures on sculptural vases all show this approach. The Leda (no. 62) is particularly characteristic, since the figure, whose anatomy is covered but not concealed by blowing drapery, is conceived fully in the tradition of the Rich Style. There is, however, a breadth and amorphousness to the modelling that contrasts with the slenderness and geometric sharpness of some of the famous late fifth century Nikes or the marble torso in the exhibition (no. 2).

The Late Classical style often manages to reconcile this polarity, but it still remains a major issue. Refinement, grace and slenderness are mitigated by a sense of generous volume in the figures on the Kerch Style hydria (no. 25). The marble lekythos (no. 6) also presents a harmonious and fluent blend of these elements. Many artists, however, continued to render figures in extremely refined and slender terms. Praxiteles brilliantly manipulated these figural types for his seemingly playful Apollos, gods of love, satyrs or demigods, as the fragmentary torso included here (no. 4) can perhaps suggest. This Praxitelean taste emerges on the popular level in works like a rather androgynous head engraved on a gold ring (no. 157). The treatment of Eros on gems and rings that might be connected with the "Latest Classical Group" is a brilliant manifestation of this sensibility, whether one thinks of the silver ring with the flute-playing Eros or, best of all, the victorious Eros signed by the master gem-engraver Kallippos (nos. 160, 162).

Fourth century artists also succeeded in blending the elegant and the formidable in images of long-haired youthful gods or heroes. Apollo is presented with locks streaming down on his neck on an intaglio and a lead token (nos. 155, 134). On a coin of Megara, which is probably based on an Apollo by Praxiteles in a sanctuary of the city, the god's rope-like locks are looped more loosely over his headband (no. 99).[12] All these portrayals of the god have an almost predatory fierceness of expression.

Refinement versus substance is also an issue that is important for decorative, non-figurative art. The vegetal ornament that is so much a part of Greek design follows

10. Pliny, *Natural History*, xxxiv, 65

11. See below, p. 44, footnote 3.

12. On the hair style which appears in several heads of Dionysos known through Roman copies and ascribed to Praxiteles (the Chatsworth Dionysos, Dionysos "Sardanapalos") see C. Picard, *Manuel d'archéologie grecque: la sculpture*, 4, 2, 1 (Paris 1954) p. 316ff., fig. 132f. On Apollos by Praxiteles at Megara, see Pausanias, I, xl, 3; xliv, 2; Picard, *op. cit.*, p. 344, n. 1.

both directions, often in contradictory fashion. At the beginning of the century, the ornament of vases was icily precise and elegant. Slender palmettes and vine scrolls coil in irregular areas around handles leaving large areas of surface empty. Very quickly these motifs spread out and become ever broader and fleshier. Filler elements take up what is left of the background to create a densely packed texture of pattern. The fully developed version of this approach, which is seen in vases of the Kerch Style, has been called the "Tapestry Style."

Concomitantly, a new system of ornament was developed that was simultaneously more naturalistic and more geometric. Wreaths or vines, rendered with much use of added clay and originally gilded, circle the vase. These illusionistic additions maintain an elegant restraint and slenderness. Both systems can be seen in the Kerch Style hydria, no. 25. The handle areas are packed with massive palmettes and scrolls, while a much tighter and more naturalistic olive wreath surrounds the neck. The wreath recalls the real gold wreaths at times placed on metal ash urns. Eventually, these wreaths become the sole ornament and are set against the lustrous but plain black surface of the vase, as in nos. 42 and 48. This system of ornament outlives the red-figure technique. Added clay ornament and overpainting or gilding continue to be used throughout the Early Hellenistic period. The more lively and less illusionistic effects of that time have been named "West Slope" decoration or "West Slope Ware."

The same issues can be raised with the ornament of bronze vessels. The early amphora handles have the icy elegance of the Erechtheion. The hydria attachments have a florid, curvilinear richness and fullness. The inlaid silver ivy vine encircling the sprinkler is a close parallel for the decoration of West Slope Ware.

The reaction against the extreme refinement of some Rich Style artists, however, remained vivid throughout the century. Euphranor, who worked at Athens as both a painter and sculptor, contrasted his portrayal of Theseus with one by Parrhasios; Parrhasios's hero looked as though he dined on roses while Euphranor's own clearly was nourished on beef.[13] Even Euphranor did not fully capture the mood of the times; although he was considered "the first to have represented the grandeur of heroes...he rendered the bodies on the whole too slight and the heads and limbs too large."[14] An assertion of the massively powerful physique appears in many works of the mid-century or later; one might mention major grave reliefs like the Illisos stele,[15] or, to restrict oneself to works in the exhibition, the bronze mirror (no. 139) or the krater with the apotheosis of Herakles (no. 20). A comparably majestic effect for less pretentious subjects may be found in the seated girl on the grave relief (no. 11). She wears a high belt that tends to increase the long fall of drapery and to suggest height. Her tight melon-coiffure creates the effect of large limbs and small head that seems to have been much prized. Fleshy bulk could also be pushed to willfully grotesque extremes. The infantile flabbiness of the baby Dionysos in a figural vase is an amusing prelude to the startling anatomic accuracy of the obese Mossynoecians.

Complexity and subtlety of pose were an evolving concern for artists throughout the century. Contrapposto, the articulation of a body through a balanced contrast of relaxed and tensioned members, had become a highly developed system in the second half of the fifth century. In works like the marble torso of a muscular youth (no. 1), contrasts have been pushed to a jarring extreme. In the course of the fourth century, this angularity is softened. Figures of youths pouring wine make use of strong shifts of axis, but with a more curvilinear fluency or with a more relaxed fullness. The sculptural vase with Dionysos (no. 63), on the other hand, shows a very balanced straightforward contrapposto hardly different from that of High Classical statues. Only a relaxed and gentle quality makes it a distinctly fourth century interpretation. Complexity increases in many three-dimensional works and with it often comes instability. The pouring youth is a good example. The Praxitelean torso and the terracotta fat lady go a step further toward twisting movement and gestures that enclose space.

Two-dimensional works are particularly adventurous in the use of complicated poses. Twisting poses appear at a very early date in works like the silver ring engraved with a dancing maenad (no. 146). Two-dimensional media make use of ever more sinuous, curvilinear compositions. Often, the figures develop the complex poses of the sculpted friezes in the latest monuments on the Acropolis. Crouching postures and feet propped up on rocks (as in nos. 16 and 21) are borrowed as much from this source as is the Nike sacrificing a bull. Sinuous curvilinear designs also appear in the new vase forms of the century, like the cup-kantharos.

Illusionism and idealism form another pair of antitheses that sets the art of the century on a dynamic course. Observation of concrete reality had long been a major component of Greek art. In the fourth century, the encounter with reality took on a new dimension. Objects were no longer described as they were in an "objective" way but instead, in words attributed to Lysippos, "as they appeared to be."[16] The act of seeing became important in itself. An illusionistic presentation of form is pervasive in

13. The anecdote is repeated by several Roman authors; see below, p. 27 , footnote 16.
14. Pliny, *Natural History*, xxxv, 129; O. Palagia, *Euphranor* (Leiden 1980) p. lf.
15. *Hellenistic Art*, p. 243
16. Pliny, *Natural History*, xxxiv, 19, 65

the art of the time; objects are created for their visual effect when seen from a certain point of view. Sculptural vases are composed as little scenes with landscape settings vividly colored. Only the visible front side is important; backs are neglected. Red-figure vases have added colors and applied clay reliefs to increase the painterly effect. In relief vases, the applied clay becomes the dominant element. With the original colors intact, the illusionistic intent would have been more evident than it is at present. Sculptors become concerned with light and shade. Reliefs are composed like framed pictures, and as the figures stand out in ever greater depth, deep shadow becomes an even more important ingredient in the composition. Drill channels tear into marble to produce shadow-catching lines. Surfaces are modelled with contrasts of smooth polish and rough texture to create the illusion of flesh and hair. The observation of the natural world remains an artistic concern and expands its range of subjects. Still lifes of simple objects like shells or knucklebones maintain their popularity, while portraits of recognizable individuals become a major theme, particularly at the end of the century.

This illusionism is, however, tempered or even contradicted by pattern-making on a geometric framework. The ideal world, the divine world or the mythological world were much too pervasive in the imagination of the period for artists to be satisfied with a passive record of mundane reality. At times the new illusionistic techniques were rejected in favor of overtly old-fashioned ones. The stiff elegance and contrived patterns of the Archaic period were often revived both because of their charm and because of their suggestions of religious tradition. Images of Athena the warrior goddess attacking in a stiffly erect posture continued to be painted on Attic vases (nos. 31, 32). The ancient black-figure technique survived with her and even had a modest new popularity because of its sparkling and colorful effects. The archaistic Athena spread far beyond Athens; the motif was taken up on the coinage of Ptolemy of Egypt (nos. 125, 126). The sphinx, a mythological monster borrowed from pharaonic Egypt centuries before, was revived with old-fashioned geometric precision in a sculptural vase of fourth century Athens (no. 66). With her patterned wings and her delicate proto-Hellenistic anatomy and head, the sphinx presents a most delightful and harmonious blend of two characteristic and contrasting styles of the fourth century, the archaistic and the illusionistic.

Polar opposites govern the art of the time in small scale and in large. Polarities had already emerged vividly in the fifth century, typified perhaps by the contrast on the Acropolis between the straightforward and symmetrical Temple of Athena Nike and the ornate and asymmetrical Erechtheion. The contrast between progresssive and retrospective had, however, hardly become the conscious ambivalence seen in the fourth century. This balancing of the modern and the post-modern, which then, as now, may only have been a nostalgic idea of the pre-modern, casts a shadow across the course of Greek art, but it also adds a fascinating extra dimension to the art of the fourth century, public or private.

Marble Sculpture

Marble sculpture was one of the two most characteristic Athenian art forms during the Classical period. Not only did a major source of raw material exist nearby in the quarries of Mt. Pentelikon, but the wealth and the cultural aspirations of Athens led to one of the great ages of temple building and sculptural embellishment. The vast majority of the material used was the fine-grained marble from Mt. Pentelikon. The less-desirable grade of Pentelic marble can be rather easily recognized from its coarse flaws or veins of greenish, micaceous crystals (as in nos. 4 and 11). Softer-toned, larger crystalled marble from the Aegean islands was employed for some of the more prestigious statuary (as in no. 12).

In the last decade of the fifth century, the crises of the end of the Peloponnesian War inevitably created a situation highly unfavorable for the continuation of major public sculptural projects in the manner of the previous half century. Many accomplished sculptors seem to have emigrated in search of commissions, but sculptural activity in Attica by no means came to an end. There were simply too many good artists around, and sculpture was too deeply entrenched in cultural patterns. Civic and religious practice led to private dedications in sanctuaries. Victorious athletes continued to be commemorated with statues, and votive figures were offered to the gods. Public commissions for the embellishment of previously-built structures also continued at a somewhat reduced rate as Athens rapidly regained its former prosperity. Public building probably accelerated greatly around the time of the Corinthian War of 394 B.C., when funerary monuments were set up to the fallen and a new temple was dedicated to Aphrodite in commemoration of the naval victory at Cnidos.

Masterworks of the period following the end of the Peloponnesian War and through the fourth century tend to be known from much later testimony of Roman Imperial times. Roman writers described the monuments and artists of Athens, and sculptors reproduced works of our period. Among the copies are late examples of the Rich Style dating from around 400 B.C. As in the parapet of the Temple of Nike on the Acropolis, minutely detailed drapery flows like water across firm, flexible female bodies.

In the Rich Style, figures often have complex and subtle movements, and the complexity tends to increase during the fourth century. Axes shift and tilt, and figures crouch and twist. Even male figures ostensibly standing at rest can be animated with shifting stresses. Contrapposto, the play between supporting and relaxed members, becomes sharply contrasted. In a torso (no. 1) that originally had its relaxed leg pushed forward (the "Attic contrapposto"), the body sways and tilts to counterbalance the stance. With ever-varying inflections the figural type became a staple of sculptors throughout the century. This presumably early version is notable for its slender proportions and ridged musculature. The body type was frequently employed in a more gentle and suave form for athletic and funerary statues in Athens.[1] It appeared in more sober fashion, in commemorative statues at Delphi attributed to the school of Lysippos,[2] and went on to be used in a variety of statues of athletes and heroes in the waxy, blurred treatment of Hellenistic times.[3]

Many fourth century figures shift their center of gravity to the point that a support is required, whether a post, a tree trunk or another figure. They take on a new complexity as they reach out into space and twist laterally. Both features are combined in a fragmentary torso that might have originally represented a youthful demigod (no. 4). In such figures, the softness of the still-unformed adolescent anatomy is brought out. Such figures were used for wine-pouring cup-bearers, as in reliefs to heroes or in statues like the so-called Munich Oil Pourer (no. 3).

The mood of fourth century statuary is often playful. The subjects themselves may be decidedly light-weight: knucklebone players, satyrs or demigod shepherd boys like Ganymede, who was abducted by Zeus in the form of an eagle. Yet statues in this seemingly gay, informal or relaxed mood were deemed suitable for dedications in the most sacred sites; one need only think of the Hermes playfully holding the infant Dionysos carved by the Attic sculptor Praxiteles that was displayed in the Temple of Hera at Olympia.[4] The intimate, warm and caring side of divinity was brought out in such images.

Marble sculpture was produced in fourth century Athens above all for purely private needs. Grave monuments and votive reliefs, the latter set up in recognition of some perceived act of divine grace, have survived in impressive numbers. The usual form for both was a relief panel treated like a simulated building; normally, the panel was framed at the sides by a pair of doric piers (antae) and above by an architrave, topped by the edge of a tile roof. The composition suggests, in greatly abbreviated fashion, a porch (stoa) of the kind often erected in sanctuaries to shelter pilgrims or votive offerings. Some grave markers, however, were made in the form of enormously enlarged oil bottles with cylindrical bodies, long necks and a single handle (lekythoi) of the kind that had frequently been placed in tombs in the fifth century. Curiously, the form of lekythos that survived as a tomb offering in the fourth century, the squat lekythos, had a low, rounded body. Funerary art perpetuated the venerable, cylindrical form, which had disappeared from ordinary usage.

Even in some of the most modest of private monuments, the new directions in fourth century marble sculpture appear clearly. In funerary monuments, the figures often show the deceased either holding or playing with a favorite pet or a child or else bidding their loved ones good-by with a handshake. The compositions mix dignity and intimacy. In scenes where the mistress reaches into a jewel box held by a maid, the pleasures of a prosperous social position are evoked without losing warmth or tenderness. Fourth century art has a new expressiveness quite evident in funerary sculpture. Emotion breaks into these scenes in symbolic form when a Siren, a mythological creature half woman and half bird, beats her breast in mourning on the roof of the simulated building. Emotion may be shown directly when one of the figures in the farewell scene holds her bowed head in grief.

Any sense of intimacy or individuality, however, is missing in votive reliefs. The atmosphere is one of solemn formality as individuals or families of votaries with palms raised and bodies shrouded in drapery advance to salute their god or hero. The divinities are shown in larger scale and usually take no notice of their devotees. They become particularly detached as they banquet on couches and gaze directly out of the relief. A standard composition was worked out for votive reliefs to these gods or demigods who became patrons of the Underworld and of healing. The few inscribed pieces make it clear that such reliefs could be dedicated to almost any of the countless male and female heroes without distinction. They might honor such obscure figures as Eukolos, Zeuxippos, Basileia or the founding heroes of tribes like Hegemon Archegetes. They might also be dedicated to Underworld gods like Demeter and Persephone or protective divinities like Good Fortune

1. See the boy from Piraeus: F. Hiller, *Formgeschichtliche Untersuchungen zur griechischen Statue des späten 5. Jahrhunderts v. Chr.* (Mainz 1971) no. 10; Ridgway, *Fifth Century*, fig. 92; see also a funerary statue in Boston: Comstock and Vermeule, *Sculpture*, no. 59.

2. In the Daochos Group, especially Agias: see Robertson, *Shorter History*, fig. 228.

3. A statuette of a young athlete in the Rhode Island School of Design repeats the generalities of this kind of figure: the "Bebenburg Youth," said to have been found at Cnidos: the scale is essentially identical: B. Ridgway, *Catalogue of the Classical Collection: Classical Sculpture* (Providence 1972) no. 19 (dated about 300 B.C.); C. Vermeule, *S to S*, p. 120, fig. 29 (execution dated about 50 B.C.). A small-scale Herakles in Sicily also presents a version of this pose. *Antike Plastik W. Amelung* (Berlin 1928) p. 172ff., pl. 12; C. Picard, *Manuel d'archéologie grecque: la sculpture* 4, 2, 2 (Paris 1963) p. 585, fig. 246.

4. Robertson, *Shorter History*, p. 139, fig. 191

(Agatha Tyche). All must have been invoked for their curative powers.[5] The great healing hero Asklepios, who was not shown reclining, was a very popular recipient of votive reliefs.

The treatment of form evolves substantially in the course of the century, and Athens's contribution can be followed in minor as well as major monuments. The illusion of visual reality is a primary theme throughout the period. Rich Style drapery that seems almost transparent represents only a starting point. Drapery of around 400 B.C. has a sharp, linear definition. Very quickly a softer, gentler and in a sense more realistic description of corporeal form emerges. Volumes are broader and more generous. Drapery is modulated more softly and directly. Geometric definition of outline is avoided or muted. By the middle of the century in works like the votive relief to the sun and moon (no. 7), the masses of the body are shown, but the effort to describe anatomy hidden below clothing is given up as academic. However, visible anatomy, as in the majestic team of horses, is suggested with great skill. By the Age of Alexander, the play of light and shade had become a primary concern of sculpture. In works like the stele with the mistress and maid (no. 11), the figures spring into high relief, creating sharp contrasts of deep shadow and bright highlight. This contrast is developed further by drilling deep, shadow-catching channels into the drapery. Geometric outline has entirely disappeared in favor of mass, volume, chiaroscuro and optical effect.

In Early Hellenistic Attic works like the Bartlett Aphrodite in the Museum of Fine Arts or like an under-life-size head of Asklepios (no. 12), this technique has become extremely subtle and extremely tender. The creator of this approach must surely have been Praxiteles in works like the Hermes at Olympia. Earlier technique seems almost heavy-handed and literal by comparison. Transitions are gradual and indefinite. Volumes are gently amorphous. The power of suggestion creates a penetrating illusion of life and feeling.

Marble sculpture for funerary purposes had an extraordinary expansion at Athens in the Age of Alexander. Many of these monuments became of colossal size, and the figures turned into free-standing statues enclosed in stage spaces. A puristic reaction set in at the beginning of the Hellenistic period. A tightness and skimpiness appear in female costume, as gowns are belted high under the breasts, and fabrics are pulled more tightly. Hair styles reflect the new mood even more clearly. Hair is combed into rows and twisted into a braid that circles the back of the head. The composition is tight and firm.

5. In the third century, such reliefs would also be dedicated to the heroized dead. On this category of relief, see R. Thönges-Stringaris, *AthMitt* 80 (1965) p. 1ff.

In 317 B.C. conspicuous and extravagant funerary monuments were banned by Demetrius of Phaleron, who ruled Athens on the sufferance of the Macedonian military leader Kassander. While the quantity of marble sculpture at Athens was enormously reduced, fine works for civic and religious purposes continued to be produced, and the new Praxitelean techniques went on to become a major ingredient in the style of the Hellenistic period throughout most of the Greek world.

1. Torso from a statuette of an athlete

Roman Imperial Period, first century B.C. or A.D.
After an Attic(?) prototype of about 420-370 B.C.
Bequest of Benjamin Rowland, Jr. 1974.123
Height 40.5 cm. Relatively crystalline Pentelic marble.

The young athlete stood in "Attic contrapposto" with the relaxed leg advanced in front of the weight-bearing leg. The weight-bearing hip swings far to one side, and the axes of the upper body are tilted strongly to compensate.

There are numerous parallels for this kind of hard-muscled, hip-swinging youth in the High Classical period. A life-size torso in the Agora presents a close parallel in its stance and musculature, but its effect is much more massively mature and more Heraklean. The Agora piece has been variously attributed to the second half of the fifth or to the fourth century B.C.[1] It has also been considered a Roman copy.[2] The Agora torso (or its archetype) must have been famous since an apparent replica in heroic scale is in the Museum of Fine Arts.[3]

The statuette exhibited here and another small-scale replica preserved in the University Museum, Philadelphia,[4] might be miniature versions of the Agora/Boston type, but the differences seem significant and probably reflect a later and more mannered model. This piece steps out with a livelier and more elastic movement. Cornelius Vermeule has compared it to the movement of the discophoros of Naukydes, whose archetype is datable in the early fourth century. The Boston piece not only reverses the direction of movement, but it is also slimmer than the Naukydes athlete. The exact stance and proportions of the torso can be paralleled in a group of classicistic Roman statues: the Magdalensberg Youth, the Lychnouchos from Pompeii and the Idolino in Florence.[5] The classicistic figures are, however, very sleek and smooth compared to the Boston piece.

1. *EAA*, 1, p. 843, fig. 1060; H. Thompson, *Hesperia* 18 (1949) p. 233ff., pls. 49, 50; C. Gottlieb, AJA 61 (1957) pp. 161-5, pl. 61, 2; C. Morgan, *Hesperia* 32 (1963) p. 92, pl. 33; Robertson, *History*, p. 345, pl. 114b
2. For a summary of opinions, see A. Delivorrias, *Attische Giebelskulpturen und Akrotere des fünften Jahrhunderts* (Tübinger Studien 1, 1974) pp. 22-24.
3. Comstock and Vermeule, *Sculpture*, no. 142
4. B. Hamanaka in *Allentown*, p. 156, no. 76
5. Ridgway, *Copies*, p. 83, pls. 101-105

Cat. 1.

Slim proportions and vigorous articulation do appear in the youth from Eleusis in the Athens National Museum, dated to the late fifth or early fourth century.[6] This statuette could well have been a young athlete either without attributes or perhaps carrying a discus in his left hand, much like an athlete with a very similar stance and anatomy on a coin of Philippopolis minted in the early third century A.D.[7] The original behind this statuette might have dated in the late fifth century, but it could also have been later; beyond its connections to the Naukydes discophoros, there is a certain similarity to the fragmentary figures from the pediments of the Temple of Asklepios at Epidauros, dated in the first third of the fourth century (perhaps about 380-375 B.C.). There, too, rib cages are outlined, waists are nipped in and slender thighs flex with tension.[8] Timotheos, the guiding spirit of the Epidauros project, was probably trained in the Attic School.[9]

The statuette may well date from early in Imperial times. Reduced copies and variants of this type of sinuous athlete seem to have been popular in the Hellenistic period. Several are modelled in the gently indefinite style popular then. While this piece is more vigorously muscular, as in some Hellenistic and Roman images of Herakles, its workmanship still has a component of Hellenistic softness.

Published: Comstock and Vermeule, *Sculpture,* no. 152 with previous bibliography; J. Farmer, *Birmingham Festival of Arts 1976,* no. 4, illus.; C. Vermeule, *Greek Sculpture and Roman Taste* (Ann Arbor 1977) p. 32, fig. 31.

2. Torso of a woman bending forward (knucklebone player?) (illustrated, p. 1)
Roman, Early Imperial Period
After an Attic prototype of the early fourth century
Bought in Rome
H. L. Pierce Fund 01.8203
Height 22 cm. Pentelic marble.

The torso is a splendid reflection of the Rich Style of the late fifth and beginning of the fourth centuries. Bridget Hamanaka has pointed out that it presents an almost literal quotation of the pose and drapery of the "Sandal-binding Nike" from the balustrade of the Nike Temple on the Acropolis (about 420 B.C.). The shoulder fastening of her chiton has fallen on her arm as she bends forward and to the right. The drapery, which looks wet and transparent in the manner of the Rich Style, is simpler and flows more freely than in the "Sandal-binding Nike." The different treatment has suggested a date around 400 B.C. or a little later for the prototype of the torso.

Previously, the figure was thought to have been sitting or even leaning back to her left, but the careful finish of her back and the movement of the drapery away from her left arm conflicts with those interpretations. The composition is best explained if the girl leans slightly forward and to her right. Her lower body was draped in a mantle, the upper edge of which appears on her lower right back. Since the mantle was not supported by her arms, she must have been sitting or squatting. She may well have been crouching to play knucklebones, a subject that became popular in terracotta statuettes and on coins in the fourth century.

For the "Sandal-binding Nike," see Robertson, *History,* p. 350, p1. 117a; *idem, Shorter History,* fig. 169.

Published: Comstock and Vermeule, *Sculpture,* no. 151, with previous bibliography; B. Hamanaka in *Allentown,* no. 73.

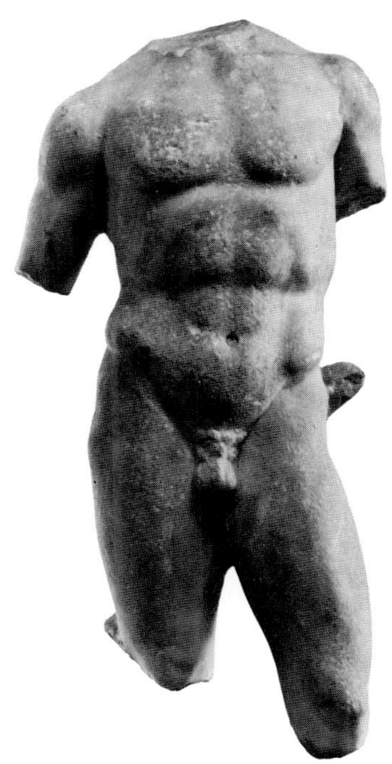

3. Head of an athlete (the "Munich Oil Pourer")
Late Hellenistic, late second or earlier first century B.C.
After a prototype of about 360 B.C.
From Athens
H. L. Pierce Fund 04.11
Height 23 cm. Pentelic marble.

6. Süsserott, p. 136f., pl. 29, 2; Hiller, *op. cit.,* fig. 11, p. 18, pl. 5
7. Bank Leu and Numismatic Fine Arts, *The Garrett Collection,* no. 843: now Museum of Fine Arts no. 1984.218. Cornelius Vermeule pointed out to me the relationship between the coin and the Naukydes athlete in its various permutations.
8. B. Brown, *Anticlassicism in Greek Sculpture of the Fourth Century B.C.* (New York 1973) pp. 8-15, 26-29, figs. 13, 26, 30
9. L. Vlad Borrelli in *EAA* 7, p. 862 (Timotheos)

Cat. 3.
Cat. 4.
Cat. 5.
Cat. 6.

This fragment comes from a type that is well known from a fairly complete statue in Munich. The youth raises his right arm to pour a liquid into his left hand. The asymmetrical pose is much like that of the cup-bearer in a votive relief in the exhibition (no. 10). This figure might also have been pouring wine for a god. His powerful physique, however, is not like that of the normal boyish cup-bearer, and he is usually reconstructed as an athlete pouring oil into his hand to anoint himself before a wrestling match. The Munich statue is also made of obvious Pentelic marble, and it is possible, but by no means certain, that the fourth century model for the copies stood in Attica. It has also been connected with the Peloponnesian tradition in the time between Polykleitos and Lysippos.

This head has been much praised for its excellent sculptural quality; it may not reflect the prototype with literal-minded accuracy, but it does display a Hellenistic freshness and fluidity of form.

Published: Comstock and Vermeule, *Sculpture*, no. 154; B. Vierneisel-Schlörb, *Glyptothek München, Katalog der Skulpturen, II: klassisches Skulpturen des 5. und 4. Jahrhunderts v. Chr.* (Munich 1979) p. 305ff.

4. Torso of a young god or mythological being
Roman Imperial Period
Inspired by a work of the mid-fourth century, perhaps by Praxiteles
Bequest of Benjamin Rowland, Jr. 1974.125
Height 74 cm. Pentelic marble.

The head was made separately and attached by a pin. The penis was carved independently. A support or strut was set into a hole in the thigh. All these signs of repair might be due to a reworking in Antiquity. A marble strut on the thigh pre-existed and was replaced by the large peg hole.

The soft adolescent anatomy and the swaying pose have justly been compared by Cornelius Vermeule to the young gods and satyrs of Praxiteles. The composition shows an additional spatial complexity since both arms reached forward and seem to have crossed in front of the torso. These "interwoven" or "spiraling" figures were rare in large-scale statuary until the time of Lysippos. His flute-playing satyr, his athlete scraping himself with a strigil and his Eros stringing a bow all have this kind of structure.

The youthful figure could well have been a young satyr or some young demigod like Ganymede. He could have been leaning on a low pier or tree trunk and pouring a libation from a pitcher into a cup or plate, like the "Phaidemos Boy" in the Vatican. The torso might also have represented Ganymede embracing the eagle of Zeus. The eagle stands beside the left thigh of Ganymede in marble groups in Naples and Florence. The Naples/Florence

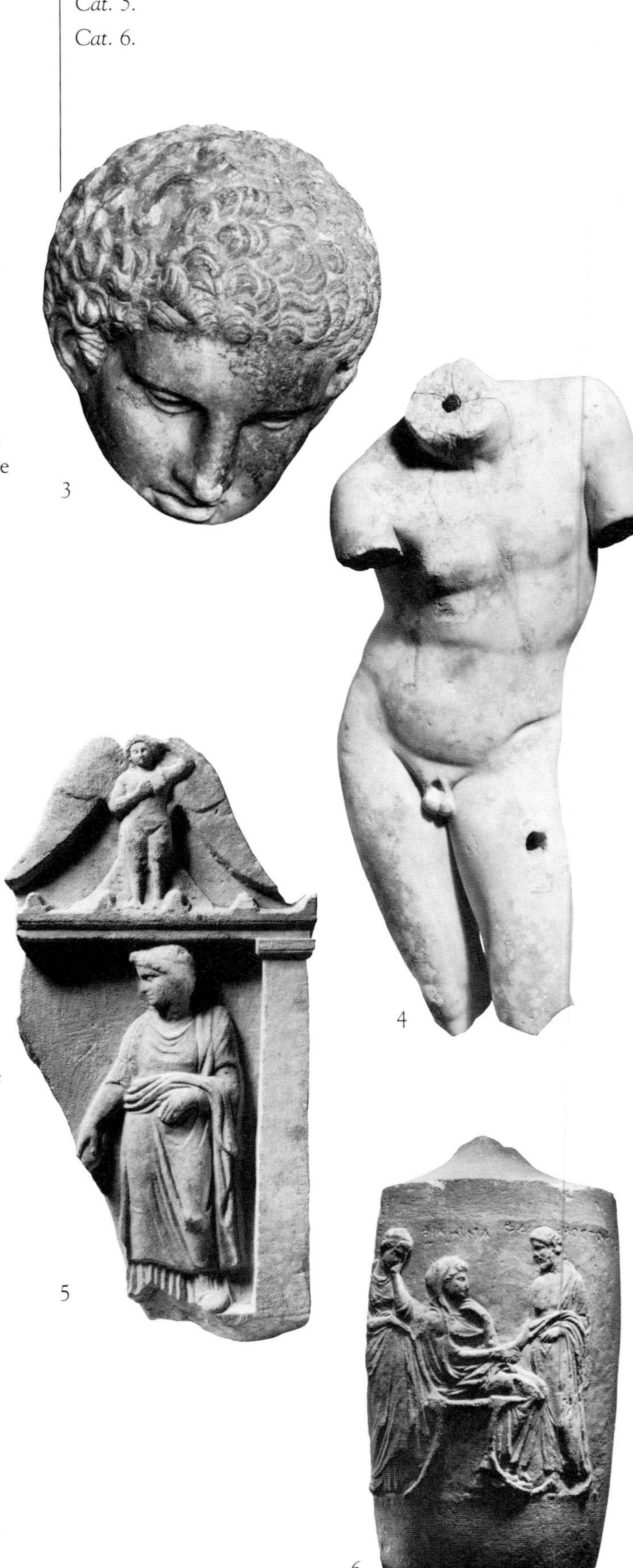
3
4
5
6

group is currently thought to be a late Hellenistic creation inspired by Praxitelean models.

For the Naples Ganymede, see W. Klein, *Praxiteles* (Leipzig 1898) p. 128ff., fig. 17; *National Museum of Naples, the Archaeological Collections* (Naples 1950) fig. 39. For the Florence example (whose right arm and shoulder are entirely restored) see G. Mansuelli, *Galleria degli Uffizi: le sculture*, I (Rome 1958) no. 111. A nude Ganymede offers the eagle a drinking horn in a small bronze group: H. Sichtermann, *Ganymed* (Berlin, n. d.) pl. 14, 2. For the Phaidemos boy, see W. Amelung, *Die Skulpturen des vaticanischen Museums*, I (Berlin 1903) pl. 5. For late fifth century renditions of Ganymede feeding the eagle, see M. Weber, *AthMitt* 91 (1976) pp. 155ff., 163ff. For the Lysippan figures, see Robertson, *History*, pl. 147.

Published: Comstock and Vermeule, *Sculpture*, no. 161.

5. Grave stele of a young lady

Around 385 B.C.
J. H. and E. A. Payne Fund 1973.169
Height 72 cm. Width 34 cm. Pentelic marble.

The woman, dressed in a chiton and himation, holds a bird in her hand. A dog or a child may have occupied the now-missing lower part of the field. The field is framed by a doric pilaster (anta) and a lintel (architrave) that is crowned by a moulding and simulated roof-tiles, whose joints are masked by antefixes. On this simulated roof stands a Siren, a creature half woman and half bird, who mourns for the deceased, pummelling her chest and head.

This modest work has a bluff, frontal composition made more complex by contrasting diagonal tugs of drapery and by a roll of drapery that divides the composition strongly at the waist. The drapery patterns repeat almost line for line those of a decree relief dated by inscription to around 387/6. The decree relief is only slightly less ungraceful, and it is very likely the two are almost contemporary.

Published: Morgan, *Brockton*, no. 13; Comstock and Vermeule, *Sculpture*, no. 67; B. Ridgway in *Allentown*, no. 78.

6. Grave marker in the form of a oil bottle (lekythos) with a couple shaking hands and a mourner

About 385-380 B.C.
Mary S. and Edward J. Holmes Fund 1972.864
Height 55.5 cm. Diameter 25 cm. Pentelic marble.
Inscribed **ΦΙΛΙΝΝΑ ΦΑ ΝΟΣΤΡΑΤΟΣ**. The neck, handle and foot of the vase are missing.

Philinna, seated in a chair (klismos) with her feet on a footstool, wears a chiton and a himation that is carried up over the crown of her head. She holds the himation in place with her left hand and shakes her husband Phanostratos's hand with her right. He is bare-chested with his lower body wrapped in a himation that continues up over his left shoulder. Behind Philinna, another woman, dressed also in chiton and himation and perhaps representing Philinna's sister or daughter, holds her head in her hand in a gesture of intense grief.

The workmanship is sketchy but intelligent. The relief is low, as usual in lekythoi. The drapery moves in graceful curves, and the figures, particularly the mourning woman at the left, have complex, shifting poses. Their lower bodies face forward while the axis of their upper bodies turns slightly to the side. A strong division at the waist marks the change of axis and divides the figure into two regions of curvilinear flow. The poses and even details of drapery patterns can be paralleled in reliefs dated by inscription to the 380s and 370s. The piece, however, seems closer to the more complex, unstable rhythms of the 380s than to the more harmonious compositions of the 370s. The drapery of the mourner is very similar to that of the woman in the preceding stele. Characteristic are the oblique line of the hem of her himation and the catenary that links the breasts. The grace and flow of the composition, however, is not simply a product of greater quality. In the mourner, the folds on the hip echo the principal lines of the composition rather than running counter to them. The drapery does not yet, however, have the easy upward movement of the famous decree relief of 375/4 (treaty with Kerkyra). The same qualities can also be seen in a beautiful lekythos in Munich that is closely related to the Kerkyra relief and that seems to represent the next step beyond this one. Even the furniture on this relief still belongs to the world of the later fifth and the earlier fourth century. The lovely, curvilinear klismos seems to drop from favor on grave monuments after around 380 B.C.

For the Munich lekythos, Süsserott, p. 112f., pl. 17, 4. For the reliefs of 387/6, 384/3 and 375/4, see Süsserott, p. 42ff., pls. 2, 4; 3, 1, 2. For other similar reliefs dated by Süsserott to the 380s, see *ibid.*, p. 110ff., pl. 17, 1-3. For the relief of 375/4, see also J. Charbonneaux, R. Martin, F. Villard, *Classical Greek Art (480-330 B.C.)* (New York 1972) fig. 239. On the fall from fashion of the klismos, see Dohrn, p. 145ff.

Published: Comstock and Vermeule, *Sculpture*, no. 74; A. Holden in *Allentown*, no. 77.

7. Two-sided votive relief dedicated to the sun and the moon

About 340 B.C.
Frederick Brown Fund 1972.78
Height 45 cm. Width 44.5 cm. Pentelic marble.

Obverse: Helios, identified by his sun-disc halo, wears the long, belted chiton of a charioteer and drives his

Cat. 7.

Cat. 7.

four-horse team. The chariot is the usual light racing vehicle with an upper railing and a pair of four-spoked wheels. The field is framed by a doric anta and an architrave topped by a moulding and a simulated roof-edge whose cover tiles have decorative terminations (akroteria). The architrave has a fragmentary inscription.

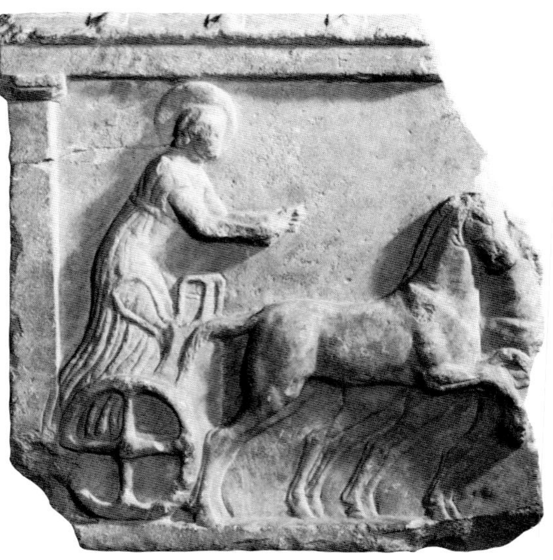

Reverse: the Asiatic moon god Men, wearing a long feminine costume, rides sidesaddle on a ram in front of a large crescent. Before him is a three-legged table filled with pyramidal and lobed cakes (*pyramides* and *omphalota popana*), clearly an offering to the god. Below the table is a rooster, Men's constant companion in Late Classical and Early Hellenistic Attic art, and a hen. A family of votaries (two men, a woman behind them and a child beside them) approaches with their right hands raised in adoration. The field is framed as on the obverse, and there are likewise traces of an inscription.

The figure of Helios is very similar to a charioteer from the Mausoleum of Halicarnassos, datable around the middle of the fourth century. Since several Athenian sculptors worked on the Mausoleum, the relationship may have been very direct.

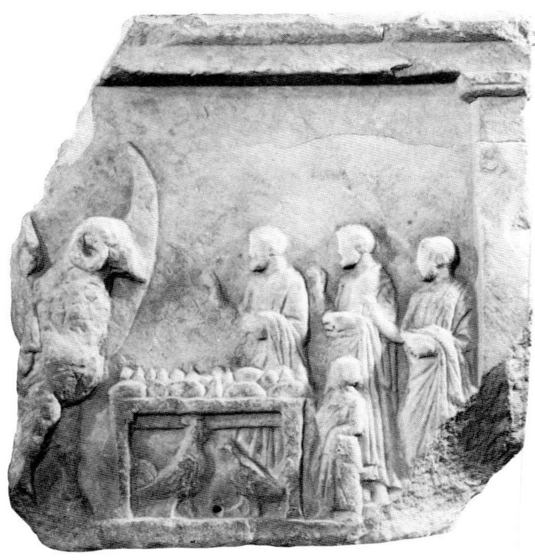

In Attica, the cult of Men was apparently practiced exclusively by foreigners. Attic sculptors, who seem to have been the first to represent the male moon god of Asia Minor, gave Men a decidedly androgynous look (evidenced here by the sidesaddle riding position), perhaps as a result of their own cultural conditioning rather than of their clients' theological specifications. The traditional moon god of Attica (and Greece in general) was female, whether Selene, Artemis or Aphrodite.

For the Mausoleum charioteer, see Robertson, *History*, p. 452, pls. 143b, 145a. On the offerings on the table, usually presented to gods or heroes of the Underworld, see R. Thönges-Stringaris, *AthMitt* 80 (1965) pp. 19, 63.

Published: Comstock and Vermeule, *Sculpture*, no. 78; E. N. Lane, *Corpus Monumentorum Religionis Dei Menis*, I, p. 1f., II, p. 171, III, pp. 1ff., 13, 38, 92, 97, note 37, 101; Vermeule, *S to S*, pp. 16, 118, 161f., figs. 19f.; D. Salzmann, *Istanbuler Mitteilungen* 30 (1980) pp. 275f.

8. Fragment of a votive relief to a hero

Second half of the fourth century
From Athens
Gift of Mr. and Mrs. William de Forest Thomson 18.436
Height 12.8 cm. Width 24.5 cm. Pentelic marble.

Within an architectural frame, a votary with raised palm salutes a hero, probably Asklepios. The bearded figure leans to his left. The mantle is draped over the left shoulder and probably cushioned the staff on which the hero leaned. The pose could well have been based on that of the Asklepios of Megara by Bryaxis, created shortly before the middle of the century (see no. 142).

Published: Comstock and Vermeule, *Sculpture*, no. 79.

9. Fragment of a votive relief to a banqueting hero or god of the Underworld

Second half of the fourth century
Presumably from Athens
Gift of Mr. and Mrs. William de Forest Thomson 19.318
Height 13.5 cm. Width 9 cm. Pentelic marble.

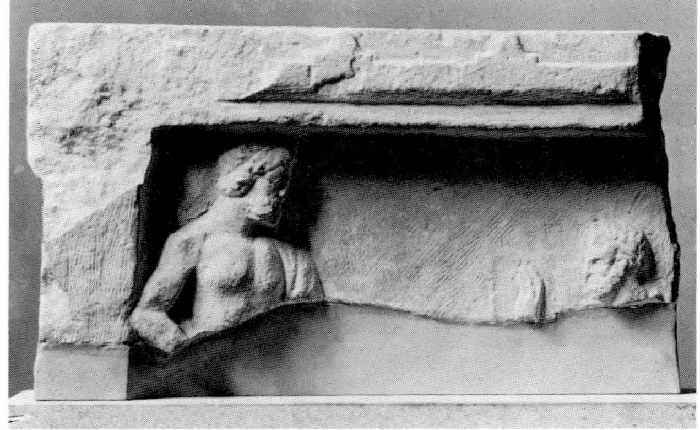

Cat. 8.

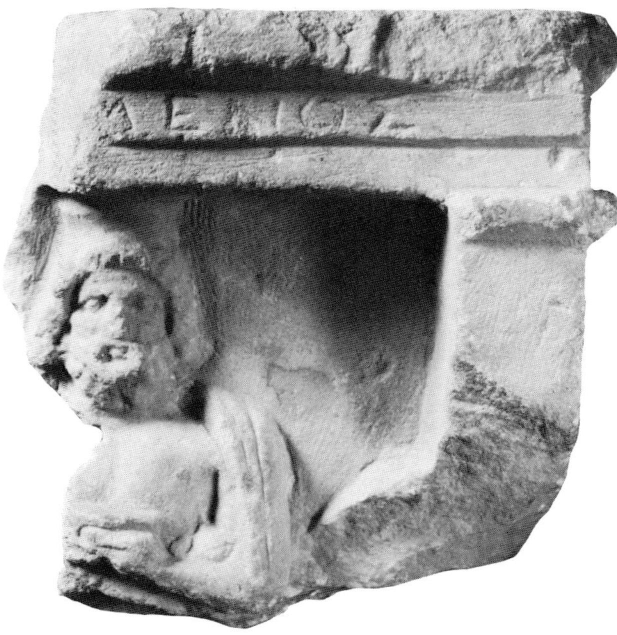

Cat. 9.

Within an architecturally framed setting is the head and chest of a bearded hero crowned with a cylindrical crown (polos), perhaps inspired by a grain measure (modius). The headdress is the attribute of Underworld divinities like Hades. The original slab would have shown him enjoying the delights of the fortunate, reclining on a couch beside a food-laden table and drinking from the cup or drinking bowl that he holds before him. He would have been accompanied by his wife, a cup-bearer and one or more other figures, usually including a votary. The inscription on the lintel, ...**ΜΕΝΟΣ**, probably is the termination of the name of the dedicant.

Compare R. Thönges-Stringaris, *AthMitt* 80 (1965) no. 87, 128, pp. 81, 86, pls. 14, 1, 15, 1.

Published: Comstock and Vermeule, *Sculpture,* no. 81.

10. Section of a votive relief to a banqueting hero or god of the Underworld

Second half of the fourth century
Presumably from Athens
Gift of Mr. and Mrs. William de Forest Thomson 19.320
Height 34.5 cm. Width 18 cm. Pentelic marble.

The relief originally showed a modius-crowned hero enjoying the delights of the Underworld as in the preceding. In this fragment, the setting is shown more fully. The youthful cup-bearer pours wine from a pitcher into a drinking bowl or cup. The supple pose reflects that of the statue known as the Munich Oil Pourer. He has filled his pitcher in the large volute krater in which the wine was mixed with water. Beside the krater appears a short stretch of the dining table, whose leg is hidden by the krater, and on it a lobed cake called an *omphaloton popanon*. The table and offerings would have closely resembled those of the Men relief.

Compare R. Thönges-Stringaris, *AthMitt* 80 (1965) no. 87, 128, pp. 81, 86, pls. 14, 1, 15, 1. For the name of the cake, see *ibid.*, p. 19, n. 73.

Published: Comstock and Vermeule, *Sculpture,* no. 82.

11. Grave stele with a girl and her maid

Around 320 B.C.
Classical Department Exchange Fund 1979.510
Height 75 cm. Width 56 cm. Pentelic marble.

The deceased girl sits on a stool with turned legs (diphros) and reaches into a jewel box held by a slave girl. Originally, another figure, of which only a shoulder is preserved, was shown in low relief on the background between the two women. The contrast in social rank between the two preserved figures is underlined by the difference in costume. The maid wears a simple chiton and her hair is held in a cloth (sakkos). The mistress wears not only a chiton, but also a himation that is draped around her legs and circles up over her left shoulder. Her hair is arranged in a melon-coiffure; it is divided into rows and pulled into a braid that circles the back of her head. The scene was originally bordered by piers (antae), of which one is preserved. The figures, however, burst this frame; the seated girl and her stool reach to the very outer limit of the marble slab.

As in many of the later Attic stelai, the principal figure, the seated girl, is shown in very high relief; her head is

Cat. 11.
Cat. 12.
Cat. 12.

worked almost completely free of the background. Such three-dimensional tableaux are common from the Age of Alexander up to the ban on pretentious funeral monuments in 317 B.C. The seated girl's costume suggests that this is among the latest stelai. Not only does she wear her belt high under the breasts, but even more important, the specific form of melon-coiffure seems to be early Hellenistic. In the Age of Alexander, braids were carried over the top of the head. Apparently only later, as here, does the braid circle the back of the head. The fashion seems to have survived well into the third century in portraits of Berenike I of Egypt (died in the 270s). After the beginning of the third century, the loop of the braid becomes smaller and lower until it is essentially a bun placed at the neck.

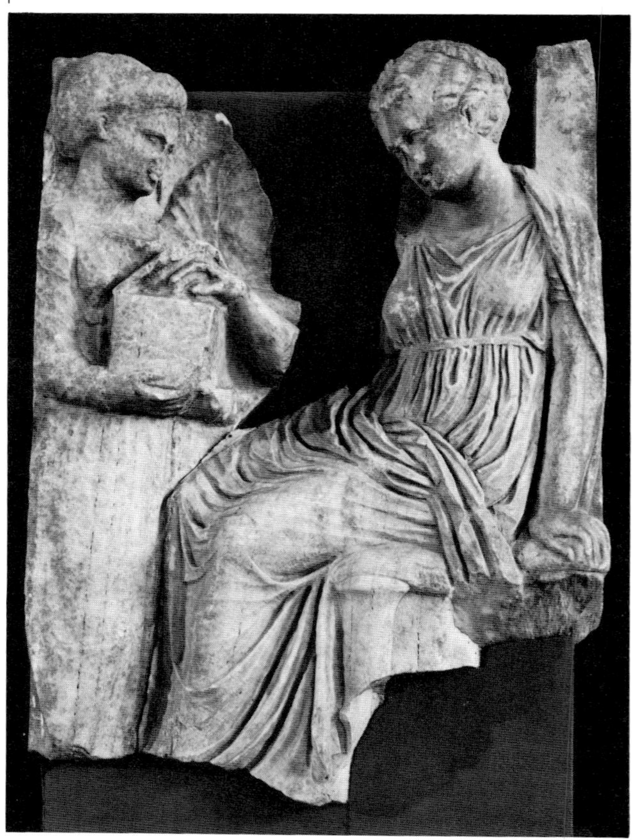

The early form of melon-coiffure appears on the base for a statue by Praxiteles at Mantinea: Robertson, *Shorter History,* fig. 197. For an intaglio in Oxford generally recognized as Berenike I wearing a melon-coiffure, see Richter, no. 627; Boardman, p. 362, pl. 1009; Boardman and Vollenweider, no. 282. For the late form of the melon-coiffure (with bun), see Artemis on a coin of Pyrrhus of Epirus of 278-276 B.C.: P. Franke and M. Hirmer, *Die Griechische Münze* (Munich 1964) p. 105, pl. 151. The fashion also appears on coins of Arsinoë II of Egypt at about the same time (285-246 B.C.): *ibid.*, p. 165, pl. 219; Brett, nos. 2267ff

Published: *The Ernest Brummer Collection* 2 (Zurich 1979) p. 206f., no. 615; Vermeule, *America,* no. 87.

12. Head of a god, probably Asklepios

Late fourth century
Greek, possibly Athenian
Loan, from the collections of Alfred E. Hamill, Ernest A. Hamill; previously, Haviland collection
Height 16.5 cm. Greek island marble, probably Parian.

The head is complete but only sketchily worked behind. It was evidently intended to be seen from the front and was more likely broken from a small votive statue than a grave relief. The conception of the head, with the locks of the beard separated by drill channels, goes back to a votive relief to Asklepios at Epidauros often ascribed to Timotheos. The softer more expressive treatment here, however, suggests a later, post-Praxitelean date. The finest heads from the latest phase of Attic funerary monuments around 320 B.C., like the head of a woman in New York, show a similar, gently amorphous handling.

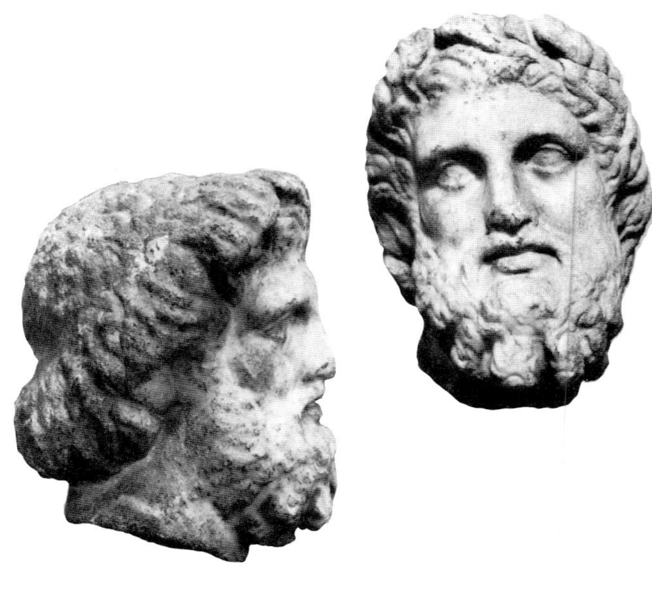

Compare the girl from the Walter Baker Collection in the Metropolitan: Vermeule, *America,* no. 95.

Cats. 14, 13.

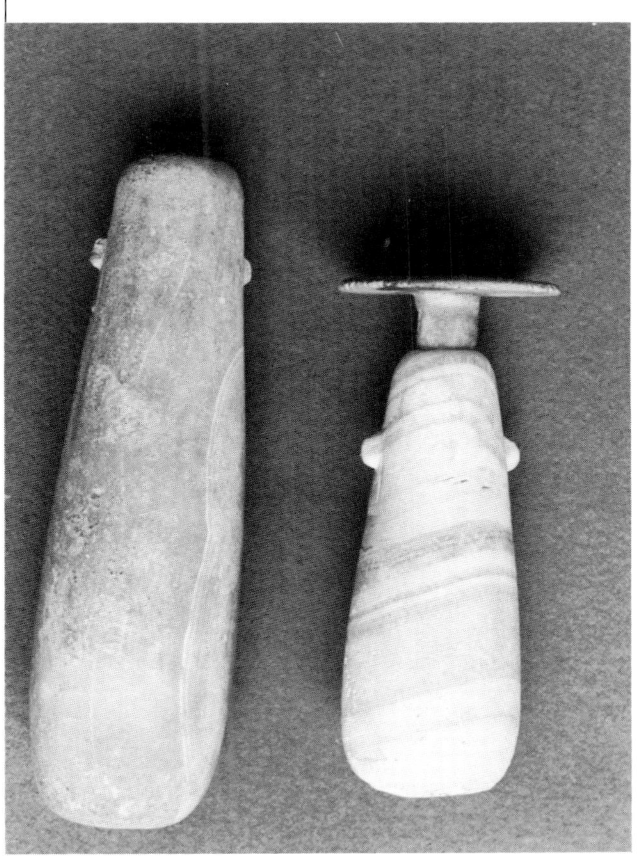

Alabaster Vases: Alabastra

White or yellowish-white stone vases with pronounced veins or banding are frequently found in Greek tombs of the fifth and fourth centuries. The stone is termed alabaster by archaeologists, but it might more properly be called calcite. Vases of this stone were traditionally made in the shape called alabastron (after the material), an elongated oil bottle with lugs on the side, a short neck and a wide, flat rim. Neck and rim were often made separately. These alabastra were almost certainly imported, filled with some perfumed oil, from Egypt. Alabastra were manufactured at Naukratis in the Nile Delta, where corings have been found in large quantities in a mid-fifth century layer.[1]

Several Egyptian alabastra in the Museum of Fine Arts almost certainly stem from graves on the northern shores of the Mediterranean. Their Egyptian origin can easily be checked by comparison with the many alabastra excavated by museum expeditions to Egypt and the Sudan.[2] Their findspots are unknown, but it can be deduced with a fair degree of probability that they were discovered in Classical lands. They were donated to the Museum in the 19th century in collections filled with Greek and Italian material but without any other apparent Egyptian products. The Museum of Fine Arts alabastra therefore provide new evidence that the trade in minor vases between Athens and Egypt was not a one-way street. The ships heading south with the various small red-figure and black glaze vases excavated at Naukratis could have returned north carrying calcite oil bottles for the tombs of Attica.

The shapes of alabastra vary widely and follow no well-understood pattern. The examples in the exhibition are perfectly compatible with fourth century dates. The fourth century Tomb III at Odos Kassandras in Athens contained a range of alabastra with varied body shapes much like the two included here.[3] The wide, hat-like rim already appears in the fifth century.[4] A fourth century tomb on Paros, however, produced an alabastron with the same type of upper termination.[5]

1. F. Petrie, *Naukratis*, I (London 1886) p. 15; J. Boardman, *The Greeks Overseas* (London 1980) p. 142f. On the diffusion of Egyptian alabastra in Greece and Italy, see also D. A. Amyx, *Hesperia* 27 (1958) p. 214.
2. I owe the identification of the material to Peter Lacovara.
3. P. Kapetanakis, *Athens Annals of Archaeology* 6 (1973) p. 279f., fig. 7
4. Compare C. Boulter, *Hesperia* 32 (1963) p. 125f., pl. 45; B. Schlörb-Vierneisel, *AthMitt* 81 (1966) p. 38, pl. 30, 4.
5. E. Baroucha, *ArchEph* (1925-26) p. 114, fig. 1

13. Alabastron of Egyptian alabaster

Fifth or early fourth century
Egyptian
Gift of H. P. Kidder 80.615, 80.619
Height of body 12.7 cm. Diameter of body 5.1 cm.
Diameter of neck 1.7 cm. Diameter of rim 6.1 cm.

The mouth, which was made separately, fits well into the body. A ridge on the neck is perfectly aligned with the upper edge of the body. The piece is strikingly similar to an alabastron from the tomb on Paros.

14. Alabastron of Egyptian alabaster

Fifth or fourth century
Egyptian
Gift of B. W. Crowninshield 81.193
Height 18.8 cm. Diameter 6 cm.

The mouth, which was made separately, is missing.

Red-figure Vases:

Fourth century Attic vase painting stands in a dubious critical position. It has the misfortune to follow two centuries of awesome achievement. In the fourth century, major personalities are much rarer, and the average level of craftsmanship is more careless than in earlier times. During the century, Attica even lost one of its most important vase markets: South Italy. In the course of the Peloponnesian War, Athenian potters and painters had migrated to Italy's southern coast, and eventually the shops they founded took over the local market. Quite characteristically, most of the red-figure vases in this exhibition that have Italian proveniences date from early in the century, before local production had become completely dominant. The fourth century even has the unenviable distinction of witnessing the end of vase painting in Athens; the craft seems to have died out in the last years of the century. Symptoms of retrenchment can be noted from its beginning, as category after category of vase disappeared. The twisted-handle amphora by the Suessula Painter (no. 15) is one of the last of its kind. The traditional kylix is continued by the Jena Painter and his followers hardly longer than the middle of the century.

The causes of the decline of red-figure vase painting are numerous. The changed situation appears shortly after the end of the Peloponnesian War in 404 B.C. It seems very likely that the potters' quarter was involved in the same crisis of confidence that affected Athenian political and intellectual life generally after the military defeat.[1] There are many signs that vase painting began to imitate other, evidently more prestigious art forms, specifically wall painting and metalwork, by introducing new and somewhat alien techiques. Apparently, vase painting suited the temper of the times less than it had in previous centuries, and painters passed much of the later Classical period devising stratagems to make vases appear other than they were.

In spite of these obstacles, important vase painters did emerge during the course of the fourth century, and several major styles succeeded one another. While to some extent the craft of vase painting had its own development, in other respects (and in a positive sense) it reflected major trends in other arts like sculpture. Although hardly any large-scale wall or panel painting survives, it seems very likely that red-figure vases also had strong links to the work of famous contemporary painters.

The first quarter of the century represents the final phase of the Rich Style, which can be traced in all branches of Greek art from about 425 to 375 B.C., but the early fourth century established its own character so strongly that it has been subtitled the Ornate Style.[2] The Boston collection is particularly strong in works of this phase, and included among them are several datable works that are important for anchoring the chronology of the period. The Suessula Painter is known to have been working at the end of the fifth century, since a fragment of one of his vases was found in the filling of a burial of Spartans in Athens in 403 B.C.[3] The Pronomos Painter must have been active around 393 B.C.[4] Most important here is the group of vase fragments from the memorial to Dexileos,

fig. 3. Funerary monument for Dexileos and his family in the Kerameikos, 394-3 B.C. Reconstruction by H. Kinch. From A. Brueckner, Der Friedhof am Eridanos *(Berlin 1909) fig. 34.*

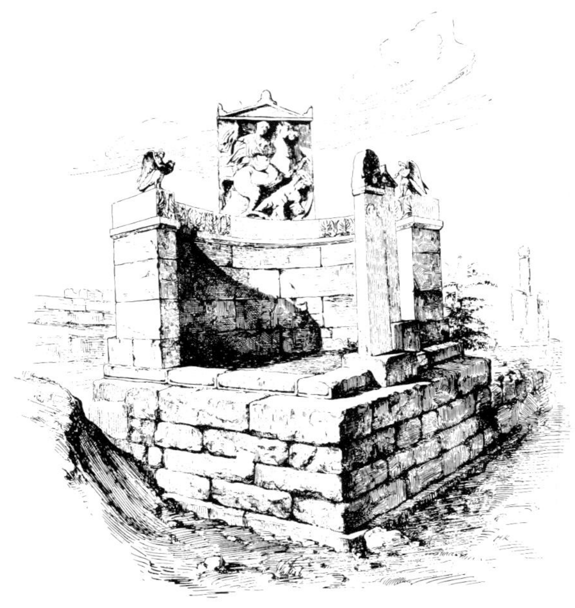

who died in the Corinthian War of 394-3. Interpretation of this find has, however, varied considerably. Initially, it was assumed that the vases were long-treasured possessions, and there is a tradition of dating them around 400 B.C.[5] Emily Vermeule has justly argued, on the other hand, that it is most likely that they were acquired no earlier than the time when the monument was built.[6] Even though many members of Dexileos's family were buried in the monument over a period of several decades, the general similarity

1. On this topic in general, see E. Lévy, *Athènes devant la défaite de 404* (Paris 1976).
2. G. Richter, *Red-figured Athenian Vases in the Metropolitan Museum of Art* (New Haven 1936) p. 207f.
3. *AA* 1937, col. 193-5, fig. 13, 3; Beazley, *ARV*, p. 852f.
4. The name Pronomos was inscribed on one of his vases. It must refer to a popular flute player who is known from a reference by Aristophanes in his *Ecclesiazousai* of 393 B.C. and from an inscription of 384/3: Hahland, p. 6.
5. van Hoorn, *Choes*, nos. 371, 372, 373, 379, 380; Robertson, *History*, p. 420f.
6. *JdI* 85 (1970) pp. 94-111. Hahland had also come to essentially the same conclusion, p. 6f.

of the various pitchers found there led scholars to consider them more or less contemporary. Only Schefold has suggested that at least one of the vases was painted in the decade after the death of Dexileos.[7] It seems to this writer that the differences in the pitcher fragments not only correspond to the hands of different artists but that they also reflect different dates ranging down to about 375 B.C.

In general, the Ornate Style of vase painting in the early fourth century is characterized by gaudy effects of polychromy and pattern. The practice had already been established in the late fifth century, when vase painters had begun to make extensive use of white paint, dilute glaze, "added clay" and gilding. White, which was applied in thick layers after the background had been glazed, was employed for flesh and various details like flowers or jewelry. Dilute glaze both added a yellowish brown tonality to the rich polychromy and also offered a medium in which a brush could create tonal modulation. It should be noted that these techniques had also been much used in the Archaic period and to a limited degree thereafter,[8] but in these previous experiences the techniques had contributed to linear description. In the later phases of the Rich Style, polychromy and relief were employed with much greater breadth and profuseness. Clay was applied over the surface like cake frosting in thin lines and dots, not just to articulate certain details but also to create broad areas of sculptural modulation on the surface (particularly for wings). These areas of relief were frequently gilded (an apparent novelty of the Rich Style), making the vase quite literally metallic. Terracotta vases thereby became precious sculptural objects comparable to silver vessels, which frequently in this period also made use of gilding. Patterned garments were another feature of this style, and boldly painted rows of crennellations or bands of wave pattern gave weight and emphasis to the figures. All these enrichments tended to break down the consistency of the drawing, but they created startling, eye-catching and occasionally almost magical effects. In some respects these devices are almost comparable to Byzantine icons with gilded or silvered backgrounds or overlays. Even today, the impulse resurfaces in photographic postcards with silvered or embroidered figures, where the inconsistencies give a relic-like preciousness to central features.

These occasionally gaudy enrichments also could serve a more serious purpose. The variety of colors made it possible to rival the effects of painting on walls or panels. Figures were frequently conceived in terms of broad, colorful silhouettes (as in nos. 16, 22) rather than in terms of sharp linear detail. Dilute glaze applied with a brush could be modulated very much as in the brushwork of a conventional painting. Modulated brushwork is much in evidence in the work of the Suessula Painter and the followers of the Pronomos Painter (nos. 15, 18). Even gilding conforms to representational and illusionistic rules. It is used for objects that were in reality golden, above all jewelry, which can at times include golden wreaths. The wings of Eros, frequently gilded in vase painting, were gold-colored according to Euripides.[9]

The imitation of tonal painting is also evident in the frequent efforts to create a landscape setting. Figures are spotted around at various levels as if on a rocky hillside, and some figures are even truncated by these largely invisible natural protuberances. Bushes, flowers and parts of buildings are strewn about rather arbitrarily to provide some non-human components of a visual field.

In the late fifth century, large-scale painting had emerged into a new prominence, and evidently tonal values came to predominate over linear description. Plato complained about the illusionistic trickery of Apollodoros, an Athenian painter famous for his "shadow painting."[10] Skillful brushwork, an essential means to these illusionistic ends, was made much of.[11] The free brushstrokes of dilute glaze on the shields of the Suessula Painter must be an effort to rival these controversial new techniques. The limitations of vase painting are such, however, that no truly consistent chiaroscuro could be created. The potters were fated to reinterpret the new illusionism in decorative and symbolic terms, and consequently, their craft was condemned to a second class status. From that time on, much vase painting took on the role of a backward folk art in the larger setting of Athenian creativity.

Many vase painters, however, continued to exhibit great resourcefulness and continued to follow the fashions of other major art forms with great facility. The innovations of large-scale sculpture, particularly relief sculpture, were eagerly reflected in the potters' quarter. Contrapposto, the rhythmic arrangement of weight-bearing and relaxed limbs, becomes almost as evident in figures on vases as it does in marble sculpture. War monuments supplied compositions to the Suessula Painter. The Nike Temple on the Acropolis seems to have had an especially pervasive influence. The crouching, willowy figures of the temple's friezes were echoed again and again. Gracefully undulating gestures used with restraint in the Nike Temple parapet become a hallmark of vase painting. Spectacular compositional units from the parapet, like the Nike sacrificing a bull, were made the centerpiece of vases like the

7. Schefold, *UKV,* p. 158

8. Robertson, *History,* p. 421

9. *Iphigenaia in Aulis,* 549; *Hippolytos,* 1270: cited in Trumpf-Lyritzaki, p. 129, note 166. According to Schefold, gold and white were connected with the ideal world of the gods, and this symbolic significance had much to do with their increased use; see J. Bibauw (editor), *Hommages à Marcel Renard,* 3 (Brussels 1969) p. 511f.

10. Plato: Schefold, *KV,* p. 8; Robertson, *History,* p. 411

11. Pliny states that Zeuxis, who worked at the beginning of the fourth century, "led forward the already not unadventurous paintbrush...to great glory" (xxv, 60f.) (Rackham translation): Robertson, *History,* pp. 411, 485.

lekythos, no. 22. Even major glyptic works from distant cities may have had their influence; the magnificent coinage of Syracuse may well have been the ultimate source for the chariot scenes of early fourth century vase painting.

Most of these observations apply as well to the great vase painters of the late fifth century, headed by the Meidias Painter and the Dinos Painter, as they do to the painters of the Ornate Style in the period following the Peloponnesian War (404-ca. 375 B.C.). The Ornate Style, however, usually distinguishes itself by the effort to attain a new volume and solidity. The attenuated elegance of many late fifth century painters (particularly the Meidias Painter and his circle) was generally given up. Figures stand erect or are aligned in symmetrical compositions of superimposed rows or circular constellations. Often figures are compact and massive. This is particularly true in the work of the Pronomos Painter and his circle (as in the fragment with the goddess on a lion, no. 18, or in less closely related works like the bell krater by the Painter of London F90, no. 19). Bold, simple silhouettes become popular, and female figures are often defined in terms of oval shapes that terminate in a skirt ballooning in a bell-like outline. Linear pattern becomes less elegant; line is scratchy, broken and less geometric. The outer contour of figures undulates subtly as it is defined by brushwork that fills in the background. The rejection of geometric perfection may well be related to a new fascination with the world of illusion. Nature is random and irregular, and geometry exists only in the ideal world prized greatly by logicians and philosophers of the period. The prestige of brushwork and tonal modulation may even be reflected in the way backgrounds are only loosely brushed in in vases like the krater with the veneration of Herakles (no. 20).

Different stylistic currents coexisted within this broad framework. The simple style descended from the work of the Dinos Painter can be followed from the rather light-weight work of the Suessula Painter to the more massive figures created by the followers of the Pronomos Painter or the followers of the Meleager Painter (the Painter of London F90). Angular poses and gestures are common in this group. The "simple current" also included workshops like the "Fat Boy" group that produced quite crudely painted vases probably intended for export markets. In many vases of this current, like the palaestra scenes on the kylix, no. 21, poses are easy and natural, and drapery falls loosely and allows basic volumes to emerge.

In evolving fashion, the more consciously elegant current descended from the Meidias Painter also continued. The Painter of the Athens Wedding imitated the Meidias Painter quite closely, but made use of more stable, static compositions. The lekythos with Aphrodite and Anchises was related to the late fifth century master but made use of simpler, more colorful volumes. This style, too, may be related to the work of painters of walls and panels. According to the Roman writer Quintillian, Parrhasios of Ephesos, active at Athens in the late fifth century, did not follow the new fashion for defining forms in terms of light and shadow, but rather "examined lines more subtly." Martin Robertson has suggested that Parrhasios may have had a position comparable to that of Botticelli around 1500 A.D.[12] The elegant contours of figures on the vases just mentioned, the graceful poses and the flowing linear patterns of drapery (in the Painter of the Athens Wedding in any case) all have something in common with the work of the Italian Renaissance master. Even the very delicate, languid characterizations are not un-Botticellian.

In changing terms throughout the first quarter of the fourth century, these delicate figures, perhaps to be described as the "Meidian" or "Parrhasian" ideal, remained pervasive. Boys in early adolescence with slender physiques and pinched facial features reappear constantly. At times, this type, which was probably intended to evoke the sweetness and innocence of well-brought-up youth, was misapplied to mature heroes like Herakles, as in the kraters, nos. 17, 20. In later vases of this elegant current, the slender figures in sinuous poses establish a weightless, curvilinear pattern across the surface of the vase that is again quite Botticellian. Smaller vases, like the Nike lekythos or the chariot race pitcher, represent this phase of the Ornate Style.

In the 370s, a distinctly new style emerged in the potters' quarter at Athens. It is called the "Kerch Style" from the fact that enormous quantities of such vases, including the finest pieces, have been found in the Graeco-Scythian areas on the northern shores of the Black Sea. Easier, more graceful rhythms came to dominate as vase painters developed a new, curvilinear fluency. Volumes are very expertly suggested. When broken lines are used they do not have the harsh angularity that they had had early in the century. Fan-like patterns of line model form more discreetly. The effort to rival landscape painting is given up, and architectural props, vegetation and truncated figures recede in importance. This fuller yet graceful style has been connected with the reforms of the painter Pamphilos, who reasserted the value of good drawing and geometry in ways that were to form the backbone of the succeeding Classical tradition.[13]

The first phase of the Kerch Style, represented by the Painter of the Oinochoes (no. 24), differs only subtly from some examples of the Ornate Style. The easy movements and softer draperies of such a vase are only a step

12. For a discussion of the evidence for Parrhasios, see Robertson, *History*, p. 412f.

13. Schefold, *KV*, p. 8. On this painter, see also Robertson, *History*, p. 484f. On the Kerch style, *ibid.*, p. 436

beyond the slightly contrived figures of the kylix with the palaestra scene. The Jena Painter and his circle, from which the kylix stems, is in fact thought to have had a major role in the formation of the new style.[14] However, in a mature Kerch Style work like the hydria, no. 25, forms are softer, more volumetric and more delicately handled.

In the last phase of the Kerch Style during the Age of Alexander, technique changes once again. Forms are modelled with short, choppy lines, and artificially arranged curvilinear fold patterns are avoided. Artists succeed in creating illusionistic effects with purely graphic means. In the krater with the apotheosis of Herakles, a dashing spray of lines effectively indicates the strains of muscles, the pulls of drapery and the semi-transparent effects of bodily hair and sideburns. These techniques surely reflect a new translation of painterly illusionism into the graphic medium of vase painting. The influence of Alexander's court painters is evident in the use of figures seen from behind, a device that gained Apelles considerable renown.[15]

Even the figure types show a new conception. The fragile youths and maidens of the beginning of the century are replaced by beefy muscle men and robust females. How much this reflects the work of Macedonian court painters may be inferred from the central unit of our late krater, no. 26. The weighty seated Athena is very similar to the same figure on tetradrachms of Lysimachus (nos. 121, 122). Some of these ideas probably originated in Athens itself. The Athenian painter and sculptor Euphranor, active in the Age of Alexander, contrasted his work with that of earlier times in just this way. For him the heroes painted by Parrhasios looked as though they had been fed on roses. His own heroes dined on beef.[16] The contrast between the treatment of Herakles on the kraters in the exhibition (nos. 17, 20 and no. 26) could hardly be summed up more succinctly.

Ornament plays a not insignificant role in fourth century vase painting. As in the fifth century, ornamental bands circle the vase like architectural mouldings and form ground lines for the pictures. Complex compositions of palmettes and scrolls fill in irregular areas around handles. In the course of the fourth century, these traditional forms pass from being elegantly slender to being full and fleshy. Eventually in the Kerch Style, the decorative forms swell to eliminate background areas almost completely. These densely packed masses of palmettes and scrolls have been called the "Tapestry Style."[17] This highly patterned treatment of the classical repertory of form is not paralleled in architectural sculpture or in mosaic pavements of the fourth century, indicating how, in many respects, the traditions of vase painting were quite independent from those of other arts and crafts.

The subject matter of red-figure pottery is one of its most interesting and characteristic features. To some extent the subjects are dictated by the traditions and the usage of individual vase types. Scenes from Athenian festivals like horse races or happy processions are at home on pitchers of the form called the chous. This kind of pitcher was prominently connected with the wine drinking in the great pan-Hellenic spring festival named Anthesteria. One day of the festival was even called "Choes" after the pitchers. Wine cups (kylikes) were traditionally decorated with athletic scenes. The hydria was a water jar used by women, and it is natural that a goddess should be the central figure: here Ariadne. Kraters, used to hold the wine at a symposium, naturally featured Dionysos, the god of wine. Tales of Herakles were also a long-standing tradition on such pots.

The intended markets may also have had a certain influence on the selection of subject matter. The legend of the griffins and Arimasps had the far north as its setting. The tale gained great popularity at just the time the northeast corner of the Black Sea became the primary destination for figure-decorated Attic pottery. Somewhat surprisingly, the Argonauts, the first voyagers to the Black Sea, are not popular, but one vase here (no. 15), showing a battle with rock-throwing warriors, is apparently connected with their saga.

The selection of mythological tales, however, also reflects a changed outlook within Greek culture, and the way these tales are presented is equally characteristic. Herakles is rarely shown as the muscular adversary of improbable monsters. Instead, moments from his saga are chosen that present him as the mortal who attains the delights of eternal life. He arrives at the far-off and idyllic land of the Hesperides, which was thought of as a kind of terrestrial abode of blessed souls. He is introduced into Olympos and is venerated as he enjoys the delights of the gods. Ariadne is also popular as a mortal who after adversity attains divinity. Here she is shown as the happy spouse of Dionysos and a formidable goddess riding on a lion (if a recent interpretation is correct). Of these scenes, only the apotheosis of Herakles had been popular previously, and the focus of the earlier versions of the story had been the physical transit: the departure in a chariot or the arrival accompanied by a cortege. In the fourth century, enjoyments of the delights of paradise and paradisiacal repose form the focus of attention. It has been suggested that this new area of concentration reflects a more wide-spread belief that these delights were open to all men who had struggled and suffered.[18]

14. Schefold, *KV*, pp. 7, 9
15. See cat. no. 26. On Apelles, see Robertson, *History*, p. 492ff.
16. Pliny, *Natural History*, 35, 129; Plutarch, *Moralia*, IV, 346A; O. Palagia, *Euphranor* (Leiden 1980) p. 57; Robertson, *History*, pp. 412, 434
17. P. Jacobsthal, *Ornamente griechischer Vasen* (Berlin 1927) p. 203f.
18. Metzger, *Représentations*, p. 230

Cat. 15.

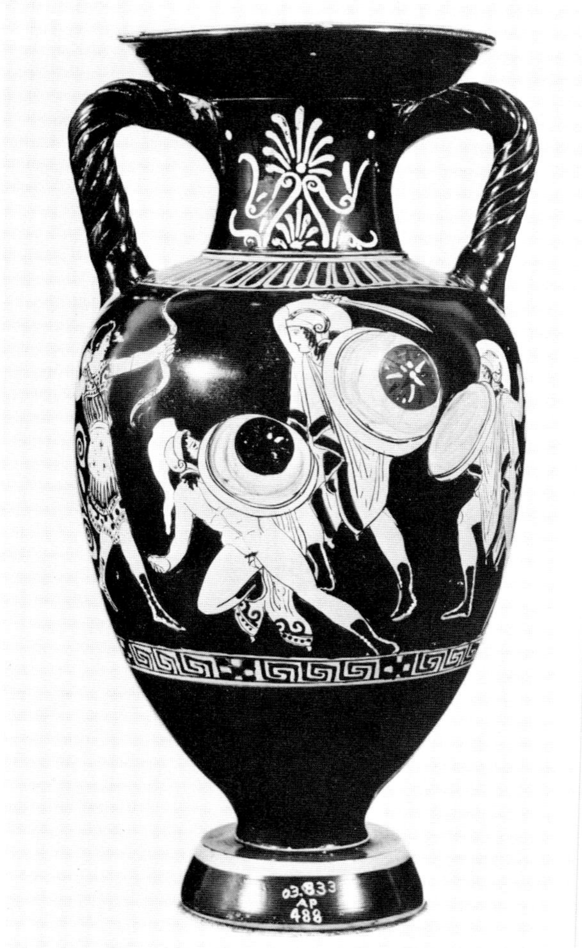

Dionysos, a god who suffered, has a pervasive influence. Not only is he a frequent subject, but his retinue of satyrs, silenoi, maenads and nymphs is introduced into scenes where Dionysos himself does not properly belong. His thiasos becomes the very personification of the delights of paradise. His invincible power is celebrated, as in the *Bacchai* of Euripides, produced in 406 B.C.[19]

Eros is another figure who is almost emblematic of the century. Rarely had he appeared until late in the fifth century, when he becomes the almost inseparable companion of his mother Aphrodite. He often appears alone and at times almost seems to replace her. The theme of love and a company of Erotes, probably standing for Eros (love), Pothos (longing) and Himeros (desire), invade Herakles's exploit in the land of the Hesperides, and they become the companions of the adolescent Dionysos. The situation seems to reflect the new attention to Eros in Socratic discussions reflected and recorded in the *Symposium* or *Phaidros* of Plato.[20]

The focus of traditional myths was redirected by the addition of these secondary figures, who take on an almost symbolic role. An allegorizing approach is pervasive, even in scenes that purport to deal with everyday life. Nike is used again and again to underline the meaning of a scene and to transfer the proceedings onto a higher level of existence. She accompanies not only Herakles on his entrance into Olympos but also a victorious charioteer in an annually-recurring race. She becomes the principal actress in a sacrifice of a bull to Aphrodite, presumably after a historical military exploit.

15. Jar with twisted vertical handles (amphora)

Front: battle with stone-throwing warriors, perhaps the Argonauts fighting the giants of Cyzicus
Back: Dionysiac revel (maenad and satyr)
Attributed to the Suessula Painter, about 400 B.C.
Found at Suessula in South Italy
Francis Bartlett Fund 03.833
Height 35 cm. Added white: stars on shields, crests of two helmets and plumes, sandals, palmettes on neck; on the reverse: leaves in maenad's hair and fruit on tray. Dilute glaze: modelling of shields.

Three of the warriors engaged in this skirmish are nude except for cloaks. Their defensive armor consists of an Attic helmet and a shield. The fourth is an archer wearing an elaborately patterned short tunic (chitoniskos) and a traveller's hat (petasos) slung over his shoulders. All wear boots. Only one of the nude warriors wields a sword; the other two are reduced to the seemingly desperate expedient of throwing rocks.

That both a defeated and an attacking warrior throw rocks suggests that their swords have not merely been dropped or broken in the course of the battle. They are probably a different quality or race from those with more sophisticated weapons. Giants, the primitive and animalistic adversaries of the Olympian gods, can be armed with helmet, shield and stones exactly as these warriors are. The archer and the swordsman here do not, however, seem to be gods; they are probably mortal Greeks. They could well be the Argonauts, who battled giants who inhabited the area around Cyzicus on the Propontis. The giants attacked with rocks and were repelled by the more sophisticated weapons of the Argonauts.

The central pair of figures, one lunging forward and the other fallen backward, is extraordinarily similar to the two warriors on the roughly contemporary grave relief of Stratokles in the Museum of Fine Arts. Not only are the poses similar, but the figures overlap and fuse into a single

19. On this relationship, see Metzger, *Représentations*, p. 404; Schefold, *Göttersage*, p. 335.
20. Metzger, *Représentations*, p. 371; Schefold, *Göttersage*, p. 196

unit in the same way. The grouping goes back even earlier to the Athenian relief of 430-425 B.C. in the Albani collection in Rome, which probably was an official state memorial to Athenian war dead. On the vase, however, the action is expanded beyond the central duel by adding a supporting figure at either side.

On the Stratokles relief, see Comstock and Vermeule, *Sculpture*, no. 64. On the Albani relief, see Ridgway, *Fifth Century*, pp. 144-5, figs. 104-5. For giants fitted out exactly like the stone-throwers on this vase, see the masterpiece of the Suessula Painter in the Louvre: Robertson, *Shorter History*, fig. 147; E. Pfuhl, *Malerei und Zeichnung der Griechen* (Munich 1923) fig. 584. For the fight between the Argonauts and the giants, see Apollonios of Rhodes, *The Voyage of Argo* I, 989ff.

Published: Beazley, *ARV*, p. 852, no. 3; *idem*, *ARV*[2], p. 1344, no. 4; L. Caskey and J. Beazley, *Attic Vase Paintings in the Museum of Fine Arts, Boston* III (Boston 1963) no. 173, p. 87ff., suppl. pl. 28; Beazley, *Paralipomena*, p. 482, no. 4; G. Bakalakis, *Antike Kunst* 14 (1971) p. 76, note 15.

16. Ovoid, one-handled oil bottle (squat lekythos)

Aphrodite and Anchises watched by Eros
About 400 B.C.
Found in a grave in the northwestern part of the Peloponnesos
Gift of E. P. Warren 95.1403
Height 13.4 cm. Added white: flesh of Aphrodite and Eros. Dilute glaze: details of Anchises's body. Added clay: Anchises's belt and ornaments on his cap, Aphrodite's bracelet, necklace, earrings, hair ornaments, Eros's wings, bush, bases of palmettes on rear of vase, berries in wreath above figure zone. Traces of gilding on the berries.

The painter seems intent on capturing the mood of an amorous moment. The two lovers exchange sultry glances while Eros voyeuristically parts the branches of a bush to spy on them. The lower part of Aphrodite's body is wrapped in a mantle. The Trojan prince Anchises holds two hunting spears and wears oriental costume: a Phrygian cap, a short tunic (chitoniskos), trousers, boots and a cloak.

Underneath the handle is an ornamental composition of palmettes and vine scrolls that recalls a roof ornament (akroterion). Two palmettes are mounted above one another. Stylized vines frame the lower and support the upper palmette before they undulate off to each side.

The grave in which the lekythos was found also contained an acorn lekythos in the manner of the Meidias Painter (MFA 95.1402) and two magnificent gold pins (MFA 96.717-18). The funnel-shaped, even slightly concave mouth of this vase is a later form than the full, convex mouth of the acorn lekythos.

Cat. 16.
Cat. 16.
Cat. 16.

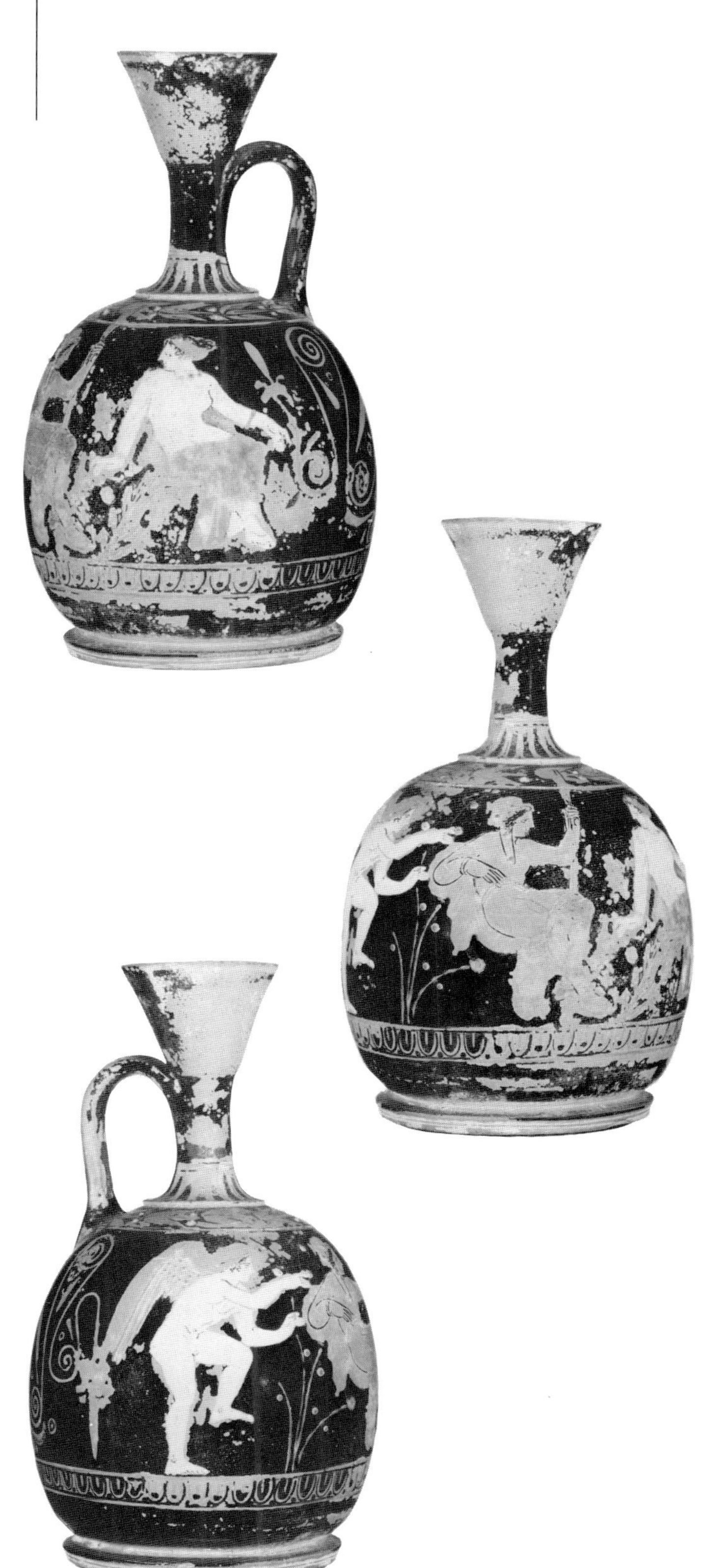

For the find, see *Annual Report* 20 (1895) p. 22, nos. 47, 48; 1896, p. 31, no. 1. Another lekythos mistakenly takes its place in succeeding discussions of the find: P. Jacobsthal, *Greek Pins* (Oxford 1956) p. 71; L. Caskey and J. Beazley, *Attic Vase Paintings in the Museum of Fine Arts, Boston* III, p. 79. For the date, see Metzger, *Représentations*, p. 20, n. 4 (citing an opinion of Beazley). Metzger considers the hero Adonis, who, however, is usually shown nude. As was already noted when the vase was first mentioned in 1895, Aphrodite's lover in oriental costume probably is the Trojan prince; see also Schefold, *Göttersage*, p. 287f., figs. 410-12.

17. Fragmentary bell-shaped mixing bowl (bell krater)

Fruit-gathering: probably Herakles in the Garden of the Hesperides
Attributed to the Painter of the Athens Wedding, about 400 B.C.
Catharine Page Perkins Fund 95.26
Height 35 cm. Diameter 35.6 cm. Added white: fruit, jewelry; strokes of white added carelessly to the wreaths.

The scene has the character of an amorous outing in the countryside. A party of young men and women surrounds a leafless tree, whose branches are loaded with globular fruit. Small bits of foliage spring up from the ground to complete the rural setting. A seated youth pulls down a branch, and an Eros shakes the tree's trunk. Another Eros with fruit in his hand flies up to a branch. Two of the girls reach for the fruit. At the left, a youth rests his hand affectionately on a girl's arm.

The three long-haired young men are nude except for mantles, on which they sit or which they tuck between their legs and under their arms. They wear festive wreaths. The girls are bejewelled with necklaces, earrings and bracelets. The hair of each is tied with a ribbon in an individual arrangement. One has leaves inserted into the ribbons in the manner of a festive crown. They wear chitons, and two, who pluck the fruit, are wrapped in himations, which keep their left hands busy. The other two are free of encumbrance and carry baskets in their left hands.

Below the scene is a meander interrupted by checkerboard squares. The underside of the lip is decorated with an olive wreath.

Although Herakles cannot be positively identified, the scene closely parallels some fourth and late fifth century representations of Herakles's exploit of bringing back golden apples from a tree that was nurtured by the nymphs called the Hesperides and protected by a formidable serpent. Herakles is shown as a beardless youth frequently identifiable only by his club. He, two companions and three or four Hesperides flank a tree loaded with fruit. One must assume that in this vase, Herakles is the central youth shaking a tree branch. His right hand must have

Cat. 17.
Cat. 18.

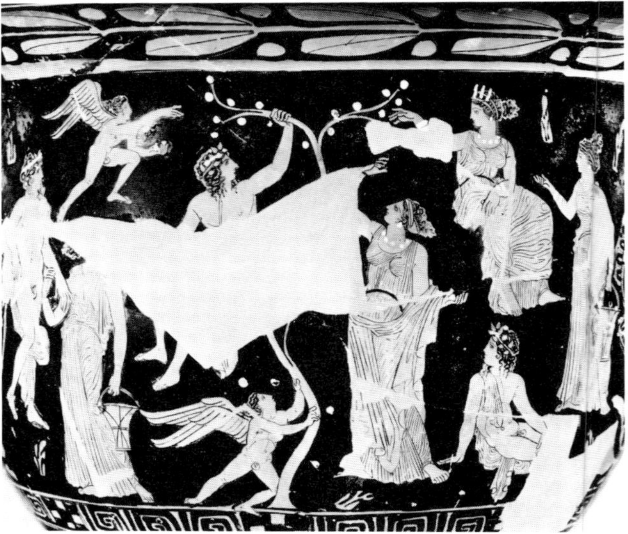

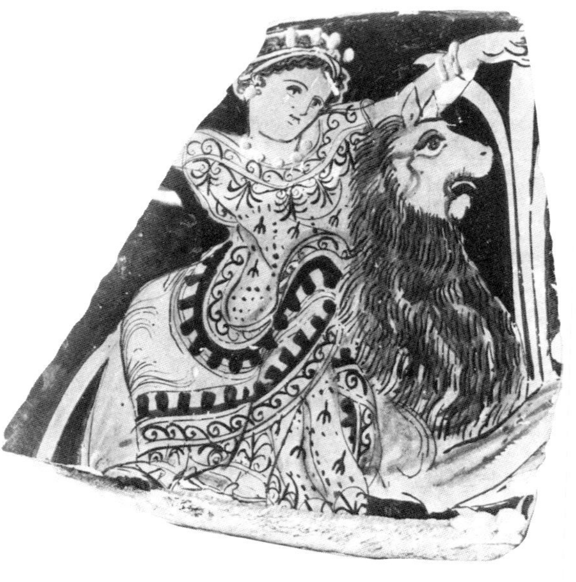

supported his upright club placed behind his knee, as in a treatment of this theme by the Meidias Painter, the master of the Painter of the Athens Wedding. On the Meidias Painter's hydria in the British Museum, the Hesperides are inscribed with their names, Chrysothemis, Asterope, Hygieia and Lipara, and Herakles's companions are labeled Iolaos and Klytios. One might assume that the same cast of characters is shown here. On the other hand, the situation has been made even more idyllic on this vase, where the theme of heroic combat has been completely eliminated. No serpent twines around the tree, and Herakles's companions have set aside their spears. Instead, a new, amo-

Cat. 19.

rous element has been introduced. The boys and girls hold hands, and Erotes help with the apple-gathering. One might then suggest that the seated female with the festive crown at the upper right is Aphrodite. A very similar amorous rendering of Herakles in the Garden of the Hesperides dating from the mid fourth century is also in London.

On the painter, see E. Paribeni in *EAA*, V, p. 570 *(Nozze Ateniesi, Pittore delle) (..un senso formale di inconsueta solidità e rigidezza).* For other treatments of the myth, see Metzger, *Représentations*, p. 202ff., pl. 27.

Published: Beazley, *ARV*, p. 842; *idem*, *ARV²*, p. 1317, no. 2; J. Ziomecki, *Les représentations d'artisans sur les vases attiques* (Warsaw 1975) p. 14, n. 4, fruit harvest 13.

18. Fragment of a plate with a goddess, perhaps Ariadne, riding a lion

Circle of the Pronomos Painter, around 393 B.C.
Bought in Greece
James Fund and Special Contribution 10.187
Length 9.6 cm. Much dilute glaze in the lion. Added clay used for bracelets, necklace and crown of the rider.

Published: Hahland, pp. 10, 15, pl. 17b; M. Nilsson, *Geschichte der griechischen Religion*, I (Munich 1941) p. 802, Appendix, p. 688 (identifying the rider as the "Asiatic Great Mother"); F. Vian, *Répertoire des Gigantomachies* (Paris 1951) no. 397, pl. 45; Metzger, *Représentations*, p. 140, pl. 19, 2; Beazley, *ARV²*, p. 1337, no. 10; *idem*, *Paralipomena*, p. 481; A. Delivorrias, *Attische Giebelskulpturen und Akrotere des fünften Jahrhunderts* (Tübinger Studien 1, 1974) p. 108, note 473; Robertson, *History*, pp. 423, 579, 695, note 168, 731, note 210, pl. 133c; J. C. Carter, in *Studies in Classical Art and Archaeology: A Tribute to Peter Heinrich von Blanckenhagen* (Locust Valley, N. Y. 1979) p. 149, note 38.

19. Mixing bowl with quasi-cylindrical body (kalyx krater)

Front: Dionysos with Erotes, nymphs and satyrs (the triumph of Dionysos)
Back: Eros presents a necklace to a draped youth, a second youth stands behind Eros
Attributed to the Painter of London F90, about 390-380 B.C.
Bequest of May Sheppard Jordan 21.271
Height 31.75 cm. Diameter 33.2 cm. Added white: bodies of the Erotes, pillar on which an Eros leans, wreaths, jewelry, ribbons, leaves of thyrsos. On the back: headband of one youth, ground line, dots between hands of Eros and above hands of second youth. Dilute glaze: detail of white figures.

Eros accompanies Dionysos, who carries his staff, the thyrsos, and throws his arm around Eros's shoulders. The pair strides forward together in balletic poses that suggest running or dancing. Ahead of them kneels a smaller Eros, and behind them, another Eros leans on a pillar. Around this central group, three satyrs or silens and three nymphs (the personifications of caves, streams and other natural features) extend ribbons and necklaces as an act of homage. All the figures are crowned with festive, leaf-trimmed headbands. The nymphs wear chitons with heavily embroidered collars and hems. In the upper row, the central nymph and the satyrs at the far right and left are partly concealed by the rocky terrain.

The nymphs are undoubtedly Dionysos's nurses, the nymphs of Nysa, traditionally three in number, as here, and located by the Homeric tradition on a mountain in Phoenicia (*Homeric Hymn 1: To Dionysos*, 8–9). The silens were the children or alternatively, the companions of the nymphs. Dionysos is, however, no longer a child but an adolescent. The situation recalls the words of the Homeric hymn that "when the goddesses had brought him up, a god oft hymned, then began he to wander continually through the woody coombes, thickly wreathed with ivy and laurel. And the Nymphs followed in his train with him for their leader" (*Hymn 26: To Dionysos*, 7-10). Strikingly, winged geniuses of love are added to the procession, as if to make manifest the longings of the maturing god.

A leaf-and-tongue passes between the handles. An olive wreath decorates the underside of the lip.

Published: Beazley, *ARV²*, p. 1417, no. 2; E. Vermeule, *AJA* 70 (1966) p. 22.

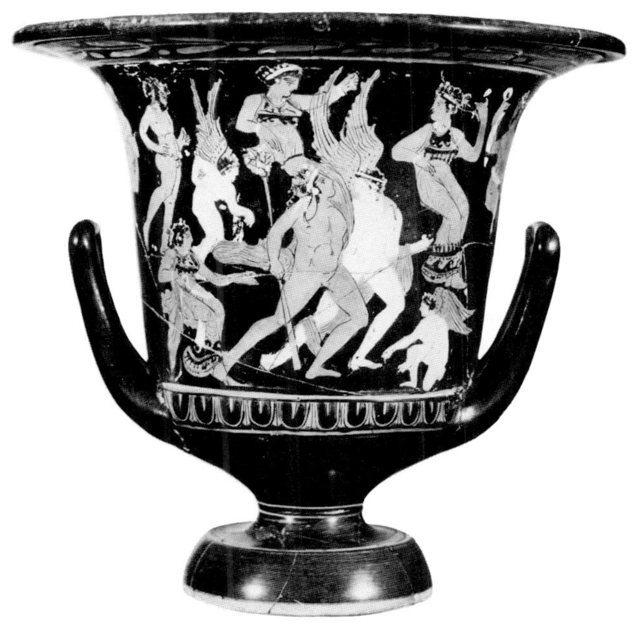

Cat. 20.

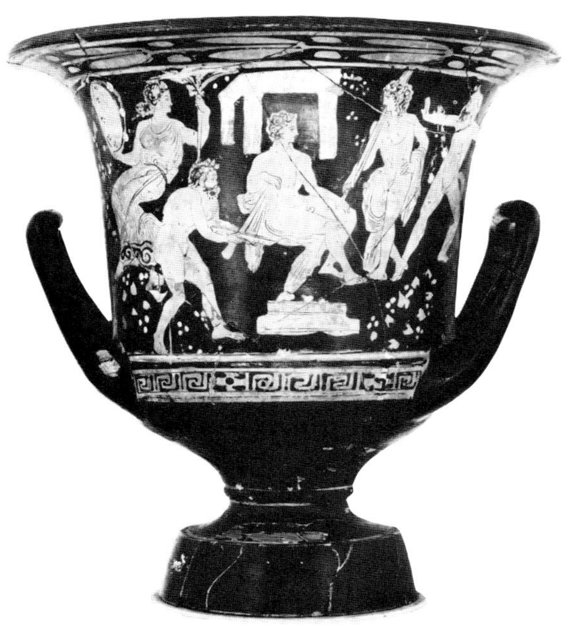

20. Mixing bowl with quasi-cylindrical body (kalyx krater)

Front: the veneration of the divinized Herakles
Back: three draped and gesturing youths
First quarter of the fourth century B.C.
Bequest of May Sheppard Jordan 21.272
Height 31.5 cm. Diameter 32.2 cm. Added white: columned structure above Herakles, wreaths, flowers on background, cymbals around rim of maenad's tambourine, food on satyr's tray and on low pedestal before him, ribbon over arm of silenos.

A beardless and very youthful Herakles is seated on his cloak on the ground and leans on his club. Behind him is a shrine with four columns. Herakles's equally youthful and even more long-haired companion Iolaos leans on a pair of spears. Behind Iolaos, a satyr seems to recoil in astonishment as he presents a huge fillet for the ornamentation of Herakles or his shrine. The satyr in the foreground seems about to empty his tray of fruit onto the low platform before him, which recalls the funerary table of Athenian cemeteries, the trapeza. The seated maenad wears a chiton with embroidered hem and carries a tambourine. She also supports a branching, leafy staff, an attribute that suggests that she personifies a grove. The outdoor setting is evoked by the leaves and flowers that upholster the background. A normal altar appears over the left handle.

A meander interrupted by checkered squares borders the scene below. An olive wreath decorates the underside of the rim.

fig 4. Shrine of Herakles Alexikakos. N. Road; 3. Herakles heroon base; 4. Wine press; 5. Temple; 6. Lesche. From Travlos, fig. 351.

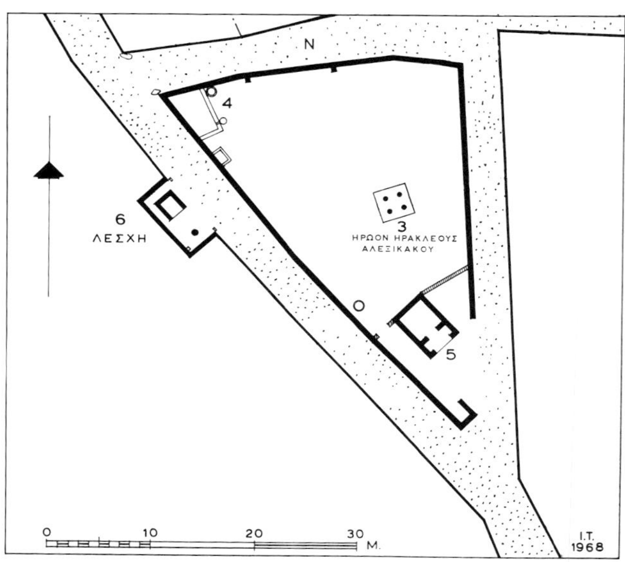

The essential purpose of this and several similar vases is to show the hero resting in a paradisiacal setting after his labors, his sufferings and his divinization. The presence of the altar and the members of the Dionysiac retinue, who render homage to Herakles, make the blissful, otherworldly locus evident. At the same time, an Athenian would very likely have recognized that the *mis-en-scène* was based on the arrangement and rituals of a specific Athenian shrine dedicated to Herakles: the shrine of Herakles Alexikakos. The site, which has been excavated not far from the Agora, consisted of a large, walled, open-air enclosure. At the entrance was a small temple, and at the center of the enclosure was a four-columned monument, the identifying feature that appears in this and several other vases. A winepress was found in one corner of the precinct, and this piece of equipment may help to explain the actions of the satyr on the vase. Apparently, wine, or at any rate grape juice, was prepared on the spot and was to be consumed in celebration of the divinized hero and his companion.

The shrine appears in more explicit fashion on marble votive reliefs of the fourth century. An example with Herakles and Hermes in the Museum of Fine Arts not only shows the four-columned shrine, which is inscribed as that of Herakles Alexikakos, but it also includes a krater for mixing wine and water. Again the link between Herakles and wine drinking in the shrine is stressed. The shrine was founded during the great epidemic of 430 B.C., and it seems likely that the ritual banquets (and possibly also ritual sleep) that took place there were intended to evoke Herakles as a healing divinity and as a guide to a happy afterlife, in the event that the hoped-for cure did not come about.

Cat. 21.

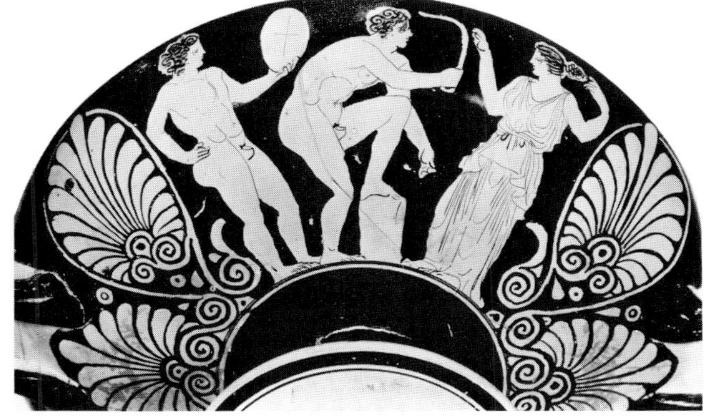

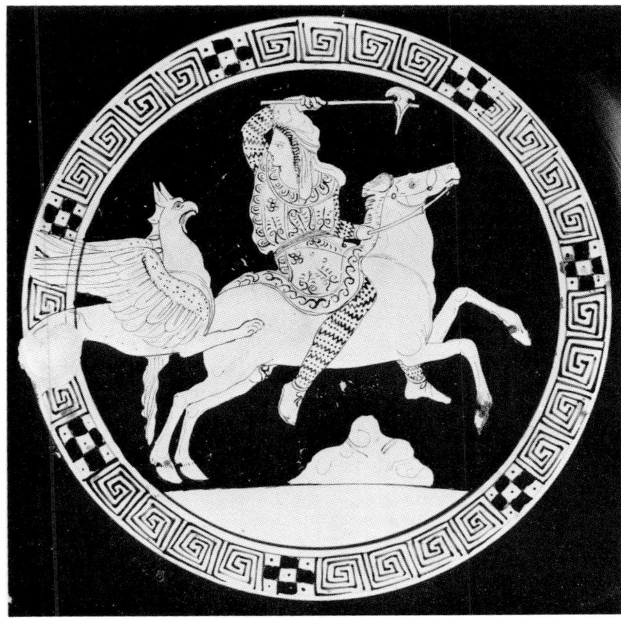

The scene on the reverse of our vase seems to show an animated conversation. A pillar and two wreaths hanging from the background provide a rudimentary setting. Two of the youths apparently carry doughnut-like objects suspended from strings.

For a discussion of similar representations of the cult of Herakles, see Metzger, *Représentations*, p. 224ff., pls. 29, 2 and 31, 2. On the precinct of Herakles Alexikakos and its relationship with these vase paintings and reliefs, see Travlos, pp. 274-6. On the relief in the Museum of Fine Arts, see Comstock and Vermeule, *Sculpture*, no. 77.

Unpublished. The attribution to an Attic workshop is due to D. Trendall.

21. Shallow drinking cup with horizontal handles and high foot (kylix)

Interior: a mounted Arimasp fighting off a griffin
Exterior: on each side, two athletes and a girl
Attributed to a follower of the Jena Painter, early fourth century B.C.
Found at Cumae in South Italy
H. L. Pierce Fund 01.8092
Height 11.4 cm. Diameter 27.3 cm.

According to legends reported by Herodotos and Aristeas of Proconnesos, the Arimasps were a people that lived in the far north in a region bordering the lands of the Scythians (in modern Russia). They enriched themselves by stealing gold guarded by griffins.

The Arimasp is fitted out in oriental fashion; he wears a long-sleeved, patterned tunic and trousers (anaxyrides); his head is covered with a Phrygian cap, and he wields an axe. His horse springs away in wild-eyed terror as the griffin's claws sink into his hindquarters. The youthful rider displays serene detachment as he coils for a retaliatory blow, which the griffin views with upraised head. The scene is framed with a meander interrupted by checkerboard squares.

On the exterior, the two scenes, which are set in the exercise yard (palaestra), are slight variations of one another. The left-hand athlete on one side holds a javelin, on the other, a discus. The central athlete has apparently finished his exercise and is cleaning himself with a strigil. The girl advances towards him with outspread arms as if to crown him with a ribbon of victory, which was presumably to be added in white paint. No trace of the paint remains, and this detail may never have been completed.

Palmettes springing from scrolls surround the handles. The side and lower surface of the foot are beautifully finished with a series of black glaze lines and reserved bands.

On the legend, see Metzger, *Représentations*, p. 327ff.

Published: Beazley, *ARV*, p. 884, no. 6; *idem*, *ARV*², p. 1518, no. 6 ("a heavy-handed imitation of the Jena Painter").

22. Ovoid oil bottle with one handle (squat lekythos)

Nike sacrificing a bull between a warrior and a warrior goddess, probably Ares and Aphrodite
First quarter of the fourth century, perhaps about 390 B.C.
Said to be from Eretria
H. L. Pierce Fund 98.884
Height 15.2 cm. Diameter 8.4 cm.
Added white: bull and flesh of female figures. Details of white areas added in dilute glaze, and brush strokes model the shield. Added clay: details of wing, hair ribbons and necklaces of Nike and Aphrodite, spears, wreath on hel-

Cat. 22.
Cat. 22.
Cat. 22.
Cat. 22.

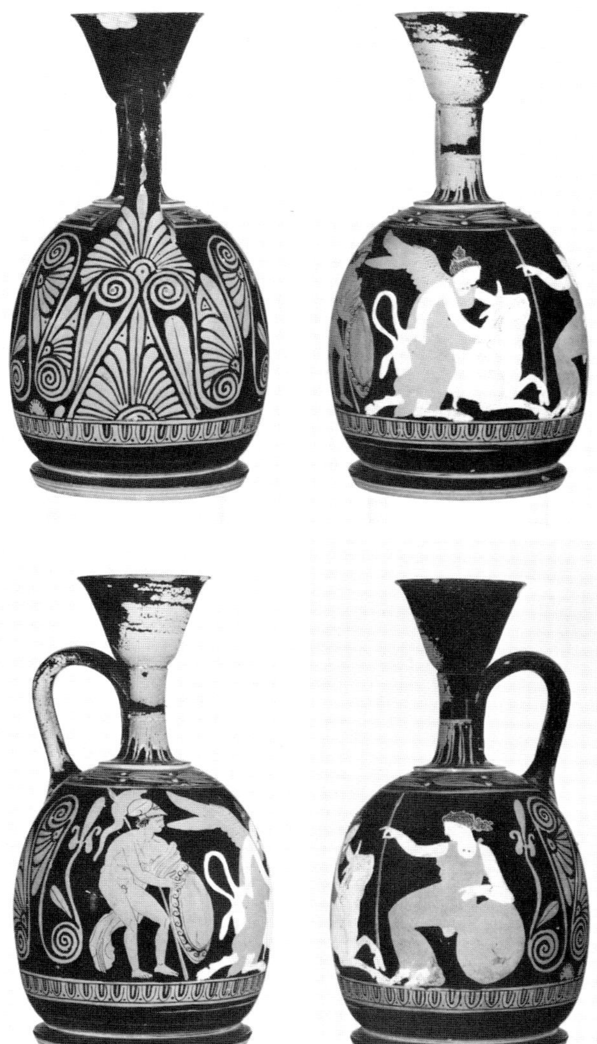

met, olives in wreath above the figures, centers of scrolls below handle.

The Nike pulls up the head of the bull with her left hand and prepares to give the *coup-de-grace* with the knife held in her right. The warrior wears a Corinthian helmet on the back of his head and steadies a shield, whose rim is decorated with a wave pattern, placed on the ground in front of him. A spear rests against his shoulder. The seated woman at the right is dressed in a chiton and steadies her spear, which passes through a loop made by her thumb and index finger. Both Nike and the seated figure wear necklaces with two beads, and the latter had a bracelet in dilute glaze.

A leaf band circles the vase below the figures. An olive wreath tops the body, and a tongue pattern (the cyma dorica) decorates the neck. A complicated mass of palmettes and scrolls springing from undulating bands occupies the rear of the main zone under the handle. A lotus blossom terminates each band. Large petals and reserved triangles fill in the free space. An acanthus leaf curls up from the ground.

The vase presents a striking example of the influence that temple sculpture on the Acropolis had on art of the early fourth century. The bull sacrifice is clearly derived from the reliefs of the Nike Temple parapet, where a similar group appeared. A pair of bronze mirrors of the end of the fifth century also show the motif and must derive from the parapet. The figure of the seated goddess in the lekythos reflects the Nike parapet less closely. In the parapet, Athena is seated on a rocky outcropping and rests her arm on a shield much as this goddess does. The stooping warrior of the lekythos echoes figures in the parapet and in the frieze of the temple itself.

The compositional motifs almost certainly were not inspired by the temple of Athena Nike directly. Only with difficulty, could the seated goddess be identified as Athena. The absence of aegis and helmet and the very light, feminine chiton all militate against the patroness of Athens. A better candidate is Aphrodite. The weapons would be appropriate for Aphrodite as venerated in the Piraeus, whose temple was built by the admiral Conon after he defeated the Spartan fleet off Cnidos in 394 B.C. Aphrodite was the patron goddess of Cnidos, who must have been regarded as favoring the Athenians on the day of the battle. Ares, the god of war and a frequent companion of Aphrodite, is the logical identification for the warrior on the other side of the bull.

Judging by this lekythos, the sculptural program of the temple at Piraeus was strongly influenced by that of Athena Nike, and the Aphrodite temple may have had an important role in diffusing victory motifs. It seems likely that the mirrors with bull sacrifices were inspired by the monument, since objects of female beautification were normally under the patronage of Aphrodite.

On the Nike Temple parapet, see R. Kekulé von Stradonitz, *Die Reliefs an der Balustrade der Athena Nike* (Stuttgart 1881) p. 11; R. Heberdey, *Österreichische Jahreshefte* 21-22 (1922-24) p. 33, fig. 32; R. Carpenter, *The Sculpture of the Nike Temple Parapet* (Cambridge, Mass. 1929) pp. 42f., pl. 17. For the influence of this monument on vase painting, see H. Schoppa, *AA* 50 (1935) pp. 34-50; E. Vermeule, *JdI* 85 (1970) p. 99, note 13. For the mirrors, see Züchner, KS 62, 63; M. Weber, *AthMitt* 91 (1976) p. 159f., note 35, pl. 51, 2. For Nike sacrificing a ram on fourth century coins, see A. Bellinger and M. Berlincourt, *Numismatic Notes and Monographs* (American Numismatic

Society) no. 149 (New York 1962) pp. 16-17, pl. 5, 11. On the Temple of Aphrodite at Piraeus, see Pausanias, I, 3.

Published: Metzger, *Recherches*, p. 113, no. 30; *idem*, *Revue des Études Grecques* 81 (1968) p. 154; *idem*, *Représentations*, p. 355; P. Alexandrescu and S. Dimitriu, *CVA*, *Roumanie* 2, p. 33, under no. 5.

23. Fragmentary pitcher (oinochoe)

Victorious four-horse chariot at the finish of a race
390-375 B.C.
From the funerary precinct of Dexileos in the Kerameikos, Athens
H. L. Pierce Fund 98.935
Height (as restored) 15.8 cm. Added clay: wreaths, Nike's bracelet, details of bridles.
Added white: pillar marking finish and its platform, body of flying Nike, wreaths. Dilute glaze: leaf moulding on platform.

At the left, a young judge wearing a wreath leans on his staff and observes the finish. He stands on the platform that carries the quadrangular pillar marking the finish line. The charioteer, who wears a long belted and spotted chiton, reins in his team. A Nike flies overhead carrying wreaths of victory. A young groom leaps up to seize the bridle of one of the horses to help bring the chariot to a halt. The figures stand on a ground line that is decorated with a leaf pattern. The band finishes just beyond the figures.

These and other fragments of pitchers were found in a family burial plot dominated by the magnificent marble stele to the memory of Dexileos, who died in the Corinthian War of 394/3 B.C. At least three members of Dexileos's family were buried in the plot. The dates of these burials are unknown, but one must have been after 357 B.C. Some of the vase fragments are painted in a rough style that continues that of the fifth century. Others, like the following, stand on the threshold of the more curvilinear and fluent Kerch style of the middle years of the fourth century. Stylistically, this piece seems to take an intermediate position.

The chariot scene on the vase offers an unusual insight into the working methods of vase painters at the time. At first glance the inspiration seems to come from relief sculpture. The groom leaping up to stop a quadriga recalls the famous relief found at Phaleron on the coast of Attica, now in the Athens National Museum. Closer examination, however, suggests that vase painters may have had small objects like gems and coins (or more probably casts thereof) close at hand while they worked. The figure of the charioteer reining in the team almost repeats the charioteer on an intaglio now in Boston that was bought in Athens and is thought to be of Attic manufacture. The rather swan-like necks of the horses have their closest parallel in the team on the gem. On this (and other early fourth century vases with chariot scenes), the horses do not, however, toss their heads. For this detail, one must turn to a more exotic glyptic source. Quadrigae with all heads aligned forward are found on the huge silver coins (dekadrachms) of Syracuse of the early fourth century. The best parallel is in an issue of dekadrachms designed by Euainetos around 390 B.C. These prestigious and high quality numismatic works may well have been responsible for the change in fashion in the Athenian potters' quarter.

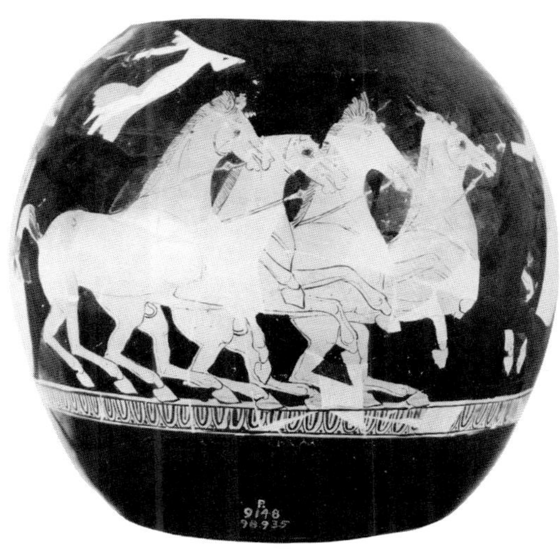

Cat. 23.

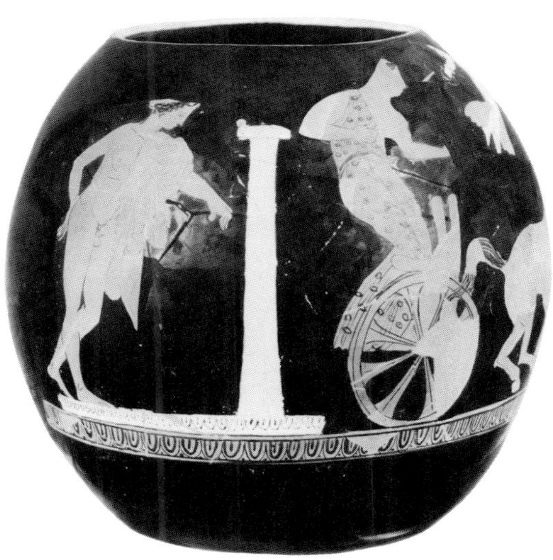

Cat. 23.

Cat. 24.

On the relief from Phaleron, the intaglio and dekadrachms of Syracuse, see C. Vermeule, *JHS* 75 (1955) p. 108ff., figs. 9, 11. For the date of the dekadrachm of Euainetos, see C. Lorber in *Wealth of the Ancient World: The Nelson Bunker Hunt and William Herbert Hunt Collections* (Fort Worth 1983) no. 86.

Published: Hahland, p. 6, pl. 24; van Hoorn, *Choes*, no. 372, pp. 32, 111; Metzger, *Recherches*, p. 69; E. Vermeule, *JdI* 85 (1970) p. 98f., no. 2, figs. 4-6; Robertson, *History*, pp. 420-1, 695, note 161, 822; R. Garland, *BSA* 77 (1982) p. 136. Schefold dates the earliest Dexileos pitcher (i.e., the one most in the style of the fifth century) (98.934: Bacchic revel) in the span 390-380; see Schefold, *UKV*, p. 158.

24. Fragmentary pitcher (oinochoe)

Parade with a rider and a lyre player
Attributed to the Painter of the Oinochoes
Early Kerch Style, about 385-370 B.C.
From the funerary precinct of Dexileos in the Kerameikos, Athens
H. L. Pierce Fund 01.8255
Height (as restored) 14 cm. Diameter about 18 cm. Added clay: headband.

A rider wearing a cloak and carrying a torch is preceded by a young man wearing a headband decorated with ivy leaves who clears the way for the rider with a staff. Behind the rider is a young man who succeeds in playing a lyre as he runs after his companions. The ground line below the figures is ornamented with meanders interrupted by checkerboard squares.

The event represented seems to be the komos or happy parade during the festival of Anthesteria. Only the "gilded" youth of Athens would have been able to appear on horseback for the event.

Treatment of anatomical details, facial features, and ornament is much like the well-known pitcher in Leningrad by the Painter of the Oinochoes. The drapery with its sketchily curvilinear folding patterns and weighted corners is particularly similar. Another pitcher from the precinct of Dexileos appears also to be by the painter (MFA 01.8254: pairs of lively youths and girls, perhaps satyrs and nymphs).

For the Painter of the Oinochoes, see Schefold, *KV*, pp. 9, 12, pls. 4a, 5; *idem*, *Göttersage*, p. 268f., fig. 383.

Published: van Hoorn, *Choes*, no. 380, pp. 32, 113, fig. 112; E. Vermeule, *JdI* 85 (1970) p. 108f., figs. 10, 11.

25. Three-handled water jar (hydria)

The meeting of Dionysos and Ariadne
Close to the Hesperides Painter
Kerch Style, 370-350 B.C.
Said to have been found at Athens
Catharine Page Perkins Fund 95.22
Height 31.6 cm. Diameter of rim 11.2 cm. Added clay: curls of hair, earrings, necklace, fibulae at shoulders and bracelets of maenad at upper right, headband of satyr, berries in wreath of Dionysos and Ariadne, necklace, bracelets and ornament on rim of tambourine of Ariadne, hair of Eros, ornament at top of cap of Hermes, berries in wreath around neck of vase. Traces of gilding on added clay, especially on berries around neck and on hair of Eros. Added white: body of Eros. Dilute glaze: detail in white area and hair; very thin washes model the bodies and the vase on the ground line.

Dionysos, who holds a shawl and his leaf-tipped staff (thyrsos), turns back as the other figures call his attention to Ariadne seated at the lower left. Eros bends forward before him and almost pats Ariadne on the head in his eagerness. At the far left, Hermes, the guide of souls, clad in a shawl and his traveller's hat (petasos) beckons to Dionysos. At the lower right, an animalistic satyr, holding a panther's skin, cautiously crouches and extends a hand toward Ariadne much as a spaniel might tentatively approach a suspicious object. A maenad perched comfortably at the upper right observes the proceedings leaning on her tambourine. Her hair is confined in a sakkos. She wears a peplos and holds a thyrsos. Ariadne is seated on a stool beside a mixing bowl (krater) of wine. Her lower body is draped in a himation, and she looks out coquettishly from behind her tambourine.

The representation ambiguously combines two moments of the Ariadne story. Ariadne is shown as the wife of Dionysos, happily enthroned and carrying the paraphernalia of the Dionysiac retinue (a tambourine) as she awaits the return of her consort. On the other hand, Dionysos is guided to Ariadne by numerous divine attendants as if it were the moment when he first discovered her

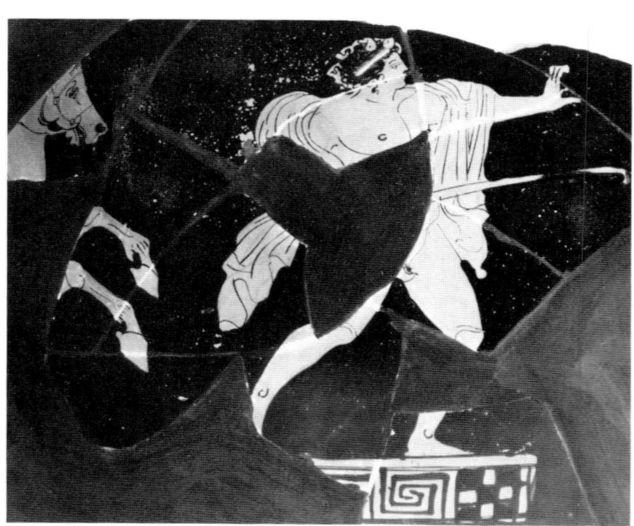

Cat. 25.
Cat. 25.

asleep and abandoned by Theseus on the island of Naxos. The guides, however, help to energize the narrative, which in a less adorned fashion becomes a frequently banal commonplace of fourth century vase painting.

In the fourth century, Dionysos's love for his wife must have taken on almost emblematic significance as the ideal example of a beautiful, faithful and vividly erotic domestic relationship. In his account (written about 380 B.C.) of a famous banquet and conversation of Socrates, Xenophon concludes the event with a pantomime rendition of the reunion of Dionysos and Ariadne. The image was evidently the ideal way to launch the guests back to their wives in the proper frame of mind. This portrayal of happy domesticity in the divine sphere has a special appropriateness on a hydria, a shape to be used above all by women in drawing water for the family.

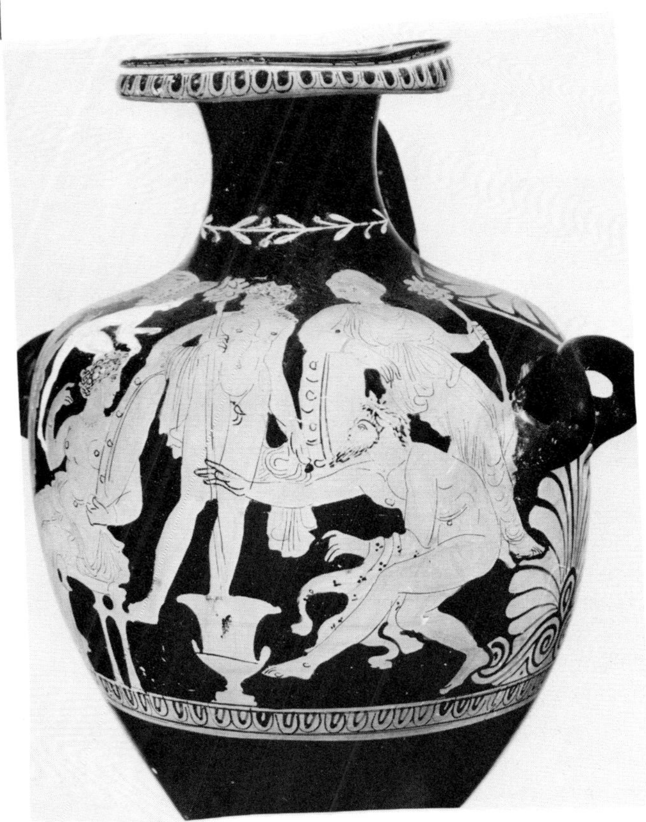

Tongue ornament follows the rim and forms a ground line for the figures. An olive wreath with gilded fruit decorates the neck. A double palmette fills the space below the rear handle. From it spreads out in each direction a scrolling band that encircles a palmette and then a half palmette. A palmette springs up from scrolls below each lateral handle. Various circles and petals fill in the intervening spaces.

For a comparable figure style, see Schefold, UKV, no. 184 (similar to Hippolytos Painter) and nos. 474 and 514 (both early works by the Hesperides Painter perhaps in the Hippolytos shop). On the happily married god of wine, see Xenophon, *Banquet* (Todd translation, Loeb edition, 1968) 9, 2ff.; Schefold, *Göttersage*, p. 268, figs. 382-384.

Unpublished.

26. Mixing bowl with quasi-cylindrical body (kalyx krater)
Front: apotheosis of Herakles
Back: conversation between three draped youths
The L.C. Group (Group of the Late Calyx-Kraters), about 320-310 B.C.
Gift of E. P. Warren 13.416
Height 44 cm. Diameter 35.5 cm. Added white: flesh and garment of Nike, flesh, shield, crest and Medusa (on breast) of Athena. Dilute glaze: detail in white area.

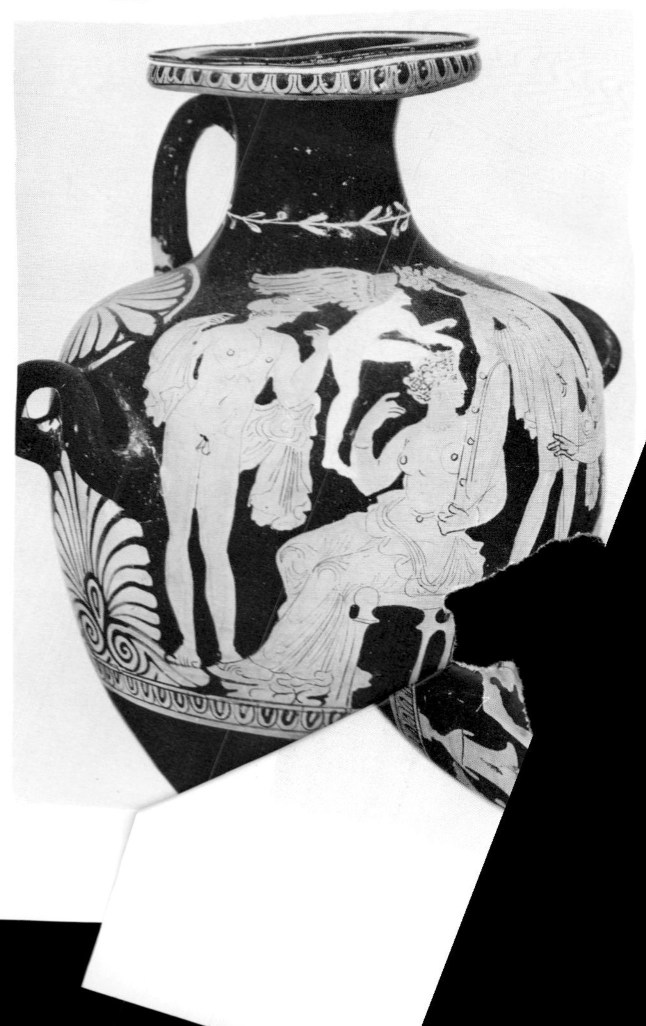

Herakles leans on his club as he is crowned with the wreath of immortality by his divine wife, Hebe. Nike flies before him as if to introduce him to his seated Olympian patroness Athena, who has her customary armament of spear, helmet, aegis and shield. A rocky protuberance below her shield might even evoke Mt. Olympos. Behind Athena is either Herakles's companion Iolaos or else Hermes, the guide of souls (an idea suggested by what might be the traveller's hat hanging behind his neck). He leans with his left elbow on the back of Athena's throne (which is not otherwise indicated) and seems to beckon with his right hand to Herakles. Over the left handle, a dancing maenad beats her tambourine. Her presence underlines the paradisiacal associations of the scene.

On the reverse, the central youth is entirely wrapped in his cloak while his two companions extend an arm to gesture. Their apparent conversation takes place in a rocky landscape behind which appear two doric columns and an enigmatic rectangular panel. The discussion might thereby seem to be set outside a mountain sanctuary.

A tongue pattern decorates the rim of the krater, and a laurel wreath circles below it. On the front, a scrolling vine passes between the handles. On the back, the vine is replaced by a laurel wreath. Pairs of reserved lines circle the foot and the stem of the vase.

A Homeric hymn to Herakles (xv) evokes the hero's apotheosis, which is the moment when he is granted Hebe as consort. Herakles is addressed as an intercessor for mankind in the Olympian courts, a role that makes his divinization a subject of special importance. The prominence of Athena, his patroness, and a maenad, here a symbol of Olympian bliss, is, however, a product of the fourth century tradition of vase painting.

The late, elongated kraters of this group seem to have been heavily exported to Boeotia, but they apparently did not reach markets much farther afield. The pose and placement of the figure of Herakles, however, suggest that the artist was not entirely out of touch with mainstream artistic currents of the Age of Alexander. Not only does the muscular figure of Herakles leaning on his club vaguely evoke the weary Herakles by Lysippos, but even more remarkable is the view of the hero from behind. This viewpoint, which previously had been reserved for an occasional accessory figure rather than a principal, could well have been inspired by a famous painting by Apelles, the favorite painter of Alexander. In a picture briefly mentioned by Pliny the Elder, Apelles showed Herakles from the back and yet was able to capture his character perfectly. Apelles's painting is not otherwise known, yet the departure from conventional composition in our vase can hardly be explained without reference to some such painted masterpiece.

For the painting by Apelles, see Pliny, *Natural History* (Loeb edition) book 35, 94. For a previous and not gener[...]pted attempt to identify reflections of the painting, see J. Six, *JdI* 20 (1905) p. 170ff.; M. Swindler, *Ancient Painting* (New Haven and London 1929) p. 270, note 11.

Published: Schefold, *UKV*, no. 233, pp. 26, 139 (for the "Meister der Kelchkratere"); G. H. Chase, [...] *Antiquities: A Guide to the Classical Collec-* [...] p. 97, fig. 112; A. W. Byvanck in *Studia* [...] (Leiden 1951) p. 18; Metzger, *Représen-* [...]1; C. Vermeule, *Greek, Etruscan &*

Cat. 26.

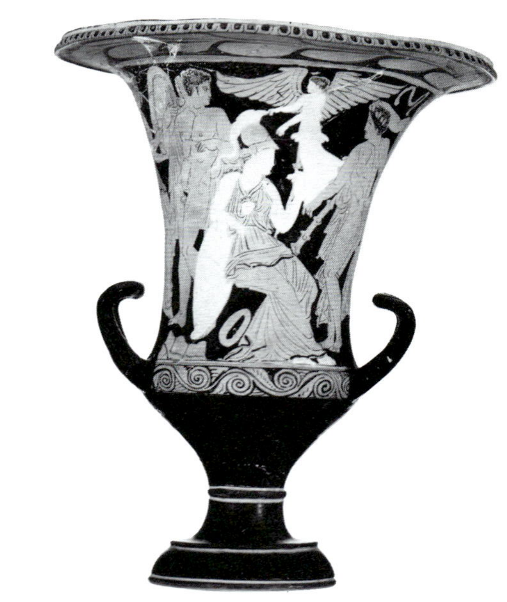

Cat. 26.

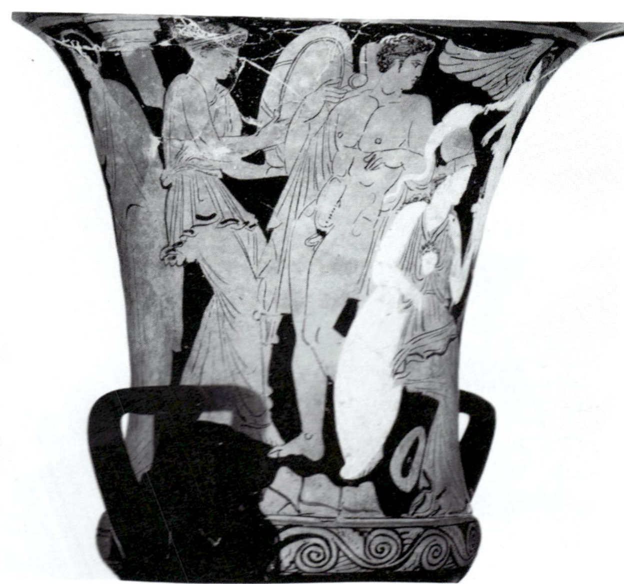

Cat. 26.

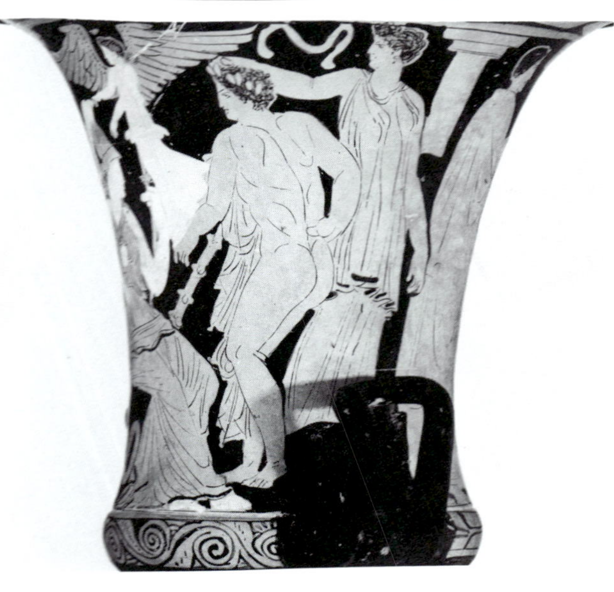

Cat. 27.

Cat. 28.

Cat. 28.

Roman Art: The Classical Collections of the Museum of Fine Arts, Boston (Boston 1972) pp. 139-140, 149, fig. 128; Beazley, *ARV*^{2}, p. 1456, no. 5 (L.C. Group); E. Simon and H. Seifert, *AA*, 1968, p. 167; Burn and Glynn, *Beazley Addenda*, p. 191; A. W. Byvanck, *BABesch* 30 (1955) pp. 32-33, no. 315; *idem*, *BABesch* 20 (1945) pp. 30, 32; C. Vermeule, *S to S*, pp. 42, 48, 103, 124, 203, fig. 57.

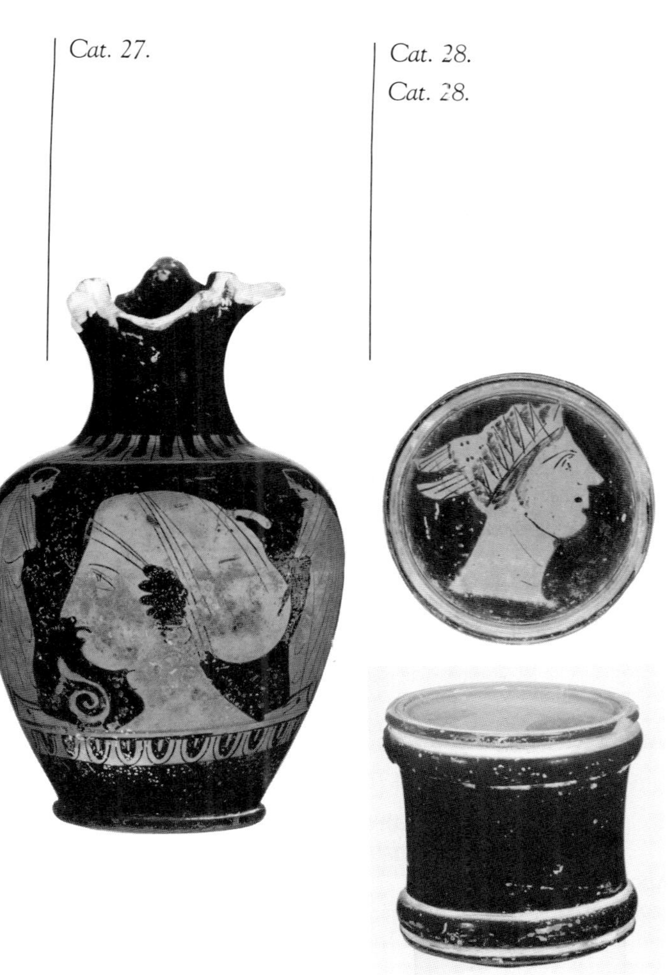

27. Pitcher with trilobe mouth and angled shoulder (shoulder oinochoe type 2)

Head of a goddess, probably Persephone, flanked by standing men
F. B. Group, fourth century
Gift of Mr. and Mrs. William de Forest Thomson 19.296
Height 18 cm. Diameter 11 cm.

The large female head has its hair in a sakkos. A scroll of foliage appears before her. The head is flanked by two youths who are tightly wrapped in their mantles (himatia). A band of tongue pattern is above the figures, a band of egg pattern below. Stylistically, the pitcher is a routine production of a kind frequently exported to Italy.

The scene could be a very abbreviated rendition of the return of Persephone to her mother Demeter after her abduction by Hades. The myth was connected with the annual return of vegetation to the earth and was part of the nucleus of legends around which the mysteries of Eleusis (located on the coast of Attica) developed. In this context, however, the dignified young men cannot be readily explained. They may be meaningless stock figures of the kind frequently seen on the rear of vases or they might be young initiates or worshippers like those seen on votive reliefs in marble.

An alternative explanation might be that the head represents Gaia, the earth mother, who in other mythological contexts is shown rising from the ground. The two dignified young men might then evoke the words of a Homeric hymn: "Through you, O queen, men are blessed in their children and blessed in their harvests, and to you it belongs to give means of life to mortal men and to take it away." (*Hymn 30: To Earth The Mother of All*, 5–8.)

For the interpretation of similar large female heads flanked by figures as Kore (Persephone), see Schefold, *Göttersage*, pp. 69-72, figs. 82, 88. For the earlier interpretation of this kind of scene as a terrestrial birth of Aphrodite (a tale not known from surviving mythology), see Metzger, *Représentations*, pp. 72-80, pls. IV, 2 and VI.

Published: Beazley, *ARV*^{2}, p. 1490, no. 164 (Fat Boy Group).

28. Cylindrical box with cover (type D pyxis or box pyxis)

On the lid: head of Hermes
Fourth century B.C.
Possibly found in Athens
Gift of E. P. Warren 96.679 a, b
Height 6.0 cm. (with lid), 5.2 cm. (without lid). Diameter of lid 6.6 cm.
Letter Λ incised on underside of lid. A small χ may be scratched inside the bowl. Αϑ is written in ink on the bottom.
Dilute glaze: Hermes's hair.

The lid is glazed inside and out. Reserved bands frame the tondo and highlight the channel between the two mouldings of the edge. Reserve bands also bracket the thick torus at the base of the bowl. The top of the bowl and the top of the step on which the lid rests are also reserved, as is the bottom.

Hermes has wings springing from his head, and he wears a headband from which triangular rays project. The forms suggest the radiate crown of the sun god, but they are more likely to be a stylization of a festive crown trimmed with olive leaves. The pyxis was a receptacle for cosmetic powder or trinkets. Hermes, a patron of prosperity, would be a suitable guardian for a jewelry container.

On the shape and its use, see *Agora* 12, pp. 173, 177-8. The profiles of nos. 1311-2, 1314 are very similar to this one.

Published: D. von Bothmer, AJA 85 (1981) p. 354.

Cat. 66.

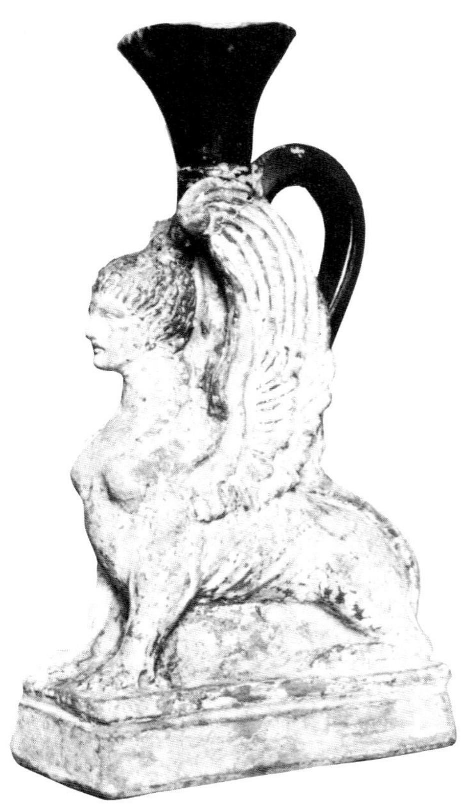

66. One-handled oil bottle (lekythos) in the form of a sphinx

Third quarter of the fourth century
Gift of Barbara Deering Danielson 1982.655
Height 11.8 cm.

The beautifully modelled figure crouches on a pedestal with an upper moulding. Her tail curls up her back to touch the base of the handle. The precisely detailed wings have an archaistic stiffness. Her hair, from which two braids hang down, is tightly pulled up to a bun on the top of her head. The arrangement comes close to that of Early Hellenistic Tanagra figurines.

The color is unusually well preserved. Over a white ground, the lips and hair are red brown, the braids yellow, the wings blue with a yellow leading edge. The ground panel and the area below the sphinx's body are blue, and the pedestal is rose. The handle and mouth of the vase have a lustrous black glaze.

The sphinx, a benevolent guardian of tombs, is bound up with the sepulchral use of many of these vases.

For the treatment of the vase mouth, wings and hair, see Trumpf-Lyritzaki, no. 110, 138, pls. 7, 16 (both 3rd quarter 4th century). On sphinxes, see *ibid., pp. 58ff., 139, pl. 22.*

Unpublished.

Terracotta Sculpture

Sculptors in clay, called coroplaths ("modellers of girls"), occupied a secondary position in the artistic hierarchy in the fourth century. For intellectuals like Plato or Isocrates, coroplaths were as common as the clay they worked.[1] Often their works were, in fact, cheap substitutes for sculptures in more valuable materials, and since they were made from moulds, they could exist in numerous copies. Yet this humble stratum of Athenian craftsmen produced many fine works and displayed a unique brand of creativity. Many of their favorite themes can hardly be paralleled in large-scale sculpture. Athenian coroplaths, moreover, set fashions that were followed by their colleagues throughout the Greek world.

The period began with very high levels of achievement. Terracottas were produced that were often vivid little tableaux. In compositions for funerary purposes, like the masterful no. 67, an altar and a funerary monument provide the setting for a mourning figure. The delicate mood and supporting environment of white ground funerary lekythoi of the late fifth century have been translated into three dimensions. The expressiveness of this terracotta also rivals that of large-scale fourth century funerary sculpture in marble. A remarkable tableaux of later date extends this tradition into the realm of myth and tragedy. A mother is shown in an outdoor setting abandoning her presumably divinely-fathered children (no. 68). The mother may have been either Tyro, the subject of a tragedy by Sophocles, or Antiope, the heroine of a play by Euripides. In either case, the tragic and heroic content and the theatrical inspiration are evident.

Most Athenian tomb figures of the first half of the century reflect very different sources of inspiration. The tone is often cheerful, and figures are drawn from the world of lighter entertainment. Dancers perform the squatting Persian dance in Eastern costume. While these dances might be presented on secular occasions, their association with the cult of Dionysos is probably the motive for the inclusion of such figures in tombs.[2] Figures of music-making Pans and Silenoi in tombs are even more evidently connected with Dionysos.[3] A much looser association between Dionysos and the world of entertainment is embodied in the figures of comic actors that became popular in the fourth century. Figures began to be made that

1. Plato, *Theaetetos*, 147; Isocrates, *Antidosis*, 2
2. See the figures of goddesses, musicians and dancers from the tomb of Hipparete in the Kerameikos: *Deltion* 18 (1963) p. 29; D. B. Thompson in *Histoire et archéologie* 81 (March 1984) p. 32f., fig. 1f.
3. *Ibid.*

captured the freewheeling, bawdy spirit and the equally bawdy costumes of the comedies of Aristophanes, performed, of course, in theatres sacred to Dionysos.

Other terracotta figures were drawn from the world of popular entertainments. Dolls that were equipped with the castanets of entertainers might well have been used as marionettes. The simulated noise-makers, in any case, play quite cleverly on the rattling sounds produced by the movements of jointed clay figures.

Like figures of actors, another category of entirely secular figures displays a taste for the grotesque combined with cruelly sharp observation. A remarkable series of terracotta women who are both nude and obese appeared in the second half of the century. The statuettes, some of which seem to show body paintings or tattooes, may have been inspired by travellers' accounts of the bizarre customs and behavior of the Mossynoecians, who lived on the southeast coast of the Black Sea. The anatomies, however, are strikingly accurate studies of semi-pathological physical conditions. It is thought that the models for the sculptors must have come from the lowest echelons of the population, perhaps practitioners of the world's oldest profession. Fourth century Athens, however, was a civilization of empirical observation, manifest in the naturalistic compilation of philosophers like Aristotle, and it was also a time of advances in medicine in the treatment centers based around sanctuaries of the healing god Asklepios or at the shrines of various divinized heroes. In the Hellenistic period, figures of grotesque and indecent females were to become quite popular, possibly just for magical or apotropaic purposes.[4]

Traditional themes like animals, which were probably intended as votive or funerary gifts, continued to be treated. Our ram (no. 69) might have magically simulated a propitiatory offering to a hero, since sacrifices of rams (as well as bulls) were especially common in the veneration of such demigods of the Underworld.[5] In any case, these studies of animals showed an acute observation; textures of fleece were effectively rendered in meticulously detailed moulds.

Craftsmanship is not only excellent, but inventive. In the second quarter of the century, a new approach emerges. Figures become smaller so that vent holes in the back can be omitted. Backs of figures can then be finished with moulds. These miniatures stand on flat, separately-made base plates. Most earlier (and even many contemporary) terracottas were open below. Bases would be moulded with the figures and frequently, as in the case of the ram, have a bulky, block-like quality.

Sculpturally, many of these terracotta figures are of great interest. Often, they have a relationship with large-scale sculpture. Seated mourning women (like no. 67) appeared in major fifth century works, like the "Penelope" from Persepolis.[6] Many poses and compositions are freer than parallels in monumental statuary. Terracotta actors strike jaunty poses and are muffled in their garments in ways that recall earlier or contemporary vase paintings rather than three-dimensional works. The twisting poses developed by the famous masters of the fourth century are taken up. The maenad of Skopas could well have influenced one of the fat ladies, who, in any case, twists even more sharply than the maenad does.

In the Age of Alexander and in the succeeding Early Hellenistic period, terracotta sculpture at Athens took a new course that was to have far-reaching ramifications in the Greek world. Figures of girls began to be created making use of the techniques hitherto employed for statuettes of comic actors. The scale is tiny, both front and back sides are moulded, vent holes are eliminated or carefully concealed, and bases are flat plates. Figures strike elegantly relaxed poses with arms braced on hips or raised pensively to the neck, and hands are completely mufffled in drapery. Little figures like the exquisite standing draped girl (no. 79) have the incisiveness of the comic actors but with a newly fashionable sweetness. This style seems in part to have been suggested by the works of the Athenian sculptor Praxiteles, famous for the soft forms, the grace and the tenderness of his works.[7] The girls frequently wear their hair pulled back in a lobed arrangement called the melon-coiffure, a fashion also seen in some of the last Athenian marble grave reliefs carved before the sumptuary laws of 317 B.C. (see no. 11). Other miniature statuettes show babies crouching on the ground and spreading out their arms in delightfully fresh and engaging poses. Girls may be dressed in ceremonial finery for their presentation to a god or goddess, as in no. 81. The custom, which almost suggests modern rites of confirmation, is also documented in the large-scale marble statues of diademed girls and boys excavated at the sanctuary of Artemis at Brauron in Attica.[8]

In the last quarter of the century, the scale of terracotta figures increases. The statuette of the girl in her finery mentioned above is a convenient point of reference since a very similar figure was found in an Athenian tomb of shortly after 325 B.C. The figures of the end of the century introduce new poses and a distinctly Early Hellenistic

4. K. Schefold, *JdI* 69 (1954) p. 218ff.
5. R. Thönges-Stringaris, *AthMitt* 80 (1965) p. 63
6. Ridgway, *Copies*, p. 8, pl. 16f.
7. Figures muffled in drapery even appear on the statue base from Mantinea by his workshop. On Praxiteles and the origin of "Tanagra figures," see D. B. Thompson, *AJA* 70 (1966) pp. 60ff.; Robertson, *Shorter History*, pp. 141f., 170, 199.
8. *Praktika*, 1950, p. 176, fig. 5; *Hellenistic Art*, fig. 239f. On the relationship of Brauron and Tanagra figures see D. B. Thompson, *AJA* 70 (1966) no. 5, pl. 17; Stella Miller, *Hesperia* 43 (1974) p. 216f., pl. 37.

taste. Silhouettes are simpler, drapery begins to pull tightly. There can be a dryness and meagreness or at times a tension, compared to the generously voluminous drapery of Late Classical times. There is frequently a light-hearted play with accessories that becomes endemic in the following century. A figure of a boy dressed in military fashion ducks his head into the top of his cloak. A girlish figure toys with a mirror. This last statuette (no. 84) represents a nymph, one of the popular new themes of the latter part of the fourth century. Because of their sympathetic roles as caring individual protectors, nymphs clearly had a hold on the affections of a large part of the population. These minor local goddesses of natural features like caves or rivers appear seated on rock outcroppings in votive reliefs and pedimental sculptures.[9] (A nymph views herself in a mirror while seated on a stool in a Late Classical engraved gem included in the exhibition [no. 156].) While the terracotta nymph here already has a certain Early Hellenistic tightness and dryness, her pose is still conceived in the terms of fourth century funerary sculpture. Like many a deceased young woman in a relief, she props herself up and reaches out to fondle a precious belonging.

The new class of terracotta figures heralded the spirit of the Hellenistic age, and the style was taken up widely. Above all in Boeotia, the region adjoining Attica, where terracotta sculpture had long played a major role, hundreds of figurines in the Early Hellenistic style were buried in tombs or dedicated at sanctuaries. A few such figures were imports from Attica, but local imitations proliferated. The cemeteries around the town of Tanagra were the site of particularly rich finds, and ever since the last century, this class of terracotta statuettes has been called Tanagra figurines. Many local Boeotian figures can be easily distinguished from Attic imports by their crude style, huge, rectangular back vents and coarse clay. In the second half of the century, however, more sophisticated workshops appeared in Boeotia, and it is far from easy to separate the products of the two regions. The problem is complicated by the variation in the "Tanagra figures" of Attica itself, where at times back vents are used, and where pale clay quite different from the red-brown clay typical of Attic vases is at times employed.

The surest guides to the contributions of Attica are the figures actually excavated there. These, unfortunately, consist largely of fragments found in wells and cisterns. As a result, even a somewhat conjectural series of attributions of figures from museum collections can help to round out the pictures of the Late Classical and Early Hellenistic periods. These figures also provide the museum-goer first-hand contact with this important artistic development led by the coroplaths of Athens.

Bibliography: The terracotta sculpture of fourth century Athens has been described above all by D. B. Thompson in *AJA* 70 (1966) p. 51ff.; *Histoire et archéologie* 81 (March 1984) p. 32ff. The picture was amplified and readjusted by Stella Miller in *Hesperia* 43 (1974) p. 211ff.

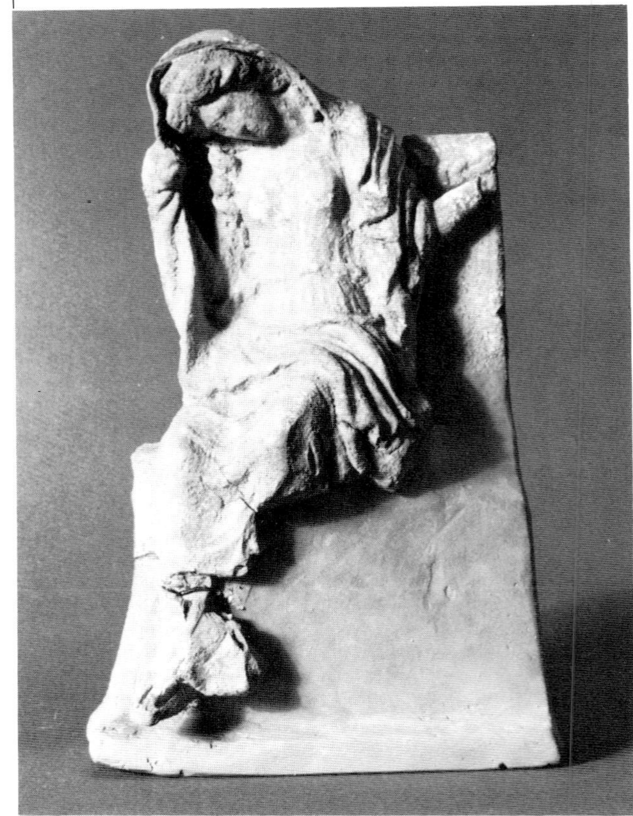

67. Woman or goddess mourning beside a stele
About 400 B.C.
Gift of E. P. Warren 90.193
Height 15.9 cm. Added white over much of the surface, red-brown in the hair. Corkscrew curls have been added, much as in the sculptural vase with the birth of Aphrodite. Rectangular vent in back of altar. Fine reddish brown clay like that of Attic vases.

A ribbon (tainia) is tied around the stele. The woman sits on an altar or funerary table (trapeza).

For the style, compare a standing woman in Munich: *Loeb Coll.*, I, pl. 33 (from Greece) dated about 400 B.C. and attributed to Attica in the brochure for the exhibition on the 50th anniversary of the death of James Loeb. See also A. Köster, *Die Griechischen Terrakotten* (Berlin 1926) p. 62, pl. 37 (from Salamis).

For the pose, see a bronze statuette of a mourning woman with a snake in her lap from north Italy (Pied-

9. See nymphs from the pediment of the Temple of Apollo Patroos in the Agora, the relief from Vari and the relief dedicated by Neoptolemos in the Agora, all datable around 330 B.C.: H. Thompson, *Hesperia* 21 (1952) p. 109f., pl. 28c, d; T. L. Shear, *Hesperia* 42 (1973) pp. 168ff., pl. 35c; O. Palagia, *Euphranor* (Leiden 1980) pp. 8, 55, figs. 2-4, 67.

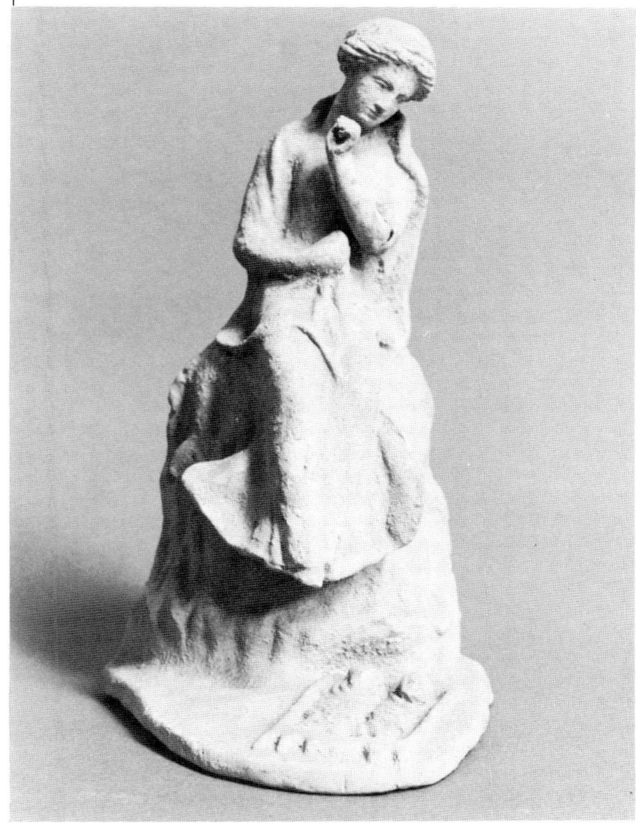

mont) in Berlin: K. A. Neugebauer, *Antike Bronzestatuetten* (Berlin 1921) p. 114, fig. 64.

A similar stone statuette in the Louvre has been identified as Aphrodite mourning for Adonis; see L. R. Farnell, *The Cults of the Greek States*, 2 (reprint, Chicago 1971) p. 695, pl. 47 (citing a description by Macrobius of a statue in Lebanon). Schefold revives the interpretation of a similar mourning figure on the three-sided relief in Boston as Demeter mourning for Adonis: *Göttersage*, p. 80, fig. 98; Comstock and Vermeule, *Sculpture*, no. 30.

68. A mother exposing her twins: perhaps Tyro, Neleus and Pelias

Fourth century
Boeotian or Athenian, said to be from Tanagra
Purchased by Contribution 01.7826
Height 18.6 cm. Open under and behind. White on face and neck, red on hair, pupils of eyes black. Fine clay, red-orange below and yellow above. The red-orange area is very similar to clay of an Attic old man (MFA 13.155), identical to clay of a woman from Kos (MFA 87.423). The yellow area is very similar to the clay of the comic actor below.

Tyro is dressed in a chiton and a skimpy himation. Her hair is rolled back over a ribbon. She looks down at her children, who are wrapped in blankets and wear babies' pointed caps. They are tucked into a cradle, which is not shown as the rustic log of the legend but as an ornate type with profiled ends known from a bronze example in the Museum of Fine Arts. Tyro launched the cradle with her children, the illegitimate offspring of Poseidon, in the river Enipeos (in the Peloponnesos). They were recovered and reared by a horse trainer, who had them nursed by animals. The children eventually returned to rescue their mother from disgrace and oppression and went on to found cities in Thessaly and the Peloponnesos.

The technique, costume and hairstyle all indicate a relatively early date for this woman seated on a rock outcropping, a compositional scheme very popular in the Hellenistic period. The unusual style could be derived from that of Athenian figural vases, some of which also have rocky settings and spindly figures. The myth has a Peloponnesian locus, but it was the subject of a tragedy by the Athenian playwright Sophocles. The terracotta, it might be noted, could well represent other analogous myths of heroes abandoned by their mother. The story of Antiope and her twins Amphion and Zethos suggests itself particularly. The twins, who had been fathered by Zeus, were left in a cave near Plataea in the frontier region between Attica and Boeotia. The Plataeans attached themselves to Attica, and Antiope was the subject of a tragedy by Euripides in the late fifth century.

In a fourth century context, this creative and poetic series is likely to have originated in Athens. Another example preserved in Athens is also said to come from Tanagra and is apparently made of Boeotian clay. The style is similar, but Tyro/Antiope wears a sakkos. The terracotta could, however, have been moulded from an Athenian figure, a not uncommon situation.

On the terracotta in Athens, see *AthMitt* 10 (1885) p. 173; P. Wolters, *JdI* 6 (1891) p. 61, p1. 2; F. Winter, *Die Typen der figürlichen Terrakotten*, I (Berlin and Stuttgart 1903) p. 140, no. 6.

For the stories of Tyro and Antiope, see C. Kerényi, *The Heroes of the Greeks* (London 1959) pp. 35ff., 71ff. For the cave of Antiope, see Pausanias, I, xxxviii, 9.

Published: Klein, p1. 3c; H. Palmer, *Archaeology* 5 (1952) p. 118.

69. Ram

Mid-fourth century
From Athens
Gift of Mrs. E. S. H. Pendergast 64.2198
Height 11 cm. Traces of white slip. Fine beige clay. Most of back and sides missing. Open under.

Cat. 69.

Cat. 70.

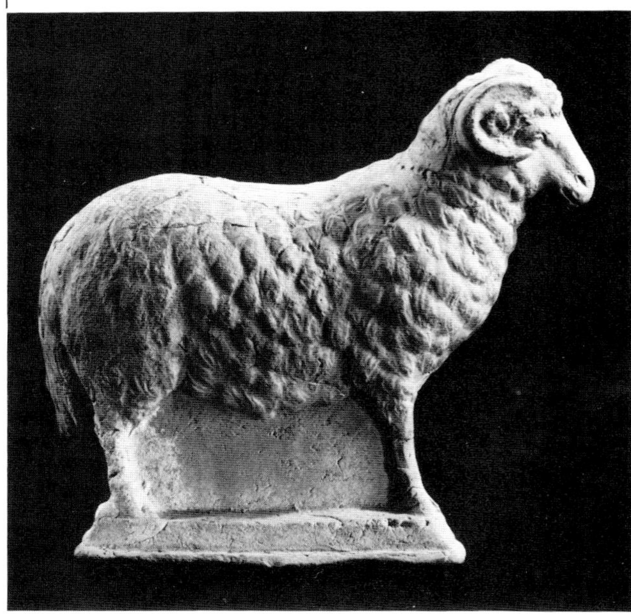

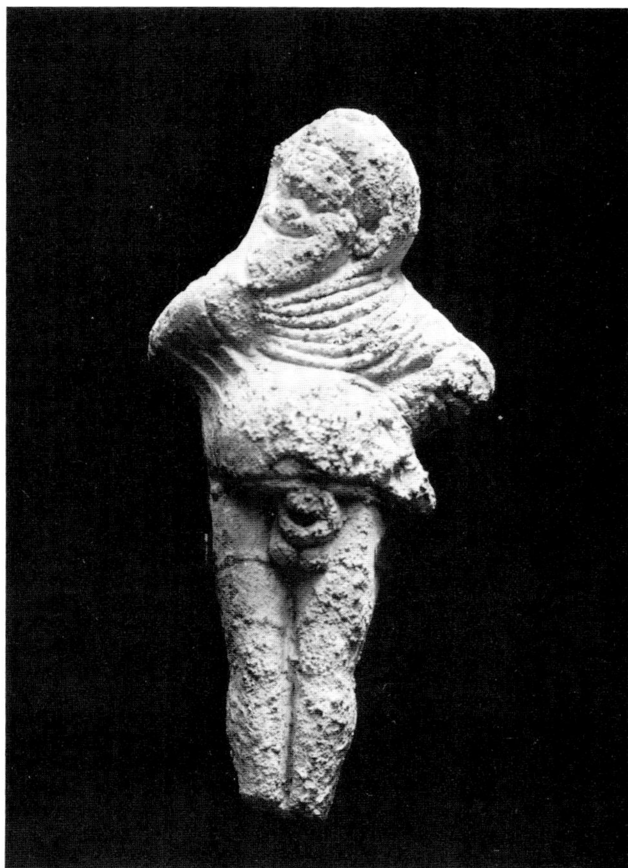

Compare a fragment of a very similar sheep excavated in a context of 338-326 B.C. on the Pnyx: D. B. Thompson, *Hesperia, Supplement* 7 (1943) p. 155, no. 99. fig. 67. For the date, see *Hesperia* 21 (1952) p. 118f., n. 12; *AJA* 70 (1966) p. 53.

Published: C. Vermeule, *Classical Journal* 62 (Dec. 1966) p. 107, fig. 16; *idem, S to S*, pp. 98f., 136, fig. 138.

70. Actor of Old Comedy
375-350 B.C.
Bought in Athens, said to be from the Kabeirion in Thebes
Purchased by Contribution 01.7758
Height 9.3 cm. Front moulded, back finished sketchily by hand. Tiny vent between the buttocks. Light yellowish beige clay.

The actor wears a short cloak (himation) wrapped over his head. The hem of a short tunic (chitoniskos) appears below it. He wears a mask and an artificial paunch and phallos.

Published: *The Theater in Ancient Art* (Princeton 1951) fig. 11; Bieber, p. 39, fig. 137; T. B. L. Webster, *Hesperia* 29 (1960) p. 271; *idem, Monuments Illustrating Old and Middle Comedy* (BICS, suppl. 23, 1969) p. 32, t.c. AT 40a; R. C. Ketterer, *Greek, Roman and Byzantine Studies* 21 (1980) p. 219.

71. Nurse or servant cradling now-missing object
Early fourth century
Bought in Athens
Purchased by Contribution 01.7896
Height 11 cm. No back vent. Small hole in base plate. Sketchily finished behind.

The woman cups her hands and tilts her head to view whatever she once held. She suggests a comic nurse, a well-established type (see the following), but her burden seems too small to have been a baby. Perhaps she carried a bird. Her hair is enclosed in the "hair-net" (sakkos) frequently worn by servants on later Classical funerary stelai. She is dressed in a chiton with sleeves and a short, shawl-like himation.

72. Actor of middle comedy as a woman with baby
375-350 B.C.
Bought in Athens
Purchased by Contribution 01.7892
Height 8 cm. Moulded in front, flat behind. Small round vent under base plate.

The actor wears the mask of an old woman and is completely wrapped in a long himation. The baby seems to be a cylindrical prop with a conical top. The actor touches his chin. The gesture suggests astonishment, perplexity or simply the act of eating.

Cat. 71.
Cat. 72.

Cat. 73.
Cat. 74.

There are several possible explanations of this figure, which is known in other better-quality replicas. She certainly evokes the mood of Aristophanes's parodies of women; she could well be one of the lazy, greedy, bibulous characters who raid their husbands' closed larders and go about with wine-skins dressed as babies *(Thesmophoriazusai*, 418-425, 730-738).

Published: Webster, *Monuments...Comedy*, p. 23, no. AT 8f.

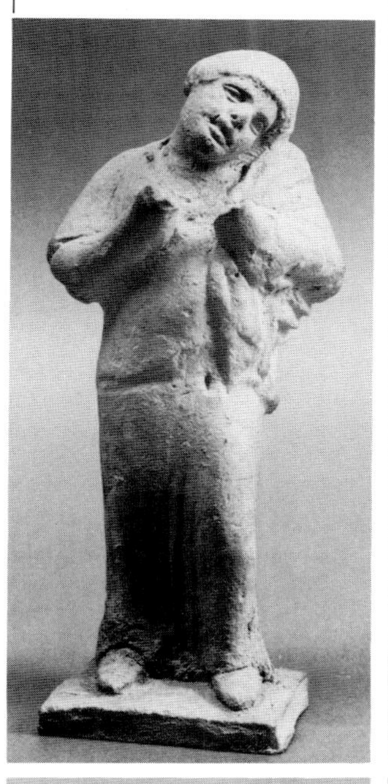

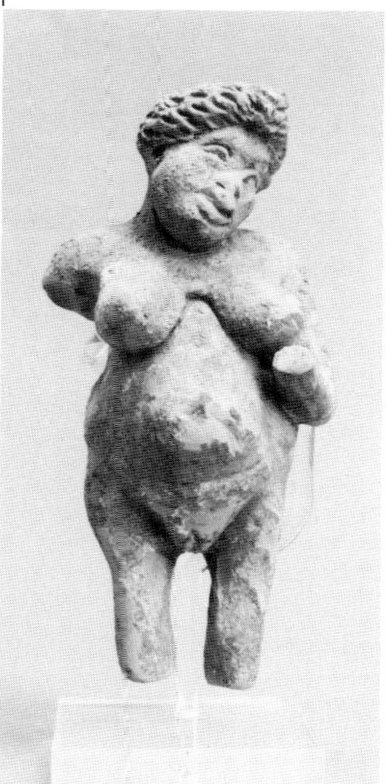

73. Nude fat lady

350-325 B.C.
Purchased by Contribution 01.7895
Height 9.6 cm. Without vent. Traces of red in hair. Body painted red-brown over a white preparatory layer.

The woman has her hair twisted into a braid across the top of her head. The dark skin tone and the facial features have a vaguely African cast. It has been suggested that this woman's projecting buttocks and spindly, bird-like legs were intended to parody a Siren.

Other such statuettes, some of which have been excavated in the Agora, have been interpreted as caricatures of foreign prostitutes. In support of this idea, Dorothy Burr Thompson has cited a fat lady in the British Museum who still retains her original painted surface; the figure seems to be tattooed as well as bejewelled. The purpose of such figures, however, would be very hard to understand. On the other hand, obese, tattooed barbarians with very silly and indecent customs (the Mossynoecians) were encountered by Xenophon on his march along the southeastern coast of the Black Sea. They fattened themselves on nuts, they engaged in sex promiscuously and publicly, and as they went about, they laughed and danced, even when alone. The Mossynoecians became popular fixtures in Greek geography, and, among other places, were incorporated into accounts of the Argonauts' legendary voyage. Perhaps these statuettes represent a kind of ethnographic comedy based on such travellers' tales.

On the Mossynoecians, see Xenophon, *Anabasis*, V, iv, 32-34; Apollonios of Rhodes, *Argonautica*, II, 379, 1019.

Published: D. B. Thompson, *Hesperia* 23 (1954) p. 91. For other similar figures and the date of the type, see *ibid.*, pp. 88, 90f., 106, no. 2, pl. 21; Higgins, p. 103, pl. 44d.

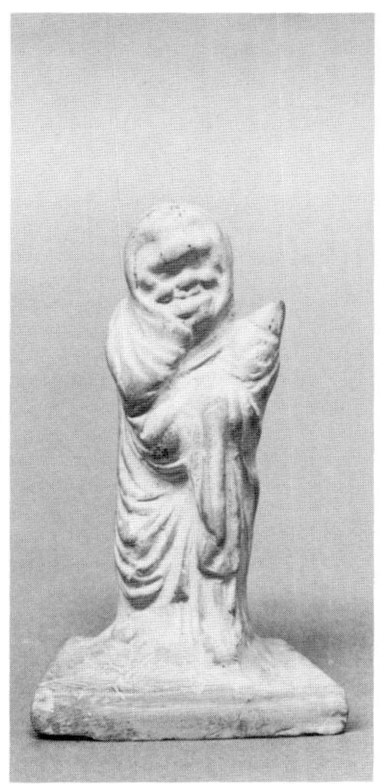

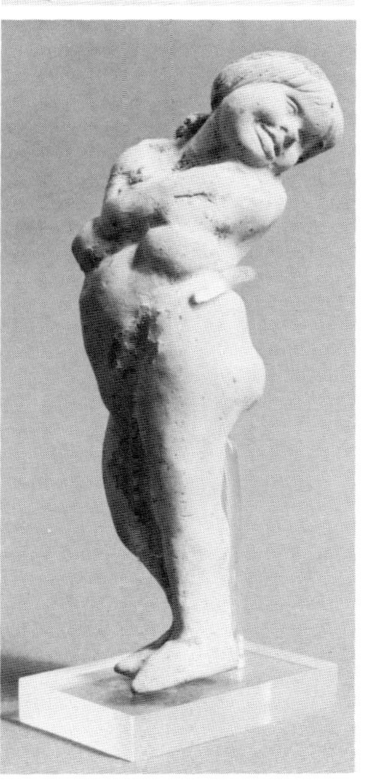

74. Nude fat lady viewing her back

Probably second half of the fourth century
Purchased by Contribution 03.915
Height 13.2 cm. Mould-made. No back vent. Traces of white ground.

Among other none-too-convincing interpretations of these puzzling statuettes of fat ladies, it has been suggested that they are caricatures of famous works of art. If so, this figure might have been intended to evoke the maenad of Skopas, famous for her spiralling pose.

This figure, it might be noted, is extremely adventurous in showing not only a twisting pose but also a backward glance, as in several middle Hellenistic sculptures. Parallels can, however, also be found in fourth century vase painting and bronze vessels.

If the figures can, on the other hand, be considered parodies of the silly, obese Mossynoecians of eastern Asia Minor, her action should be interpreted as an effort to view her body-paintings or tattooes. According to Xenophon, the backs of these people were colored especially brightly.

For the maenad of Skopas and related types, see Robertson, *History*, pp. 455f., 468, 472, pl. 143a, 149d. For fourth century maenads looking backwards and downwards, see a South Italian krater in Taranto and the reverse side of the Derveni Krater: *ibid.*, p. 429, pl. 135a; *Search*, no. 127. See also the silver ring with a maenad here (no. 146). For middle Hellenistic sculptural parallels, see Robertson, *History*, pp. 553, 564, 607, pl. 178d, 179c. For Xenophon's account of the Mossynoecians, see the previous entry.

75. Jointed doll or puppet

About 350-320 B.C.
Said to be from Attica
Purchased by Contribution 01.7883
Height 26.2 cm. Red-brown color in the hair, white on body.

The figure has a hairdo that could well be Early Hellenistic, yet the knee joints are a very old-fashioned type that had largely been displaced in the fourth century by concealed joints. She plays the castanets (krotala).

Unlike modern dolls, these figures were not intended to be dressed by their owners. In grave reliefs, these small figures are shown nude. Castanets were frequently played by professional entertainers, often courtesans. The nudity of the figures agrees with that interpretation. Jointed figures with castanets might have been puppets (neurospasta). It has been suggested that jointed dolls with the short skirts of dancers were also used for this purpose. Professional puppeteers travelled in search of an audience in Classical as well as more recent times.

A puppeteer was a guest at a famous banquet with Socrates; see Xenophon, *Symposium*, 4, 55. On puppets, see also Klein, *loc. cit.* On these dolls, see also K. Albertson, in *Allentown*, no. 123.

Published: K. Elderkin, *AJA* 34 (1930) p. 466, fig. 15; Klein, p. 15, pl. 16b; Morgan, *Brockton*, p. 52, ill. 25.

Cats. 76, 77, 78.

76. Kneeling dancer (oklasma dancer) with hands clasped

Fourth century
Formerly in the Lecuyer collection. Said to be from Athens
Purchased by Contribution 01.7888
Height 8.3 cm. Traces of blue and purple (?) color on the dancer's chiton. Solid. White slip.

The dancer kneels on a table and is clad in barbarian costume: pointed "Phrygian" cap, long-sleeved, short-skirted tunic (chiton) and trousers (anaxyrides).

Athenians of the Classical period called a kind of dance that they learned in Asia Minor "oklasma." In this dance, the performer had to bend his knees and clasp his hands. The oklasma was performed in honor of the Phrygian god Sabazios, whose cult was introduced at Athens amid considerable controversy in the later fifth century. Representations of the dance on vases with Dionysiac subjects make it clear that it was transferred to this cult as well. The table is a very commonly used prop in these scenes.

It seems likely that the oklasma dance also became a popular, purely secular entertainment. In Xenophon's account of his army's journey along the Black Sea coast, a soldier from northwest Asia Minor performed the Persian dance with crouching at a banquet.

On the oklasma dance, see Schweitzer, *Hermes* 71 (1936) p. 281ff.; J. Beazley, *JHS* 59 (1939) p. 30ff.; Metzger, *Représentations*, pp. 148ff., pls. 19a, 20b, 21a, b; Xenophon, *Anabasis*, VI, 1, 10.

Published: Lecuyer, pl. 70.

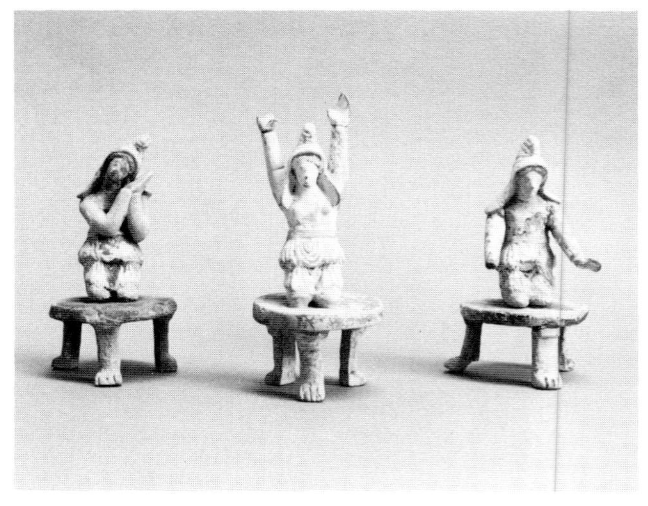

77. Kneeling dancer (oklasma dancer) with upraised arms
Fourth century
Formerly in the Lecuyer collection. Said to be from Athens
Purchased by Contribution 01.7889
Height 9.7 cm. Red-brown on hair and table, traces of blue on chiton. White slip.

Like the preceding, the dancer performs in barbaric costume on a three-legged table.

Published: Lecuyer, pl. 70.

78. Kneeling dancer (oklasma dancer) with outspread arms
Fourth century
Formerly in the Lecuyer collection. Said to be from Athens
Purchased by Contribution 01.7890
Height 8.4 cm. Red-brown on hair. White slip.

Like the preceding, the dancer performs in Persian costume on a three- legged table.

Published: Lecuyer, pl. 70.

79. Standing woman with arms muffled in drapery
About 340-320 B.C.
Purchased by Contribution 01.7899
Height 12.3 cm. White slip. Back moulded without vent. Reddish beige clay.

The hair is arranged in a melon-coiffure, and the back of her head is circled by a braid. She wears a long chiton and a short himation, which is thrown over her left shoulder, wraps around her neck snugly and hangs down in back. Her pose is a variation on the "Sophokles stance"; one arm is placed on her hip while the other is held up in front of the body.

80. Squatting child with outstretched arms
About 330-310 B.C.
Bequest of Susan C. Warren 02.38
Height 5.8 cm. Reddish brown clay. Traces of white slip. No back vent.

The girl's hair is arranged in a melon-coiffure circled by a braid. She wears a high-belted, sleeveless chiton.

Published: Klein, p. 7, pl. 7e.

81. Standing girl with tiara and tambourine (tympanon)
Around 325 B.C.
Said to have been found on Aigina
Purchased by Contribution 01.7860
Height 13.3 cm. Figure covered with white slip. Tympanon, border of tiara and hair violet. Traces of blue paint on the peplos. Irises of eyes and rim of tympanon painted black. Other black zones on tympanon and base possibly

Cat. 79.
Cat. 80.
Cat. 81.

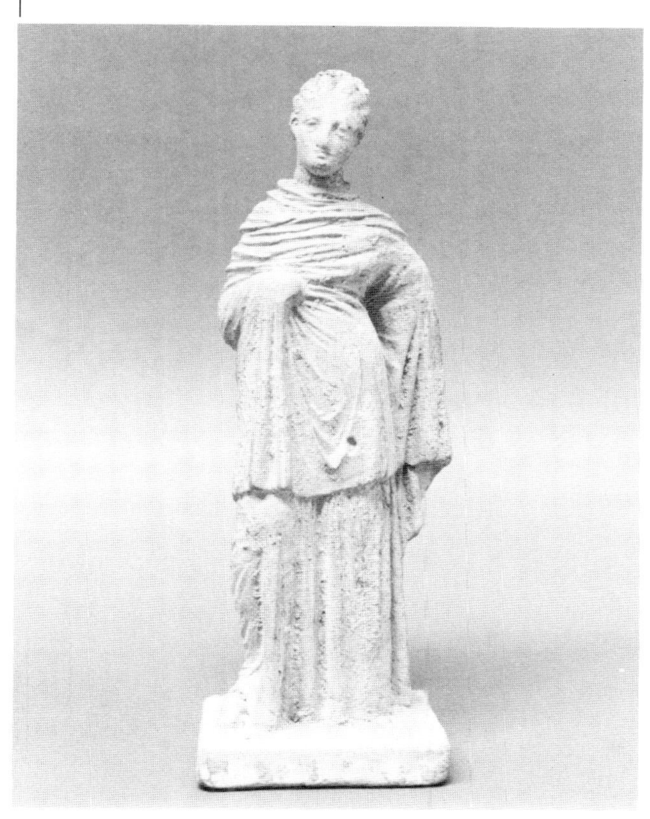

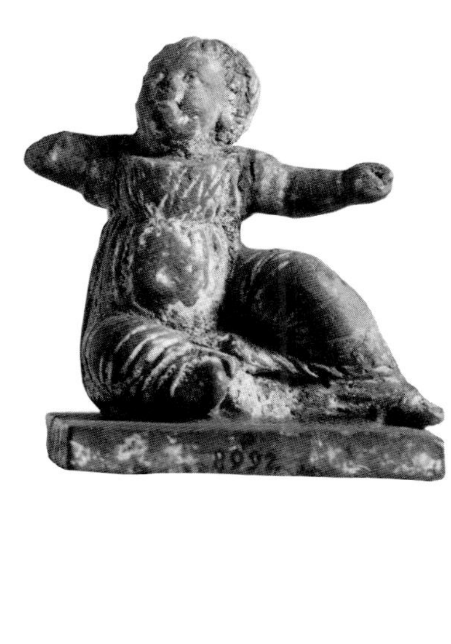

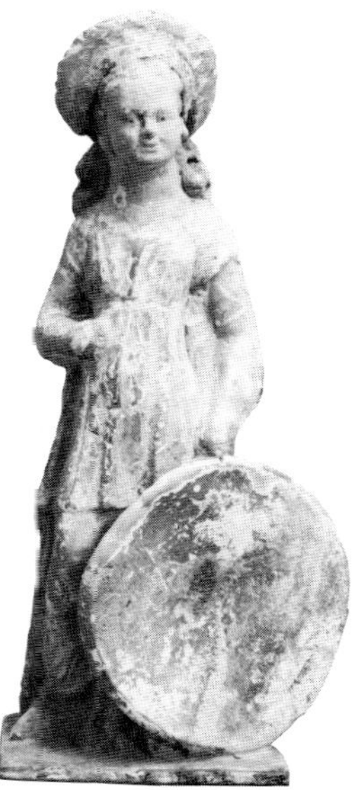

from burning. No back vent. Ribbons tying tiara (or loops of hair), tiara and tympanon added in separate strips of clay.

The girl wears earrings and a gown (peplos) with long overfold and high belt. Her hair is arranged in a melon-coiffure largely hidden by the tiara. It has been suggested that the disc is a hoop. The ornaments the girl wears, however, seem ill-suited to a situation of play, and it seems more likely that they indicate the moment of religious consecration (to Dionysos?). To be sure, playthings like dolls were dedicated at shrines before marriage.

For a very similar sketchily-modelled figure of a child with a tiara from a tomb in the Kerameikos created shortly after 325 B.C., see B. Schlörb-Vierneisel, *AthMitt* 81 (1966) p. 87, pl. 56, 6.

Published: Klein, pl. 20a.

82. Standing woman muffled in drapery

Around 320-300 B.C.
Attic or Boeotian
Purchased by Contribution 01.7833
Height 16.7 cm. Beige clay. Moulded behind without vent. Red paint on the braid of hair.

The woman has her hair arranged in a melon-coiffure circled by a braid and is dressed in a long chiton and heavy himation. Both her hands are covered, but she raises one arm from which a cascade of drapery is suspended.

The figure has the very simple contours and the tightly pulled drapery of the Early Hellenistic period. There is still enough looseness and enough relief, however, to merit a date before the century's end. The braid that reaches high onto the crown of the head is also a fourth century version of the hair style seen on the latest Athenian grave stelai.

Cat. 82.

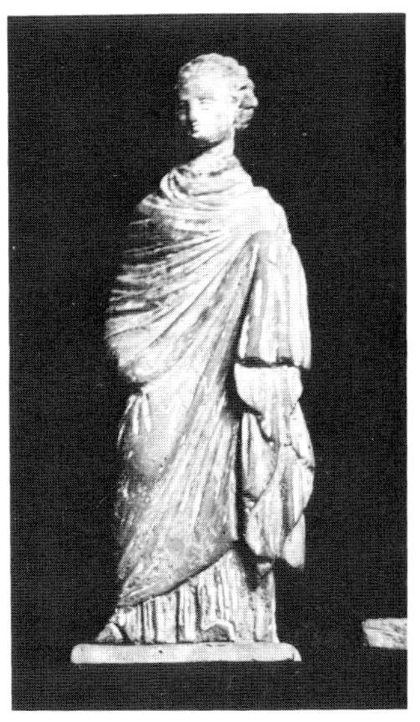

Cat. 83.

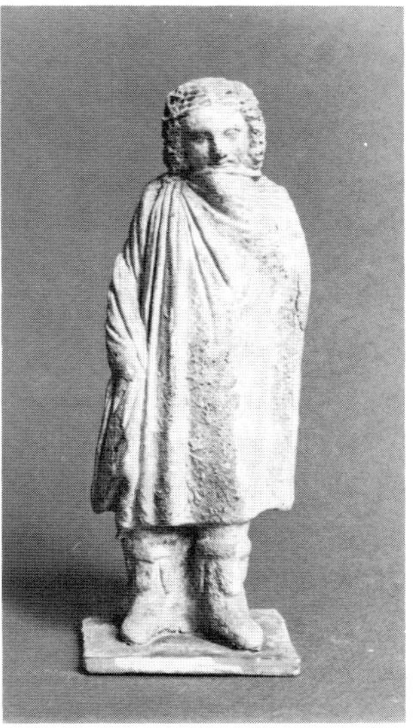

Cat. 84.

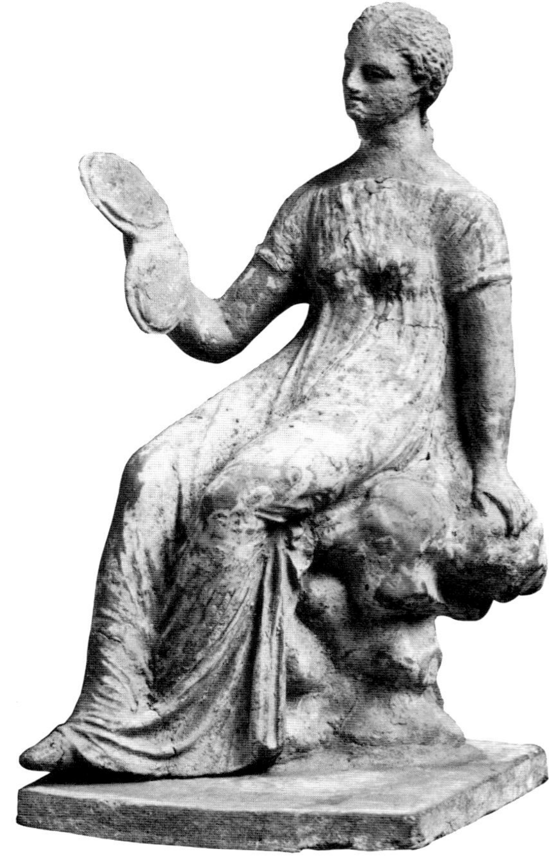

For a figure of this type dated around 300 B.C., see *Loeb Coll.*, I, pl. 42; G. Kleiner, *Tanagrafiguren, JdI, Ergänzungsheft* 15 (1942) pp. 109f.

83. Standing boy wrapped in his cloak

About 310-280 B.C.
Said to be from Athens
Purchased by Contribution 01.7795
Height 16.1 cm. No back vent. Red on hair and boots, pink on flesh, and yellow on chlamys. Fine reddish beige clay.

The boy wears military costume: boots, short tunic (chitoniskos) and cloak (chlamys). Both his hands are wrapped in his garments, and he raises his left to his chin. This costume became particularly popular throughout the Greek world during the period of Macedonian domination, but statuettes of boys wrapped up in this fashion can be traced even earlier in the fourth century. A fragmentary figure of this type has been found in the Kabeirion at Thebes and probably predates the destruction of the sanctuary by the soldiers of Alexander in 336 B.C.

For a very similar boy in the British Museum attributed to Attica, see Higgins, p. 100, pl. 41D. For a boy wrapped in his himation dating from the first half of the fourth century, see *Corinth* 15, 2, no. XVIII, 10, p. 140, pl. 27. For a find of several figures with this pose and wrapped in their cloaks in the Agora of Athens, see Stella Miller, *Hesperia* 43 (1974) p. 212f. (type I) nos. 82-7, pl. 37. For the fragment at Thebes, see B. Schmaltz, *Terrakotten aus dem Kabirenheiligtum bei Theben* (Berlin 1974) no. 203, p. 81, pl. 17. On the date and scope of the destruction of the Kabeirion, see Pausanias, IX, 25, 9f.; D. B. Thompson, *AJA* 70 (1966) p. 52; Schmaltz attempts to push a few terracottas after this date: *op. cit.*, p. 2f.

84. Nymph looking at a mirror

End of the fourth or early third century B.C.
Purchased by Contribution 01.7881
Height 16.2 cm. Covered with white slip. Red on hair, lips and decoration of mirror. Black on both parts of mirror, grey on eyes. Roughly finished on back. Without vent.

The girl sits on a rocky outcropping and is dressed in a short-sleeved, high-belted chiton. Her hair is pulled back into a ponytail. She is looking at the mirror's cover, whose relief seems to depict the head of the Medusa.

The ponytail was worn at least as early as the middle of the fourth century, as in the stele of Kallistrate in St. Louis. In such early occurrences, however, the hair is not pulled back so tightly around the face. See also the terracotta fat lady above, who wears a ponytail but has a distinct roll of hair framing her face.

For the stele of Kallistrate, see C. Vermeule, *America*, no. 69.

Published: *Museum of Fine Arts, Boston, Preview*, April 1984 (Object of the Month).

Athenian Coinage

In the great days of the Athenian empire during the second half of the fifth century B.C., the silver coinage of Athens had been awesomely abundant and widespread. The metal itself came both from the rich silver mines at Laurion in Attica and from the tribute of the states around the Aegean that were allied with Athens. This situation changed radically toward the close of the Peloponnesian War. In 413 B.C. Sparta set up a land base at Decelea in Attica that cut off the supply of silver from the mines. Two years later, Athens's allies revolted, tribute was no longer sent, and from this time, the regular minting of silver coinage almost ceased at Athens. By 406 B.C., the Athenians had been driven to melting down gold votive gifts for an issue of gold coins to finance the war.[1]

After the loss of the war in 404 B.C., the commerce of Athens limped on making use of a variety of expedients. Silver-plated bronze coins were struck. Solid silver coins dating from before 406 B.C. may have also continued to circulate. Many have been found in fourth century hoards outside Athens.[2] In Egypt, large silver tetradrachms of Athens and local imitations of Athenian coins were apparently the only generally recognized form of money through most of the fourth century.[3] The Museum of Fine Arts, in fact, possesses several Athenian tetradrachms of the late fifth century excavated in Naukratis in the Nile Delta, presumably in fourth century contexts.

Much as in modern coinage, the vast issues of coinage in fifth century Athens had been highly standardized. The imagery was a series of primary, pious civic emblems. The obverse of each coin featured the head of the city's patron Athena. The warrior goddess wears a helmet that is trimmed with the leaves of the olive tree, a distinctive product of Attica that had been her gift to the region. The reverse of most coins, particularly the larger denominations, shows the owl, a symbol of Athena. The owls had been whimsically characterized as quite a special breed by Aristophanes; they were the owls of Laurion who build "nests within your purses hatching little silver pieces."[4] The reverse is usually turned into a symbolic landscape by a branch of olive foliage and a crescent moon, appropriate for the nocturnal bird of prey. The inscription, "Athe", clearly identified the origin of the money on the reverse of all Athenian coins.

The style of Athenian coins remained constant and even old-fashioned. Both Athena and her owl are presented with the strong, geometric contours inherited from Archaic art of the sixth century B.C. As in Archaic art, the goddess's eye was shown in front view even though the head was in profile.

The mixture of plated and solid silver coinage in circulation in the late fifth and the early fourth centuries must have created a multitude of problems. The endemic irritant of counterfeiting would have aggravated the situation. Not surprisingly, coins were frequently tested by drilling and cutting, as was the case with the pieces from Naukratis, to determine if they were solid silver. In Athens itself, the confusion had become so great that a law was

1. Kraay, p. 68ff.
2. See the list of hoards and an analysis of their contents in C. Starr, *Athenian Coinage* (Oxford 1970) p. 87ff. On plated bronze, see Kraay, p. 69f.
3. Kraay, p. 76
4. Aristophanes, *The Birds*, 1106f. (B. Rogers translation)

passed in 375/4 B.C. establishing the position of "tester." Two such officials, one located in the Agora of Athens, the other in Piraeus, were empowered to make the final ruling on the authenticity of a disputed piece.

In the first decade of the fourth century, Athens rapidly improved her political and economic situation, and sometime before 391 B.C., after a hiatus of little more than a decade, solid silver coins could be issued once again. The new coinage was a deliberate revival of the old imperial money with the least possible change.[5] The images of Athena and her owl were repeated quite exactly. The only alteration was a slight modernization of the style. Athena's eye was finally shown in a manner consistent with the profile view of the head, the heavy, projecting nose was made less aggressive, and the contours of the facial features were slightly softened.

The large tetradrachm was the standard-bearer of the Athenian monetary system, but it was valuable enough to be used primarily for rather large payments. A series of smaller units was necessary for more routine transactions. As in the fifth century, fractions of the drachm along with multiples and fractions of the obol were minted in the traditional metal, silver, to satisfy everyday needs. The head of Athena remained a constant feature on the obverse of smaller coins, but slight variations on the reverse were used to distinguish the various denominations. The owl might lose his crescent moon and be turned frontally. A second branch of olive foliage might be added. The owl might even be given a double body. On the smallest units, the bird was omitted. The emblem would be the crescent moon or a new symbol, the basket. Common to all reverses, however, was the inscription that proclaimed the Athenian origin of the coin.

Considered as objects, the larger sizes of coin (the drachm and its multiples) were quite manageable, but the smaller sizes (the obol and its fractions) could well be considered elusively miniature. The tiny size, however, did have one advantage; it enabled the shopper to carry his money in his mouth, a great convenience in a civilization without pockets.[6] The practice, on the other hand, did entail the risk that the smaller change might well be inadvertently swallowed.

After the middle of the fourth century, the problems created by the small size of low denomination silver coins were avoided by introducing small change made of bronze. The inspiration for the idea must have come from the borders of the Greek world. Bronze coinage had been used in Sicily and at Olbia on the Black Sea since the fifth century. Like the silver, bronze Athenian coins also carried the head of Athena. A series of variations on the reverse is quite similar to the permutations of the reverses of the small silver coins. Stylistically, the bronze coins minted after the death of Alexander the Great take on a more cosmopolitan, Early Hellenistic character. Athena wears a Corinthian helmet and tilts her rather delicate features upwards.

The wheel of Athens's monetary and political fortunes came full circle in the first years of the third century. Athens made the effort to rid herself of her erstwhile hero, Demetrius Poliorcetes. After his disastrous defeat in 301 B.C. and during an absence of several years, she attempted to close her doors to him. He returned and put the city under siege. During this crisis, Lachares, the leader of the mercenaries who had made himself tyrant of Attica, had recourse to the same emergency financing that had been used in the last years of the Peloponnesian War. He melted down gold and silver votive offerings, including the gold foil covering the Athena Parthenos, and used the metal for coinage in 296/5 B.C. In these coins, Athena's features became a touch more refined while the composition was slightly more cluttered. The emergency issue was as unsuccessful as its precedent of 110 years earlier, since the city surrendered to Demetrius. These coins represent the end of the fourth century phase rather than a new beginning. There was apparently relatively limited minting at Athens during the following two-thirds of a century of Macedonian rule.

Bibliography: C. Seltman, *Greek Coins* (London 1955) pp. 178ff., 258ff.; Kleiner; C. Kraay, *Coins of Ancient Athens* (Newcastle upon Tyne 1968); Kraay, pp. 63-77. On early bronze coinage, see M. Jessop Price in *Essays in Greek Coinage Presented to Stanley Robinson* (Oxford 1968) p. 90ff. On bronzes of Athens, see Kroll. On silver mining in Attica in the fourth century, see R. J. Hopper, *BSA* 48 (1953) p. 200ff.

85. Silver tetradrachm

Late fifth century (before 406 B.C.)
From Naukratis
Gift of Egypt Exploration Fund 86.828
Diameter 24 mm. Weight 16.71 grams. Test hole drilled in center.
Obverse: head of Athena in crested Athenian helmet, on bowl of which are three upright olive leaves and palmette spray; horse-hair plume. Athena wears disc earrings and two necklaces, the lower of which has been obliterated.
Reverse: within square incuse, owl, body in profile, head facing; crescent moon and olive spray; **ΑΘΕ**.

Published: Brett, no. 1089.

86. Silver tetradrachm

Late fifth century (before 406 B.C.)
From Naukratis
Gift of Egypt Exploration Fund 86.827
Diameter 24 mm. Weight 16.65 grams. Test hole drilled in center.
Designs like the preceding.

Published: Brett, no. 1090.

5. Kraay, p. 74
6. Coins carried in the mouth are mentioned by Aristophanes in *The Birds*, 503; *The Wasps*, 609, 791.

87. Silver tetradrachm
393-300 B.C.
From Naukratis: different hoard from the two preceding
Gift of Egypt Exploration Fund 86.829
Diameter 23 mm. Weight 16.80 grams
Designs like the preceding.

Published: Brett, no. 1093.

88. Silver hemidrachm
393-300 B.C.
Anonymous Gift 18.681
Diameter 13 mm. Weight 2.05 grams
Obverse similar to preceding.
Reverse: within round incuse, owl facing; on either side, an olive branch; **Α Θ (Ε)**.

Published: Brett, no. 1097.

89. Silver diobol
393-300 B.C.
H. L. Pierce Fund 04.839
Diameter 12 mm. Weight 1.33 grams
Obverse similar to preceding.
Reverse: within shallow square incuse, two owls confronting with single facing head; olive twig with leaves and berry; **Α Θ Ε**.

Published: Brett, no. 1094.

90. Silver 3/4 obol
393-300 B.C.
Catharine Page Perkins Fund 00.276
Diameter 7 mm. Weight 0.50 grams
Obverse similar to preceding.
Reverse: within round incuse, three crescents enclose **ΑΘΕ**.

Published: Brett, no. 1098.

91. Silver 3/8 obol
393-300 B.C.
H. L. Pierce Fund 04.840
Diameter 6 mm. Weight 0.25 grams
Obverse similar to preceding.
Reverse: within square incuse, a basket (kalathos) on its side below **ΑΘΕ**.

Published: Brett, no. 1095.

92. Silver quarter obol
393-300 B.C.
Catharine Page Perkins Fund 00.278
Diameter 5 mm. Weight 0.19 grams
Obverse similar to preceding.
Reverse: within square incuse, crescent below **ΑΘΕ**.

Published: Brett, no. 1096.

Athenian coins of silver and gold (1:1).
Cats. 85, 86, 87.
Cats. 88, 89, 90, 91, 92.
Cat. 95.

93. Bronze coin
330-322 B.C.
Theodora Wilbour Fund in Memory of Zoë Wilbour
1965 Apparatus
Diameter 14.6 mm. Weight 3.13 grams
Obverse: head of Athena in plumed Attic helmet.
Reverse: within olive wreath, two owls over a bakchos ring (instrument of the Eleusinian cult); **ΑΘΕ**.

Compare Kroll, type B.

94. Bronze coin
About 322-307 B.C.
Theodora Wilbour Fund in Memory of Zoë Wilbour
1965 Apparatus
Diameter 15.2 mm. Weight 4.41 grams
Obverse: head of Athena in Corinthian helmet.
Reverse: within olive wreath, owl facing left; **ΗΘ/Α**.
Compare Kroll, type E.

95. Gold stater
296/5 B.C.
Catharine Page Perkins Fund 00.273
Diameter 16 mm. Weight 8.52 grams
Obverse: head of Athena in crested Athenian helmet.
Reverse: within square incuse, owl facing right; olive branch; basket (kalathos); **ΑΘΕ**.

Published: Brett, no. 1099.

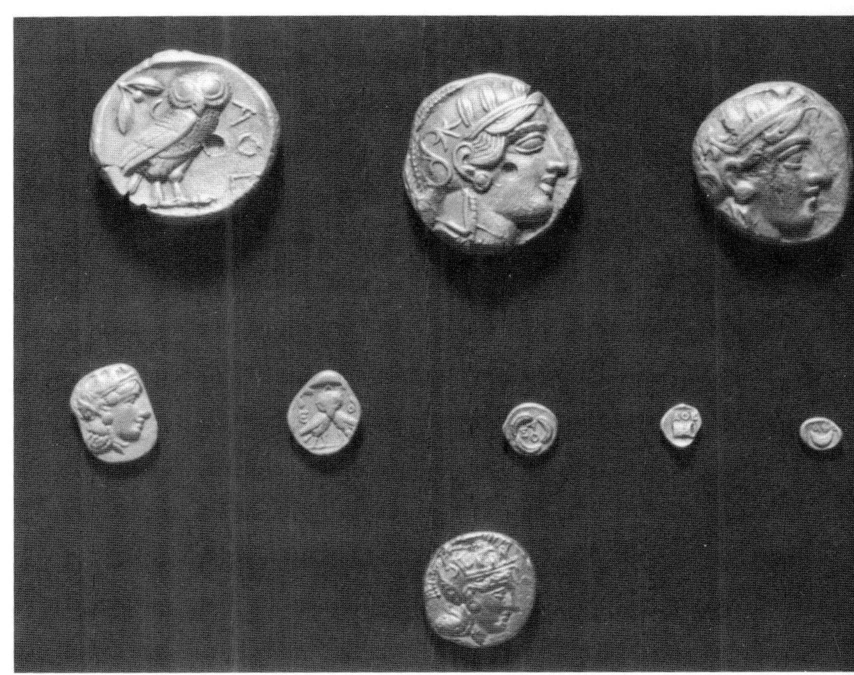

Bronze coins of Athens and Attica.
Cats. 93, 94, 98.
Cats. 96, 97.

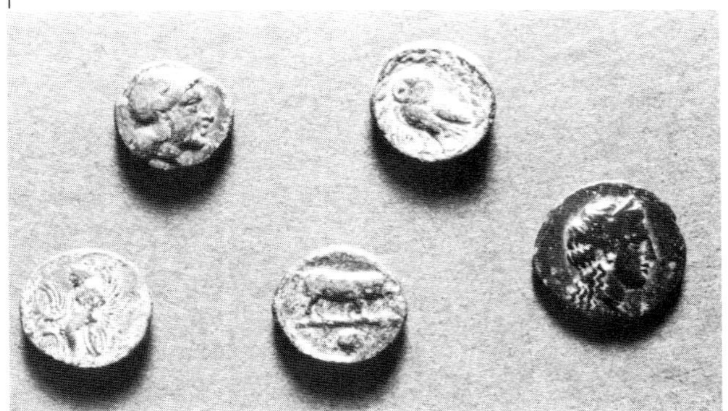

Coins of Attica

Athens was the capital of the region of Attica, the large peninsula thrusting out from central Greece into the Aegean, and she dominated the region totally. The various regions, towns and cities were given membership in the tribes of Athens and could take refuge in the metropolis in times of war. In a few cases, Athens granted the right of coining bronzes to some of these localities that had claim to some particular distinction. Most notable was Eleusis; the town's coinage celebrated the cults of Demeter, Kore and Triptolemos, whose shrines at Eleusis formed one of the most famous religious centers of Antiquity. The obverse of these coins shows Triptolemos, one of the primeval inhabitants of the locality, setting out in his winged, snake-drawn chariot to teach mankind how to cultivate crops. The reverse of these coins shows a pig, an appropriate sacrifice to the goddesses Demeter and Kore.[1] The island of Salamis just a short distance off the coast also formed a part of Attica that was permitted to issue its own coinage. Its small bronzes displayed an ancient form of shield that recalled the principal local hero, the Homeric warrior Ajax.

96. Bronze coin

Minted at Eleusis, about 350-330 B.C.
Theodora Wilbour Fund in Memory of Zoë Wilbour
65.745
Diameter 16.5 mm. Weight 3.61 grams
Obverse: Triptolemos, seated in winged car drawn by two serpents, holds two ears of corn.
Reverse: pig stands to right on a bakchos, the Eleusinian staff. In exergue, perhaps an astragal. Inscribed ΕΛΕΥΣΙ.
Compare *BMC, Attica...*, nos. 22f.; Head, p. 391; Kroll, varieties K and L, pp. 140f., 149.

97. Bronze coin

Minted at Eleusis, about 350-330 B.C.
Theodora Wilbour Fund in Memory of Zoë Wilbour
65.746
Diameter 16.5 mm. Weight 3.25 grams
Designs like the preceding except for a cockle shell in the exergue of the reverse.
Compare *BMC, Attica...*, no. 21; Kroll, varieties K and L, pp. 140f., 149.

98. Bronze coin

Minted on the island of Salamis, about 350-318 B.C.
Theodora Wilbour Fund in Memory of Zoë Wilbour
1965 Apparatus
Diameter 20 mm. Weight 3.71 grams
Obverse: female head, perhaps the nymph Salamis, wearing stephane, earring and necklace.
Reverse: shield of Ajax, on it traces of sword and sheath with strap. Inscribed ΣΑ ΛΑ.
Compare *BMC, Attica...*, no. 2.

1. P. Stengel, *Die griechische Kultusaltertümer* (Munich 1920) p. 143; R. Thönges-Stringaris, *AthMitt* 80 (1965) p. 63

Foreign Coins at Athens

In spite of varying military fortunes during the fourth century, Athens remained one of the most important commercial, cultural and political centers of the Greek world. Multitudes of foreigners must have visited the city; their presence is attested by the vast numbers of foreign coins found at Athens, which probably circulated there purely on the basis of their size. The great majority of these coins seems to have been the bronze small change of neighboring cities. Among the towns represented is Megara, which lay on the borders of Attica and generally was subject to Athens. Its coins, however, probably date from after 307 B.C., when the Macedonian King Demetrius "the Besieger" granted Megara an administrative independence from its larger neighbor.[1] Among the new issues to celebrate this relative freedom were coins displaying the head of the god, Apollo, his musical instrument, the lyre, and the tripod appropriate to his worship. In addition to the bronzes well represented at Athens, a silver coin was also minted at Megara in a beautiful, fluid Early Hellenistic style.

Bronze coins from nearby major rivals of Athens like Corinth or Thebes also appeared in Athens itself. Their

1. Head, p. 393

emblems were connected with the principal cults of the issuing city or else with myths of heroes associated with their regions. Corinth invariably displays Pegasos, who according to legend was tamed by the hero Bellerophon on the mountain overlooking the town. The trident of Poseidon, earth-shaker, horse-tamer and god of the sea, is very appropriate for a city with such an outstanding location for seaborne commerce. Boeotian coins almost always display an old-fashioned shield, whose significance is not fully understood. Poseidon, whose trident also appears on coinage of Boeotia, was the father of the primeval local hero Boeotos and the object of cult in a major shrine. Herakles was born in Boeotia and, hence, was an appropriate subject for coinage there.

Bronze coins of more distant cities also appear. Notable are several from cities or towns on the important Athenian trade route to the rich agricultural lands on the northern coast of the Black Sea. Olbia in south Russia is represented by its strikingly large and relatively early bronze coinage. A town on the north Aegean island of Lemnos issued a coin whose types seem derived from those of Athens herself. This piece and another with an Athena head from Lokris (in central Greece adjoining Boeotia) would have slipped in quite unobtrusively among Athenian bronzes.

Foreign coins of gold or silver are relatively rare. The currency law of 375/4 B.C. seems to imply that foreign silver could not circulate at Athens.[2] Alien silver coins must often have been restruck as Athenian owls, but foreign silver does make up a small part of several Attic hoards. Silver from Histiaia on the island of Euboea off the coast of Attica has been found at Athens. Dionysiac symbols, perhaps connected with some excellent vineyards, and the heifer of Euboea, whose name means "rich in cattle," are used on one coin of Histiaia. Another has an allusion to contemporary events; the nymph of Histiaia is seated on the stern of a galley to commemorate the struggles of 341/0 B.C., when a tyrant backed by the Macedonians was expelled and democracy re-established with Athenian aid.[3]

Foreign currency in precious metal also comes from quite distant regions. A most interesting hoard reputedly found in Piraeus in 1882 contained numerous electrum staters of Cyzicus of types represented in the Museum of Fine Arts.[4] Cyzicus dominated the Sea of Marmara, a principal Athenian trade route to the northeastern coasts of the Black Sea, and Cyzicus and Athens had entered into friendly relations in the last years of the Peloponnesian War. The coinage of Cyzicus is highly unusual by any standards. Its images change constantly and in many cases are remarkable artistic compositions. Some of them, moreover, seem to reflect famous works of art of the time. The Piraeus hoard, which was probably buried around 400-380 B.C.,[5] included at least one piece that reflected the fashions of Cyzicus's new ally. One design is based on the statues of the Athenian tyrant-killers, Harmodios and Aristogeiton. The image became very popular in the years immediately following the overthrow of the Spartan-backed oligarchy at Athens in 403 B.C.[6] Another member of the hoard shows a different symbol of the resistance to tyranny; the baby Herakles strangles a pair of snakes. The myth was placed on coins by several East Greek city-states who formed an alliance around 390 B.C. to throw off the domination of the king of Persia.[7] The coins of Cyzicus were rendered identifiable not only by their unusual material (electrum, a natural alloy of silver and gold used for coinage by a few East Greek cities) but also by their emblem, the tunny or tuna fish, which was worked into every obverse composition.

Other coins evoke the military campaigns of the end of the century when Alexander the Great conquered not only Greece but also the Persian Empire. Soldiers as well as traders may have brought the silver and gold coins that occasionally finished in Attica. A gold daric of the last Persian king is said to have come from an Athenian hoard. Coins of Alexander himself in both gold and silver have also appeared. Alexander's coinage displays the great deities and heroes Zeus, Herakles, Athena and Nike, who were on the one hand associated with the Macedonian royal house and on the other venerated by all Greeks. Alexander's coinage was produced in standard fashion throughout his empire and suppressed most local coinages. As an act of respect and magnanimity, however, Alexander permitted Athens and a number of other Greek city-states to maintain their own monetary systems. Athens had a specially favored position, since Alexander selected the Attic weight standard for his own coins. As a result, not only could the king's coinage be used conveniently in Athens, but Athenian coins could also move freely throughout his empire. There were, however, certain differences between the two in quality of design and in quality of metal. Zeno, the founder of Stoic philosophy, is alleged to have employed a numismatic metaphor based on the double standard, "for he said that polished and carefully composed speeches were like the Alexander silver coinage; pleasant to behold and well-rounded like that money, but

2. T. V. Buttrey in *Greek Numismatics and Archaeology: Essays in Honor of Margaret Thompson* (Wetteren, Belgium 1979) p. 39ff.
3. Kraay, p. 93f.
4. For a list of the types, see Greenwell, p. 42.
5. K. Regling, *Zeitschrift für Numismatik*, 1931, p. 26; *Inventory*, no. 47, p. 9
6. Robertson, *History*, p. 420f.
7. In spite of the anti-Persian content of these coins, the coincidence of dates recalls that Pharnabazus, a satrap of Asia Minor, subsidized the rebuilding of the walls of Athens in 393 B.C. as an anti-Spartan measure, a manifestation of the Persian kings' long-standing policy of subsidizing internecine warfare among the Greek city-states. (Plutarch, *Life of Agesilaus*, xxiii, l.) Cyzicene staters, widely used in Asia Minor, would have been a convenient means of payment.

none the better for all that. As a contrast he compared them with the Attic tetradrachms carelessly and roughly struck, yet any rate often weighing down the scales against beautifully written discourses."[8]

Alexander died in 323 B.C. but his coinage went on being minted without change for the rest of the century throughout most of his empire. The continuing production of Alexander's coins symbolized not only the legitimacy of Alexander's generals who had become his successors but also the enduring dream of a Graeco-Macedonian world unified from the Balkans to Persia.

The power struggles among Alexander's generals and the new order of the Hellenistic world that emerged at the end of the fourth century are reflected in finds of early third century coins at Athens. A few of these coins connected with personalities active in fourth century Athens have been included in the exhibition. Alexander himself is portrayed on coins of Lysimachus, one of his companions who made himself king of Thrace. Alexander is presented as a hero; he has the ram's horns of Zeus Ammon, whose son he was reputed to be. In the great naval battle off Salamis in Cyprus in 306 B.C., Alexander's heritage was almost reunited by Antigonos, one of his companions, and by Antigonos's son Demetrius "the Besieger." The victory is commemorated on coins of Demetrius minted at Salamis that show a Nike on a ship's prow and Poseidon, the god of the sea. Demetrius deserves special mention since in the latter years of the fourth century he based himself in Athens, even living for a time in the Parthenon itself. In an irony of history, he was acclaimed as king and given divine honors (the first of Alexander's successors to be so venerated) by the Athenians, the former champions of democracy and rationality. In coins that he issued in the later part of his career, Demetrius had himself shown with the bull's horn symbolic of Dionysos, his favorite divinity. The portrait may well go back to an image created in Athens in the late fourth century. Certainly his association with Dionysos stems from his Athenian period.

One of the principal adversaries of Antigonos and Demetrius was Alexander's close companion Ptolemy. Ptolemy established a solid base in Egypt from which he duelled the other surviving generals for control of the Greek world. His forays into Greece proper gave him control of Corinth in 306 B.C. Almost a decade before that time, his mint in Alexandria inaugurated the portrait of Alexander on silver. While not known from excavations in Athens, a hoard has been found near Corinth that included numerous silver tetradrachms of Ptolemy that must have been buried during the period of his control of the area.[9] These beautiful coins then would have been available in the immediate neighborhood of Athens and could have made the earliest numismatic portraits of Alexander well known in Attica.

Coins of Megara.
Cats. 100, 99, 101.

Bibliography: On the foreign coins found in the Agora of Athens, see Kleiner, figs. 16-19. On the divine honors paid to Demetrius, see Plutarch, *Life of Demetrius*, x, 3ff. Demetrius was to receive the honors due to Dionysos and to his "namesake" Demeter. The festival called Dionysia was given the name of Demetria. On his residence in the Parthenon, see Plutarch, xxiii, 3ff.

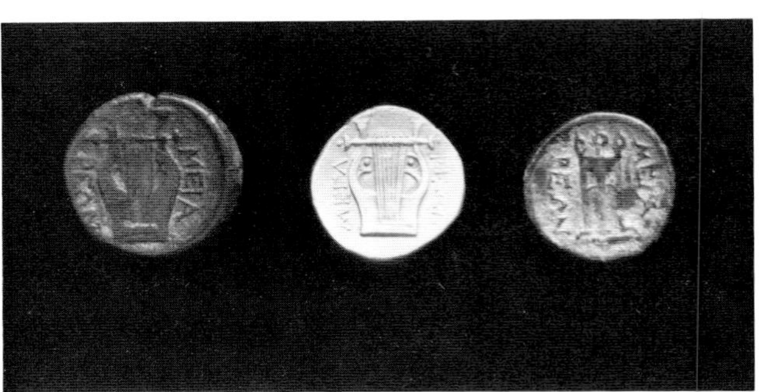

99. Silver drachm
Minted at Megara, 307-about 300 B.C.
Catharine Page Perkins Fund 01.5453
Diameter 18 mm. Weight 4.19 grams
Obverse: head of Apollo to right, laureate.
Reverse: seven-stringed lyre, ΜΕΓΑ ΡΕΩΝ.

Published: Brett, no. 1105.

100. Bronze coin
Minted at Megara, 307-243 B.C.
Theodora Wilbour Fund in Memory of Zoë Wilbour 65.749
Diameter 21 mm. Weight 6.23 grams
Obverse: laureate head of Apollo right.
Reverse: lyre, ΜΕΓΑ ΡΕΩΝ.
Compare *BMC, Attica...*, no. 12f.

101. Bronze coin
Minted at Megara, 307-243 B.C.
Theodora Wilbour Fund in Memory of Zoë Wilbour 65.748
Diameter 18 mm. Weight 3.72 grams
Obverse like the preceding.
Reverse: tripod, ΜΕΓΑ ΡΕΩΝ.
Compare *BMC, Attica...*, no. 16f.

8. Diogenes Laertius, *Lives of the Philosophers*, vii, i, 19; quoted in C. Seltman, *Greek Coins* (London 1955) p. 259.
9. G. K. Jenkins, *Museum Notes* (ANS) 9 (1960) pp. 32ff.; *Inventory* no. 85, p. 15

Foreign bronze coins at Athens: central Greece and the Peloponnesos.
Cats. 108, 104, 106, 102.
Cats. 107, 103, 105.

102. Bronze coin
Minted at Thebes in Boeotia, about 379-338 B.C.
Theodora Wilbour Fund in Memory of Zoë Wilbour 65.693
Diameter 13 mm. Weight 1.82 grams
Obverse: head of Herakles to left.
Reverse: club, caduceus to left, ΟΛΥΜ Π.
Compare *SNG*, vol. 13, no. 369 (ΠΕ); BMC, no. 194 (ΕΠΙ?).

103. Bronze coin
Boeotia, Federal mint, about 338-315 B.C.
Theodora Wilbour Fund in Memory of Zoë Wilbour 65.733
Diameter 13 mm. Weight 1.47 grams
Obverse: Boeotian shield.
Reverse: trident at right, dolphin upwards (?), ΒΟΙΩΤΩΝ.
Compare *SNG*, vol. 13, no. 179.

104. Bronze coin
Boeotia, Federal mint, about 338-315 B.C.
Theodora Wilbour Fund in Memory of Zoë Wilbour 1965 Apparatus
Diameter 14.2 mm. Weight 1.99 grams
Obverse and reverse like the preceding.

105. Bronze coin
Minted at Corinth, fourth century or later
Theodora Wilbour Fund in Memory of Zoë Wilbour 1965 Apparatus
Diameter 13.5 mm. Weight 1.71 grams
Obverse: Pegasos, traces of Corinthian Greek letter koppa.
Reverse: trident; to left, wreath; to right, N.
Compare K. Edwards, *Corinth* 6 (Cambridge, Mass. 1933) p. 15, no. 11 (partial).

106. Bronze coin
Minted at Corinth, fourth century B.C., possibly 315-310 B.C.
Theodora Wilbour Fund in Memory of Zoë Wilbour 65.751
Diameter 14.5 mm. Weight 1.75 grams
Obverse: Pegasos flying to left; below, Corinthian Greek letter koppa.
Reverse: trident, at right, uncertain symbol; below, Δ Ι.
Compare *BMC, Corinth*, no. 452. On silver these letters are used on coins of the date indicated above: *SNG*, vol. 15, nos. 93-101.

107. Bronze coin
Minted at Lokris, Lokri Opuntii, about 338-300 B.C.
Theodora Wilbour Fund in Memory of Zoë Wilbour 65.851
Diameter 14 mm. Weight 1.40 grams
Obverse: head of Athena wearing Corinthian helmet.
Reverse: bunch of grapes, ΛΟΚΡ ΕΠΙΚΝΑ.
Compare *BMC, Central Greece*, no. 71f.; *SNG*, vol. 13, nos. 65-71; Kroll, p. 153.

108. Bronze coin
Minted at Phokis, second half of the fourth century B.C. or later
Theodora Wilbour Fund in Memory of Zoë Wilbour 65.843
Diameter 15 mm. Weight 1.96 grams
Obverse: helmeted head of Athena three-quarter to right, wearing necklace.
Reverse: within wreath, ΦΩ.
Compare *BMC, Central Greece*, p. 20, no. 77; Kroll, p. 153, nos. 73f., pl. 17.

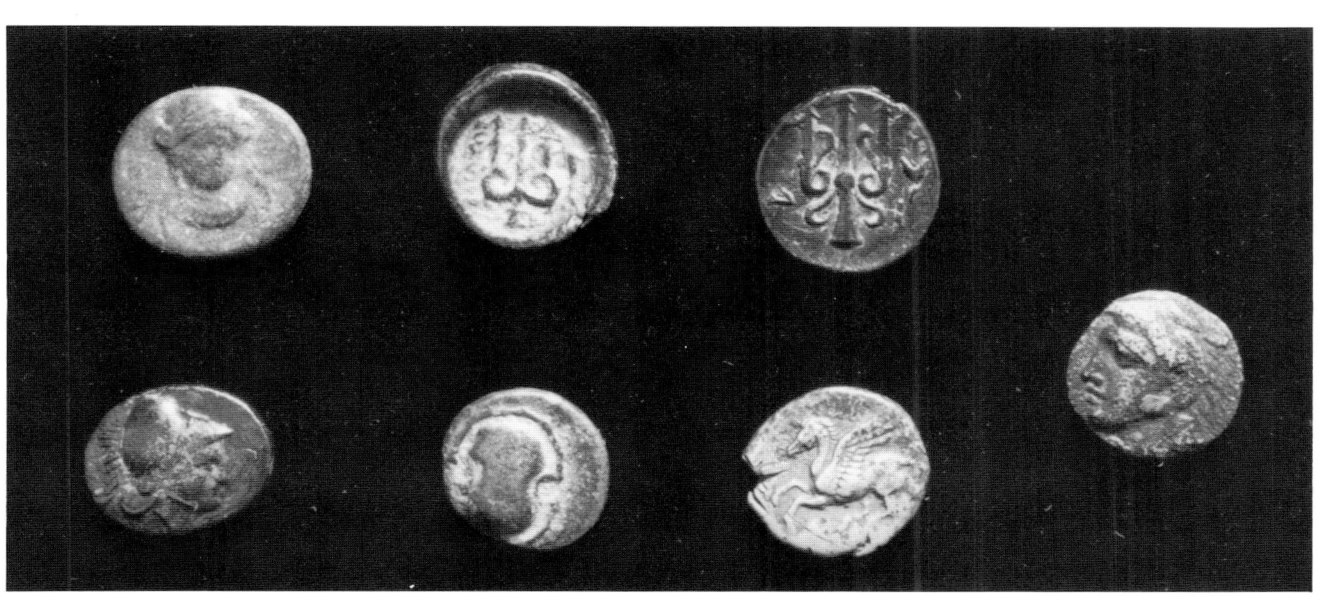

Bronze coins of distant mints at Athens. Cats. 109, 110.

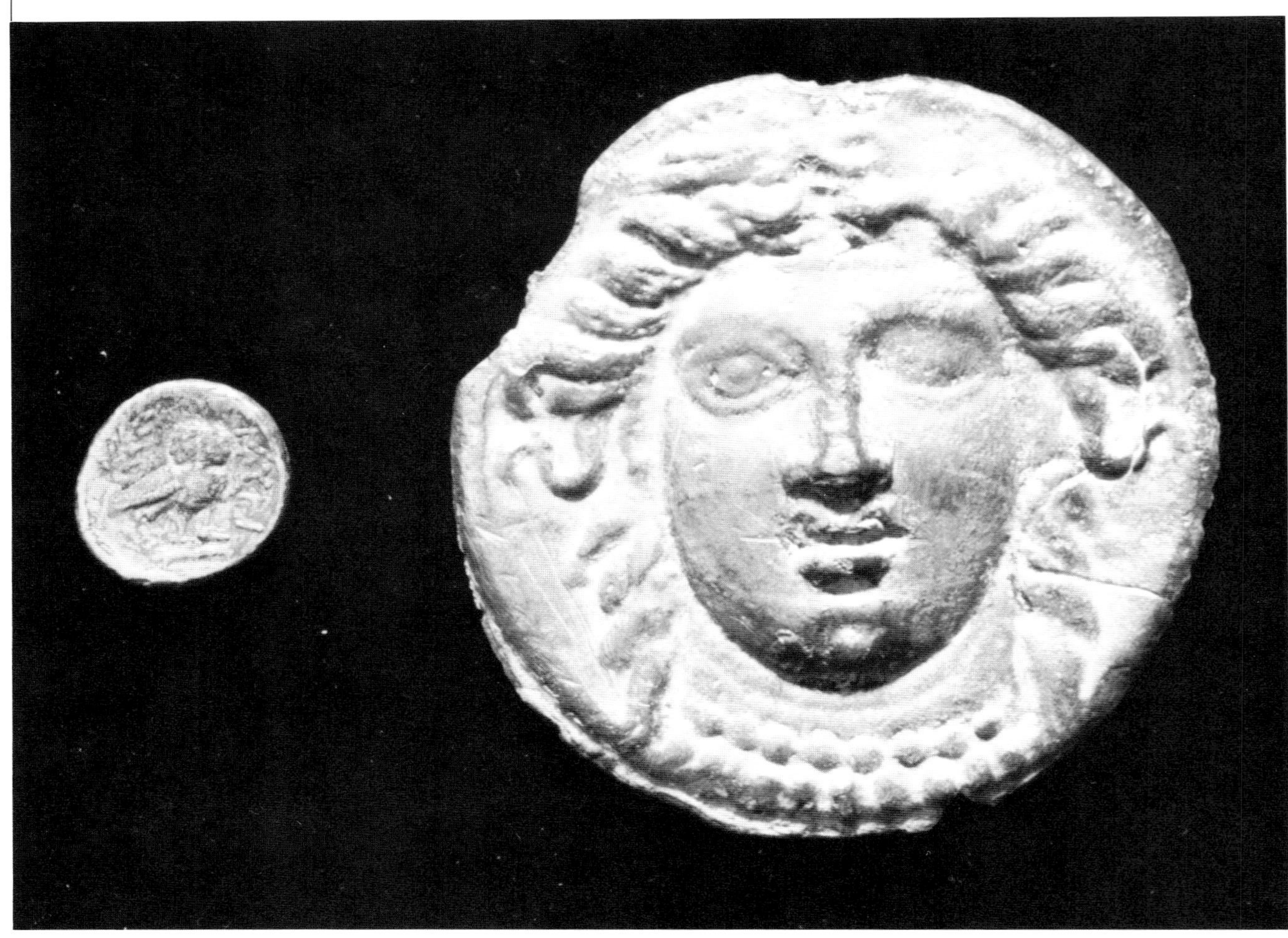

109. Bronze coin

Minted at Myrina on Lemnos, about 300 B.C.
Theodora Wilbour Fund in Memory of Zoë Wilbour 65.839
Diameter 20 mm. Weight 4.78 grams
Obverse: Athena in Corinthian helmet.
Reverse: owl facing; olive branch at left; ΜΥΡΙ.
Compare *BMC, Thrace*, no. 2.

110. Bronze coin

Minted at Olbia, first half of the fourth century
Theodora Wilbour Fund in Memory of Zoë Wilbour 58.313
Diameter 67 mm. Weight 99.25 grams
Obverse: head of Demeter facing, wearing bead necklace with pendants.
Reverse: sea eagle holding dolphin, ΟΛΒΙΗ.

For the date, see M. Jessop Price in *Essays in Greek Coinage Presented to Stanley Robinson* (Oxford 1968) p. 102.

Published: M. Comstock and C. Vermeule, *Greek Coins, 1950 to 1963, Museum of Fine Arts, Boston* (Boston 1964) no. 81.

111. Silver drachm

Minted at Histiaia on the island of Euboea, 369-338 B.C.
Catharine Page Perkins Fund 00.245
Diameter 16 mm. Weight 3.34 grams
Obverse: female head, perhaps a maenad, wearing a wreath of vine leaves and grapes, a pyramidal earring and a necklace.
Reverse: heifer walking; a grape vine with clusters of fruit; ΙΣΤΙ.

On this type, see also Kraay, no. 279, pp. 93, 357.

Published: Brett, no. 1032.

112. Silver tetrobol

Minted at Histiaia on the island of Euboea, 340-338 B.C.
Catharine Page Perkins Fund 00.246
Diameter 16 mm. Weight 2.63 grams
Obverse: similar to the preceding but hair in sphendone.
Reverse: nymph Histiaia seated on stern of galley holding stylis (naval standard) and wearing chiton and himation. Inscribed **ΙΣΤΙΑΙ ΕΩΝ**.

On the type, see also Kraay, no. 280, pp. 93-4, 357.

Published: Brett, no. 1033.

113. Electrum stater

Minted at Cyzicus in Mysia, 477-ca. 400 B.C. (probably in 403 B.C. or later)
H. L. Pierce Fund 04.1343
Diameter 20 mm. Weight 16.02 grams
Obverse: the Tyrannicides Harmodios and Aristogeiton attacking. Ground line replaced by tunny fish.
Reverse: windmill-sail incuse.

The obverse copies a famous sculptural group set up in Athens in 477 B.C. The subject had a renewed popularity at the end of the century. Robertson discusses several examples of that time, including a Panathenaic amphora of 403 B.C. and a pitcher from the funerary precinct of Dexileos (after 393 B.C.). After the Peloponnesian War, the Tyrannicides seem to have symbolized the overthrow of the Spartan-backed oligarchy at Athens in 403 B.C.

On the symbolism of the Tyrannicides, see Robertson, *History*, p. 420f. For a similar coin in the Piraeus find of 1882, see Greenwell, p. 42.

Published: Greenwell, no. 76; Brett, no. 1496: C. Vermeule in *Search*, no. 20.

114. Electrum stater

Minted at Cyzicus, possibly around 390 B.C.
H. L. Pierce Fund 04.1326
Diameter 18 mm. Weight 16.02 grams
Obverse: infant Herakles strangling a serpent in each hand, his brother Iphikles gesturing as if for help; below, a tunny fish.
Reverse: like the preceding.

For the date and interpretation of this type, see Greenwell, p. 83f.; Kraay, no. 966, pp. 264, 374. For a similar type in the Piraeus find of 1882, see Greenwell, p. 42.

Published: Greenwell, no. 63; Brett, no. 1531.

115. Electrum stater

Minted at Cyzicus, about 440-330 B.C.
Possibly from Athens
Theodora Wilbour Fund in Memory of Zoë Wilbour 58.347
Diameter 20 mm. Weight 15.85 grams
Obverse: youth wrapped in himation kneeling and throwing knucklebones; below, a tunny.
Reverse: like the preceding.

Catharine Lorber, who publishes another example of this type, notes that Cyzicene staters were the medium of exchange for the grain trade between the Black Sea and the Aegean; see Lorber in *Wealth of the Ancient World: The Nelson Bunker Hunt and William Herbert Hunt Collections* (Fort Worth 1983) p. 198.

Published: M. Comstock and C. Vermeule, *Greek Coins, 1950 to 1963, Museum of Fine Arts, Boston* (Boston 1964) no. 150.

116. Gold daric of Darius III

Minted in the Persian Empire, 337-330 B.C.
From Athens Hoard, 1929 (?)
H. E. Bolles Fund 30.50
Diameter 16 mm. Weight 8.30 grams
Obverse: king in kneeling-running pose holding spear and bow, wearing a long robe, a dentated crown and a quiver. His long beard is pointed and his hair is knotted at the back.
Reverse: oblong incuse in stylized pattern of wavy lines.

Published: Brett, no. 2205.

117. Gold stater of Alexander

Minted at Babylon, 323-320 B.C. or later
James Fund 08.345
Diameter 18 mm. Weight 8.57 grams
Obverse: head of Athena in triple-crested Corinthian helmet with coiled snake on bowl, wearing bead necklace. Traces of **M**.
Reverse: Nike standing and extending a wreath, wearing peplos blown by wind and necklace. In her left hand a naval standard. Inscribed **ΑΛΕΞΑΝΔΡ(ΟΥ) Β ΑΣΙΛΕΩ(Σ), ΛΥ**.

Published: Brett, no. 660.

118. Gold stater of Alexander

Minted at Babylon, after 317 B.C.
Catharine Page Perkins Fund 97.436
Diameter 18 mm. Weight 8.55 grams
Obverse: like the preceding, uninscribed.
Reverse: like the preceding but peplos not wind-blown and figure not wearing necklace. Inscribed **ΑΛΕΞΑΝΔΡΟ(Υ) ΒΑΣ ΙΛΕΩΣ**. Monograms: within wreath **MP**; **HP**.

Published: Brett, no. 661.

119. Silver tetradrachm of Alexander

Minted at Sikyon, 317-311 B.C.
H. L. Pierce Fund 04.730
Diameter 27 mm. Weight 17.14 grams

Foreign coins of gold, silver and electrum: types known from Attica and portraits of Macedonian kings.
Cats. 99, 111, 112.
Cats. 113, 114, 115, 116.
Cats. 117, 118, 119, 120.
Cats. 121, 122.
Cats. 125, 126.
Cats. 123, 124.

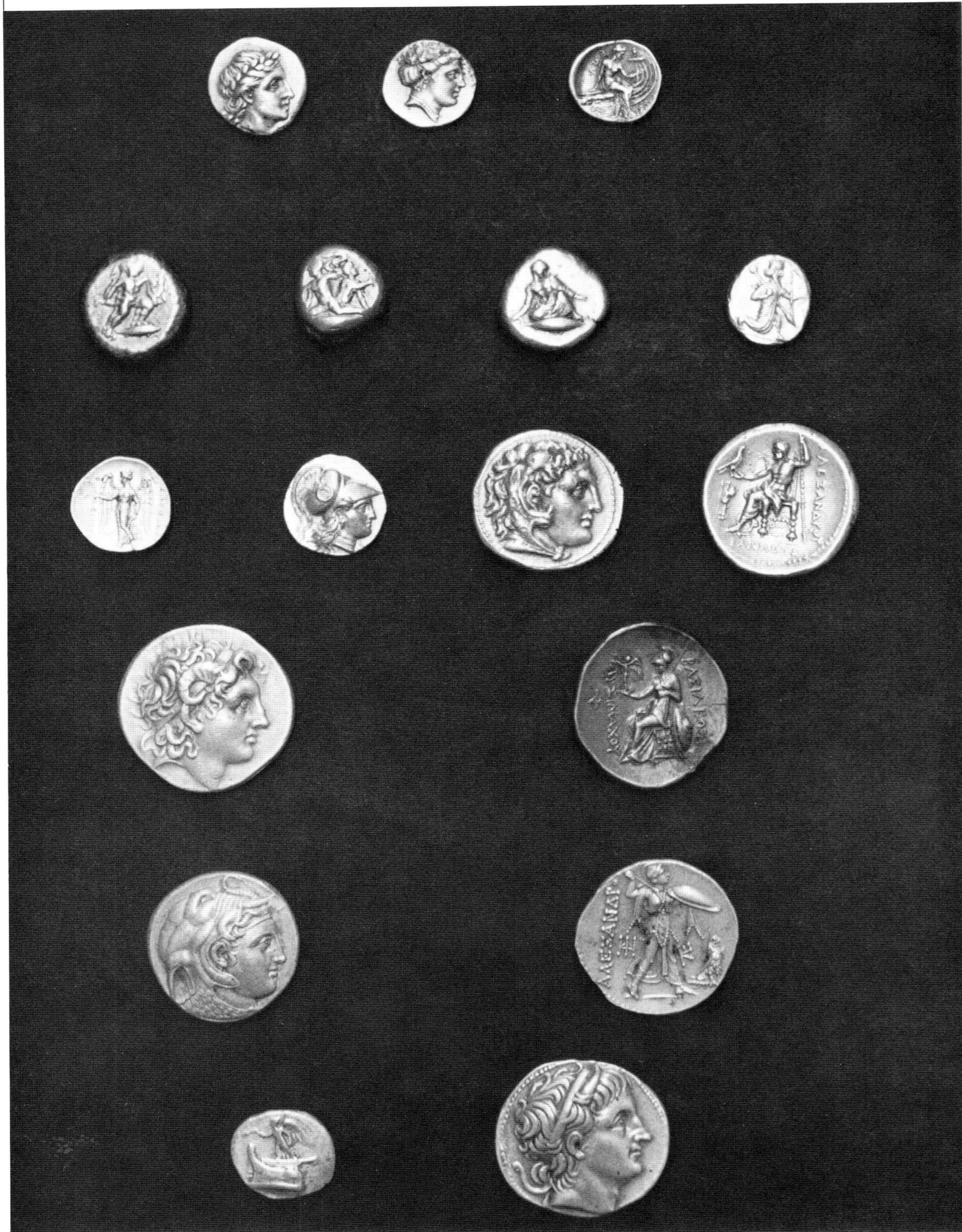

Obverse: head of Herakles, beardless, wearing lionskin with paws tied around neck; border of dots.
Reverse: Zeus seated on throne, eagle on extended right hand, scepter in left. Standing female figure, Elpis, holds flowers in right and garment in left hand. Inscribed **ΑΛΕΞΑΝΔΡΟΥ**; letters **N** and **O** below throne.

Published: Brett, no. 687.

120. Silver tetradrachm of Alexander

Minted at Sikyon, 317-311 B.C.
H. L. Pierce Fund 04.731
Diameter 28 mm. Weight 17.06 grams
Obverse: similar to the preceding.
Reverse: similar to the preceding but archaistic figure of Athena replaces Elpis; figure of Nike on each upright of throne; border of dots. Inscribed **ΑΛΕΞΑΝΔΡΟΥ ΒΑΣΙΛΕΩΣ**. In wreath below throne, **ΟΛΙ**.

Published: Brett, no. 688.

121. Silver tetradrachm of Lysimachus

Minted at Lampsakos in Mysia, about 297-281 B.C.
Theodora Wilbour Fund in Memory of Zoë Wilbour 68.47
Diameter 31.5 mm. Weight 16.68 grams
Obverse: head of the deified Alexander the Great wearing a ribbon and with the ram's horns of Zeus Ammon.
Reverse: Athena enthroned with Corinthian helmet, holding spear, shield with lion's head device and a figure of Nike holding a wreath. In field at left, a herm and monogram **Ξ**, **Δ**. Inscribed **ΒΑΣΙΛΕΩΣ ΛΥΣΙΜΑΧΟΥ**.

For the attribution to Lampsakos, see M. Thompson in *Essays in Greek Coinage Presented to Stanley Robinson* (Oxford 1968) p. 171, no. 50.

Published: M. Comstock in *Boston Museum Bulletin* 67, 349 (1969) p. 110, fig. 7; T. Hackens in *A Survey of Numismatic Research*, 1966-1971, I (New York 1973) p. 86, note 18.

122. Silver tetradrachm of Lysimachus

Minted at Alexandria Troas, 297-281 B.C.
James Fund 08.354
Diameter 30 mm. Weight 17.05 grams
Obverse: similar to preceding.
Reverse: similar to preceding but with eight-pointed star on seat and different monogram.
Compare M. Thompson, *op. cit.*, no. 150, p. 176.

Published: Brett, no. 825.

123. Silver drachm of Demetrius Poliorcetes

Minted at Tarsus in Cilicia, about 298-295 B.C.
Source unknown 18.679
Diameter 19 mm. Weight 3.87 grams
Obverse: Nike standing on ship's prow, blowing trumpet and holding naval standard.

Reverse: Poseidon striding left wielding trident. In field right and left, circled monogram **AN**; **A**. Inscribed **ΒΑΣΙ ΛΕΩ Σ (ΔΗ)ΜΗΤΡΙΟΥ**.
Compare E. Newell, *The Coinages of Demetrius Poliorcetes* (London 1927) no. 44.

124. Silver tetradrachm of Demetrius Poliorcetes

Minted at Amphipolis in Macedonia, 289-288 B.C.
Catharine Page Perkins Fund 00.173
Diameter 30 mm. Weight 17.20 grams
Obverse: head of Demetrius (with bull's horns) wearing a ribbon with fluttering ends.

Reverse: Poseidon nude with trident standing with foot on an outcropping of rock; complex monograms at left and right. Inscribed **ΒΑΣΙΛΕΩΣ ΔΗΜΗΤΡΙΟΥ**.

Published: Newell, *op. cit.*, under no. 124, cxx.-249; Brett, no. 709; *Search*, no. 22, pp. 104 (A. Herrmann), 110 (C. Vermeule).

125. Silver tetradrachm of Ptolemy I

Minted at Alexandria in Egypt, 315-300 B.C.
H. L. Pierce Fund 04.1183
Diameter 27 mm. Weight 17.07 grams
Obverse: head of Alexander with horns of Ammon and elephant skin headdress. An aegis is tied around his neck.
Reverse: Athena in a pose of attack with shield and spear. The eagle of Ptolemy in the field; two monograms. Inscribed **ΑΛΕΞΑΝΔΡΟ(Υ)**.

Published: Brett, no. 2253.

126. Silver tetradrachm of Ptolemy I

Minted at Alexandria, 315-300 B.C.
Catharine Page Perkins Fund 95.160
Diameter 28 mm. Weight 15.68 grams
Similar to the preceding but with different monograms.

Published: Brett, no. 2256.

Lead Weights, Tokens, Boxes and Seal Impressions

Weights Many objects made of lead have been found in Athens. Lead is a by-product of silver mining, and the rich silver mines at Laurion in Attica would have led to early and intense efforts to exploit the practical applications of this material. Fortunately for the health of the Athenians of the Classical period, lead was not much used for water pipes, as it was to be later in the Roman Imperial period.

The majority of the lead objects are weights, and they give us a considerable knowledge of Athenian efforts to have a coherent and standardized basis for exchange. The system was based on a standard unit (stater) subdivided into simple fractions: halves, thirds, quarters, sixths and eighths. Unlike modern systems, numerals played a small part. The fractions were written out, and to render the different denominations more visible, objects were used as symbols. The knucklebone, an object connected with a favorite game, was attached to the standard unit. Halves were marked with a dolphin in relief. Thirds had storage jars (amphorae), and their form evoked the jars of olive oil given as prizes at the great Attic festival, the Panathenaic games. Quarters were identified by the tortoise. The creature was also the symbol on the coinage of Aigina, an island that was a commercial rival of Athens, and the tortoises on Athenian weights closely resemble those on the foreign coins. It has been suggested that this unit presented some sort of link between the two rival systems. Smaller fractions were represented by the simple expedient of showing only half of the symbol, whether dolphin, amphora or tortoise.

The center for the administration of the system of weights and measures was located in the Agora of Athens, specifically in the round building (tholos), also known as the Pyrtanikon, where many lead weights have been found.[1] The weights at the tholos would have been official copies, but a host of others would have been used by merchants throughout Attica.

127. Lead weight with a knucklebone (stater, or standard unit)

Fourth or early third century
From Athens
H. L. Pierce Fund 01.8288
6.0 × 5.9 × 2.3 cm. (at edges) Weight 925 grams
Inscribed ΣΤΑ ΤΗΡ.
Compare Lang, LW 6.

128. Lead weight with an amphora (tritemorion, or one third unit)

Fourth century
H. L. Pierce Fund 01.8329
4.8 × 4.5 × 1.5 cm. (at edges) Weight 318.6 grams
Inscribed Τ (Ρ)ΙΤ Η.

The Panathenaic amphora is of the early type.

Compare Lang, p. 8, LW 20.

1. Travlos, p. 553ff., esp. fig. 701

Lead weights.
Cats. 130, 128, 127.
Cats. 131, 129, 132.

129. Lead weight with half an amphora (hemitriton, or one sixth unit)

Fourth or third century
H. L. Pierce Fund 01.8320
3.9 × 4.4 × 1.0 cm. (at edges) Weight 151 grams
Inscribed ΗΜΙΤΡΙΤΟΝ.
Compare Lang, LW 26, 28, 29.

130. Lead weight with a tortoise (tetartemorion, or one quarter unit)

Fourth century
From Athens
H. L. Pierce Fund 01.8272
3.6 × 3.7 × 1.1 cm. (at edges) Weight 152.2 grams

The tortoise has an unusually close resemblance to the tortoises on fourth century coins of Aigina.

Compare Lang, LW 34, pl. 7.

131. Lead weight with half a tortoise (hemitetarton, or one eighth unit)

Fourth century
From Athens
H. L. Pierce Fund 01.8274
3.9 × 3.7 × 0.9 cm. (at edges) Weight 131.7 grams
Inscribed across top and bottom (Η)Μ ΙΤ/ΕΤΑΡ.
Compare Lang, LW 47.

132. Lead weight (?) in the form of a shell

Fourth century?
From Athens
H. L. Pierce Fund 01.8330
Length 6.5 cm. Weight 161.3 grams Flat underneath.

The elongated, ribbed valve suggests the lima family, perhaps the common species Lima lima (usual dimensions 5 × 7 cm.). If the object was a weight, it might have been used for some household or, at any rate, unofficial purpose.

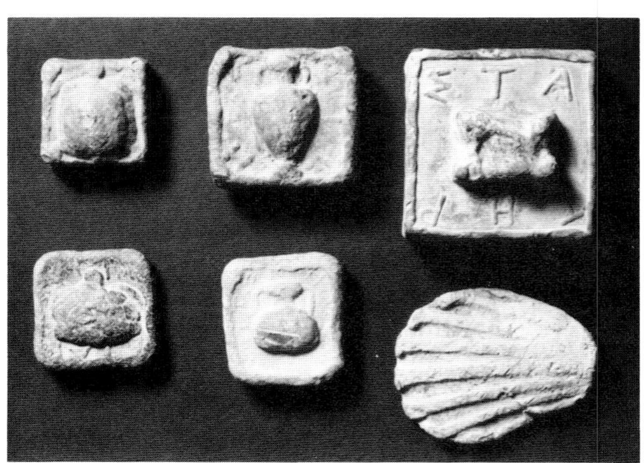

Lead tokens and a seal impression on lead. Cats. 134, 133, 136.

Tokens Many small coin-like discs of lead stamped with an endless variety of images have been found in Athens. They seem to have been counters (symbola) used in a variety of civic functions. Citizens received tokens for jury duty which they would later exchange for a meager day's pay (two obols). Tokens would record presence at the assembly or would be passed out for admission to plays or for entitlements to distribution of grain. After each event, the tokens may have been melted down and restruck, explaining the great variety of subjects found. The images were evidently impressed with official state seals. Lead tokens seem to have come into use in the second half of the fourth century in Athens. The practice was apparently not taken up in other cities until the Roman Imperial Period.

Most tokens are quite summary in style and often were crudely made. A certain percentage are, on the other hand, attractive as objects. Tokens of the fourth century tend to be rather solid and have relatively clear, simple images. Many designs are distinctly Athenian. There are frequent variations on the theme of Athena and her owl. The multitude of different designs for tokens, however, dictated a certain eclecticism in choice of subject matter. Still life subjects or animals commonly used on seals were taken up, as were designs that seem inspired by foreign coins. A long-haired head of Apollo, for instance, could well have been suggested by numismatic designs from a number of peripheral areas of the Greek world.

Bibliography: Crosby

133. Lead token with a boar

Early Hellenistic, late fourth or early third century
Gift of E. P. Warren 13.123
Diameter 15 mm.
Reverse: globe or pomegranate.
Compare Crosby, L 124.

134. Lead token with head of Apollo

Early Hellenistic, late fourth or third century
Gift of E. P. Warren 13.125
Diameter 13 mm. Flat on the reverse.

Apollo with locks of hair cascading down on his neck and wearing a laurel wreath is familiar on the coinage of the western, northern and eastern Greek world. The upward tilt of his head is an Early Hellenistic variation on the theme.

For this conception of Apollo, see Brett, nos. 191ff. (Croton); 582 (Chalcidic League); 1378f. (Kios); 1618ff. (Abydos); 1717ff. (Mytilene); 1886ff. (Miletos).

Lead Boxes

135. Cylindrical box (pyxis) with knobbed lid

Fifth or fourth century
Possibly from Crete
Gift of H. P. Kidder 81.332a, b
Height 4.1 cm. Diameter 4.8 cm.

A fragmentary pyxis of this type was found in a fifth or fourth century grave on the Pnyx. Others have been found in various sites around the Mediterranean. An example from Alexandria contained ointment, the probable function of this piece.

Compare G. Davidson, *Hesperia, Supplement* 7 (1943) pp. 96, 100, no. 27, fig. 45.

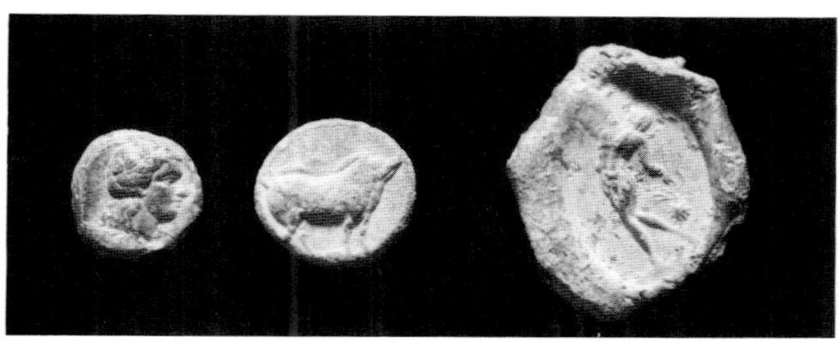

Lead Impressions of Gems

136. Imprint of a ring engraved with a dancing maenad or satyr

Early fourth century
Said to be Athenian
Gift of E. P. Warren 13.120
Length 26 mm. Length of oval field 20 mm.

The satyr carries a thyrsos in his left hand. The elongated oval imprint left by the bezel of the ring suggests a date not far from the fifth century. The nude figure in a twisting pose recalls rings of Boardman's Kassandra Group of about 400 B.C. The greater elongation and mannerism of the figure, however, anticipate fully fourth century rings like those of the Iunx or Salting Groups.

Compare Boardman, pls. 709-712, 719, 736.

Bronzeworking: Equipment for Domestic Use and Ritual

Bronzeworking in fourth century Attica is elusive. The striking accumulations of bronze armor, drinking sets and toilet articles that have appeared in tombs throughout most of the fourth century Greek world are missing from the cemeteries of Attica. Yet bronzecasting must surely have been a highly developed art form in Athens as well. Remains of major bronze statues of the period have been recovered, and installations and equipment for bronzecasting have been found in excavations in the city.[1] A precious few objects also demonstrate that bronze was used not only for major public sculpture but for a great array of functions including personal adornment. The excavations of the assembly place (the Pnyx) have yielded bronze rings, earrings, mirrors and tools.[2] All are, however, unpretentious kinds of objects found throughout the Greek world. A bronze votive snake in the Museum of Fine Arts and said to come from Athens is also on this modest level.

Bronze vessels and equipment of the highest quality had been made in the fifth century at Athens, and it is reasonable to think that the loss of the Peloponnesian War had a negative effect on this luxury craft. Certainly, other artists of talent had left the city in the last decade of the century to search their fortunes elsewhere. The case of Euripides, who fled to the Macedonian court where he wrote the *Bacchai,* is emblematic of the situation. A pair of bronze handles in the Museum of Fine Arts suggests strongly that master bronzeworkers joined the diaspora. The handles were said to have been found in Macedonia, but wherever they were actually made, the artist must have had an intimate knowledge of Athens. The ornament of S-shaped scrolls and palmettes on the handles repeats the ornamental system of the Erechtheion in the most minute and sensitive detail. The elegantly cool proportions, the contrast of convex and concave palmettes and the subtle and restrained embellishment with acanthus represent a balance of ingredients found almost uniquely in the friezes of the temple completed in 406 B.C. The Macedonian provenance reported for the handles, however, seems fully justified. The facing head of the Medusa with snakes knotted in her wild hair anticipates the masks with a corona of flowing hair in the Derveni Krater. The snakes that border the handles are a rare enrichment that is repeated in the handles of the famous Macedonian krater. It seems quite likely, then, that around 400 B.C. Athenian craftsmen were part of the melting pot that made up the heterogeneous phenomenon termed "Macedonian court art."

While they are elusive, it is clear that works of the highest quality continued to be produced by Athenian artists working at Athens as well as by Athenians emigrated to other centers. Bronze mirrors with figural reliefs are surely among the more distinguished local products. A folding mirror with a relief decoration of Aphrodite and Eros is reported to have been discovered in Attica, and several clay casts of such reliefs have been excavated in Athens itself.[3] The style of these reliefs displays what Züchner has called "the Attic clarity, the unity of grandeur and ease, the Attic grace and the freespiritedness of this citystate."[4]

Among the numerous mirrors that Züchner has ascribed to the famous bronzeworking center of Corinth are some that Martha Weber has recently taken away from that city because of their close relationship to the reliefs of the Nike Temple parapet in Athens.[5] Presumably, these mirrors are Athenian. A "Corinthian" mirror in the Museum of Fine Arts might also be reattributed since it seems strikingly similar to the mirror reportedly excavated in Attica. In the Boston mirror, Dionysos and Ariadne are seated on a rocky outcropping and turn toward one another amorously. The composition is an exception among the many two-figure reliefs, where the figures usually face one another. As in the Attic mirror with Aphrodite and Eros, the figures are surrounded by ample space. Anatomies are splendid, and the drapery is flowing yet restrained; Ariadne's costume is treated much like Aphrodite's. Recent finds of clay moulds in the Agora with almost identical figures offer further support for the Athenian origin of the piece in the Museum of Fine Arts.

A category of magnificent bronze vessels seems to have been produced in Athens. Hydriae with richly ornamented handles have been attributed to the city. The distinctive feature of these vessels is the "narrative relief" made in the repoussé technique and attached below the central vertical handle.[6] A foot and a pair of handles in the Museum of Fine Arts belong to one of these hydriae, but the figured central handle is missing. In any case, the richness of the type is evident even in the ornamental parts. Stylized floral elements in vibrantly curvilinear patterns transform these structural members into something almost alive. The handles themselves are jacketed with concave "tongue patterns" or fluting to suggest the stems of plants. Rich leaf mouldings (the Lesbian cymation) decorate the profiled feet and handle connectors. Between the leaves of the cymation are small palmettes that enhance the sense of restless movement. These palmettes had often been used in the painted ornament of East Greece before they appeared in this sculptural setting.[7] These hydriae have been found throughout the Greek world, and if the

1. C. Mattusch, *Bronze Workers in the Athenian Agora* (Exc. Ath. Ag. Picture Book, 20) p. 8ff.
2. *Hesperia, Supplement* 7 (1943) p. 96ff., figs. 44, 46
3. For the clay impressions, see Züchner, p. 222f., fig. 127; D. Thompson, *Miniature Sculpture from the Athenian Agora* (Ag. Pict. Book 3) fig. 30.
4. Züchner, KS 12, pp. 13, 222, fig. 126
5. Weber dates them to the late fifth century: *AthMitt* 91 (1976) p. 159f., note 35, pl. 51, 2.
6. For the attribution to Athens, see G. Richter, *AJA* 50 (1946) p. 361ff., pl. 22f.; E. Diehl, *Die Hydria* (Mainz 1964) p. 42; A. Andriomenou, *BCH* 99 (1975) p. 551.
7. J. Ganzert, *JdI* 98 (1983) p. 134ff., fig. 27 (Clazomenian sarcophagus), fig. 35 (supports for votive offerings, Athens)

fig 6. Crowning member of a memorial for the Battles of Corinth and Coroneia in 394 B.C. From A. Conze, Die attischen Grabreliefs 2 *(Berlin 1900) p. 253, no. 1157.*

Cat. 138.

fig. 7. Frieze from the East Portico of the Erechtheion. Drawing by G. P. Stevens. From Stevens et alii, The Erechtheum *(Cambridge, Mass. 1927) pl. 29.*

ascription to Athens is correct, Athenian craftsmanship in bronze made a major contribution to the culture of the time.

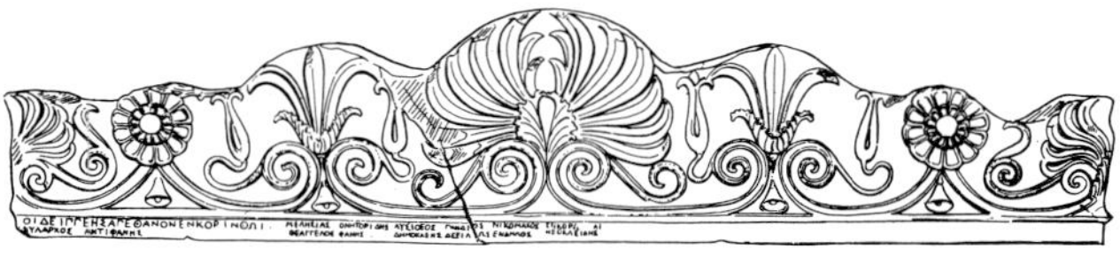

137. Snake

About 400 B.C.
From Athens
Gift of E. P. Warren 13.182
Length 14 cm.

This object probably was a offering to any of a multitude of heroes, who at times took the form of snakes, perhaps in relation to a hoped-for cure from illness. Many heroes had therapeutic faculties, above all Asklepios.

For a votive relief from Oropos showing Asklepios and Amphiaraos performing cures in the form of a snake, see Robertson, *History*, p. 376f., p1. 123b; *idem*, *Shorter History*, p. 133, fig. 181.

Published: *MFABronzes*, no. 63 (with bibliography).

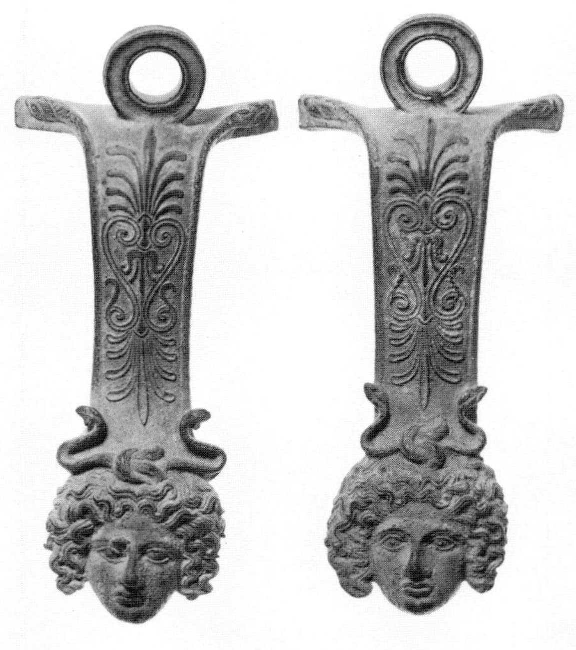

138. Pair of handles from an amphora

About 400 B.C.
Bought in Athens, said to come from Macedonia
H. L. Pierce Fund 99.471a, b
Height 15.2 cm.

A mask of Medusa formed the escutcheon at the joint between handle and the now-missing body. The formerly-fierce monster has been humanized to the point that only the snakes knotted in her hair render her identifiable. Snakes border the handles, which are surmounted by a ring to retain the cover of the amphora. The handles are embellished by a pair of S-curved scrolls and palmettes.

The heads are related to and derived from a group of magnificent facing heads from the handles of bronze volute kraters. These heads have been found at Dodona and Galaxidi (near Delphi) and attributed to a Corinthian workshop. In spite of this relationship, the handles were probably designed by an Athenian. The ornament has the

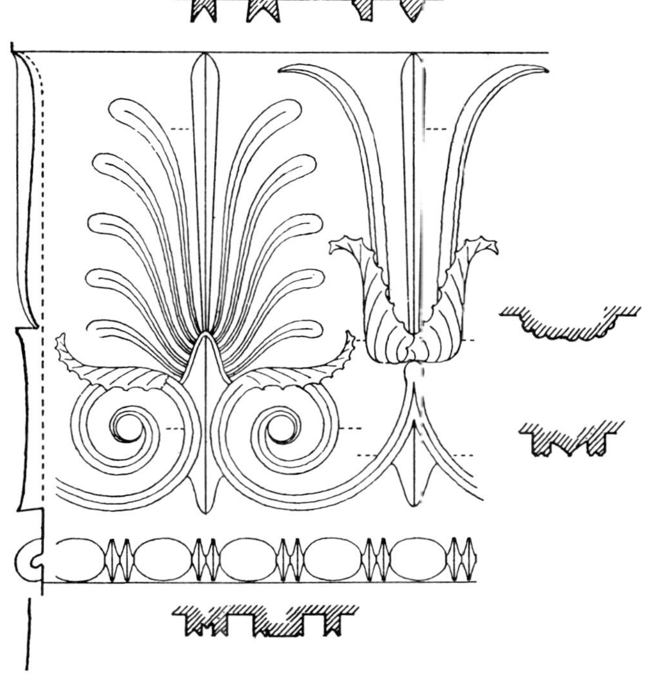

closest possible kinship with the ornamental friezes of the Erechtheion. The palmettes and scrolls have a cold elegance that is given sparkle by touches of acanthus foliage, just as in the temple on the Acropolis. The contrast between convex and concave surface and between large and small palmettes, the smaller of which spring from a calyx of acanthus, is identical. Comparisons can be followed into the smallest details, and every feature can be paralleled in the temple's frieze, which varies subtly as it passes around the various walls, antae and capital necks. Scarcely more than a decade after the completion of the Erechtheion (in 406 B.C.), ornament had become more mannered, whether in monuments at Athens like the Memorial for the Corinthian War of 394, or in Peloponnesian structures like the Heraion at Argos. Later architectural ornament became more dense, more aggressively vegetablized or more illusionistic.

For the facing heads from volute kraters, see S. Karusu, *AthMitt* 94 (1979) p. 85f., pls. 23f. For the Erechtheion frieze, see G. P. Stevens *et alii, The Erechtheum* (Cambridge, Mass. 1927) p1. 18, 29, 36 (east portico); Travlos, figs. 287, 291. For the monument of 394, see Travlos, fig. 421. For the ornament of the Temple of Hera at Argos, see Robertson, *History,* p1. 130e.

Published: D. von Bothmer, *Bulletin of the Metropolitan Museum of Art* (January, 1961) p. 145, fig. 13; *MFABronzes,* no. 426; G. Zahlhaas, H. Fuchs, *AA,* 1981, p. 581 (dated mid-4th century).

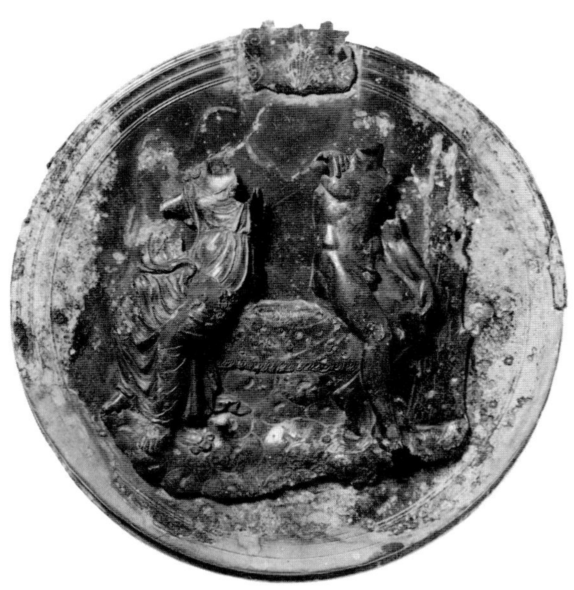

139. Cover of a folding mirror decorated with an enthroned couple

Corinthian or Athenian, about 350 B.C.
Bought at Athens
Purchased by Contribution 01.7513
Diameter 16.3 cm. Heads and arms of both figures missing.

The woman is clad in a high-waisted chiton and himation while the powerfully-muscled man is nude. A tree trunk borders the composition at the right. The pair is seated on a rocky outcropping covered with a fringed cloth or skin. A lobed structure beside the female's left foot could be a paw, reinforcing the interpretation as a skin. The couple could be Dionysos (presented with an unusually weighty physique) seated on his panther's skin in amorous conversation with Ariadne. The pair (unmistakably identified) is shown in just this grouping on an early fourth century Attic vase.

The composition has been justly cited for its elegant repose and balance. Züchner attributed it to his "simple group" of Corinthian mirrors, but in quality as well as in many details, it stands out from the other members of the group. The woman's drapery is subordinate to the underlying forms as in few other pieces. The V-shaped folds between her legs are much like the drapery of Aphrodite on a mirror found in Attica. The mirror might well be of Attic origin. Both figures can be paralleled (though not duplicated exactly) in moulds found in the Agora. Züchner himself notes the great similarity to the reliefs on hydriae, which have since been attributed to an Attic workshop. The figure of Dionysos is strikingly similar to the heroic young man on the Illisos stele.

For the other mirror, see Züchner, KS 12, pp. 13, 158, 222, fig. 126. For the vase, see Metzger, *Représentations,* p. 119, no. 23, p1. 14, 2. For the terracottas, see D. Thompson, *Miniature Sculpture from the Athenian Agora* (Ag. Pict. Book 3) figs. 55f.; *Hesperia* 31 (1962) p1. 88; *Histoire et archéologie* 81 (March 1984) p. 36f., figs. 18, 22. On hydriae, see the following entry. For the Illisos stele, see *Hellenistic Art,* fig. 243.

Published: Züchner, KS 38, pp. 33f., 201, p1. 19; B. Segall, *Berliner Winkelmannsprogramm* 119/120, p. 32f.; *MFABronzes,* no. 365; F. Brommer, *Denkmälerlisten zur griechischen Heldensage, III* (Marburg 1976) p. 50, no. 4; W. Hornbostel, *Kunst der Antike: Schätze aus Norddeutschem Privatbesitz* (Mainz 1977) p. 100.

140. Foot and pair of side handles from a hydria

Fourth century
Greek, perhaps Attic, bought in Smyrna
H. L. Pierce Fund 99.472a-f
Base, diameter 15.1 cm. Handles, length 9.3 cm. Discs, diameter 5.7 cm. One of the four attachment discs is missing.

The base is decorated with a Lesbian cymation in which the principal leaves are separated by palmettes. The handles are channeled by tongue patterns that are separated by grooves and that flare at the ends. The discs are embellished by a variation on the Lesbian cymation in which the principal leaves are separated and have an oval contour.

Published: E. Diehl, *Die Hydria,* p. 218, B 131, B 129; *MFABronzes,* no. 427.

Cat. 140.
Cat. 141.
Cat. 142.

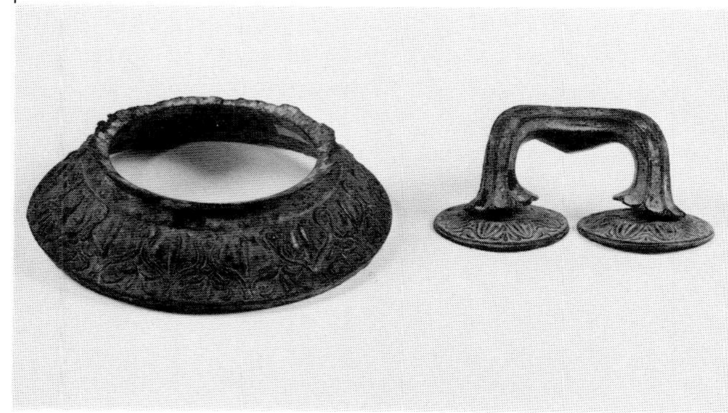

141. Onion-shaped sprinkler (perirrhanterion)

Second half of fourth century
Greek, probably Corinthian, bought in Greece
H. L. Pierce Fund 98.693
Height 15.5 cm. The upper part is held in place by a pair of flanges, which must be forced into position. The top is perforated by a hole 0.5 cm. in diameter.

An undulating ivy wreath is inlaid in silver around the body of the vase. The ivy is very similar to the decoration of Attic West Slope ware, like no. 48. Similar sprinklers have been found on the Gulf of Corinth and are attributed to Corinthian workshops.

Onion-shaped or pear-shaped sprinklers were filled with lustral water used at sacrifices and funerals. Dietrich von Bothmer has pointed out that most of the clay versions are decorated with funerary scenes.

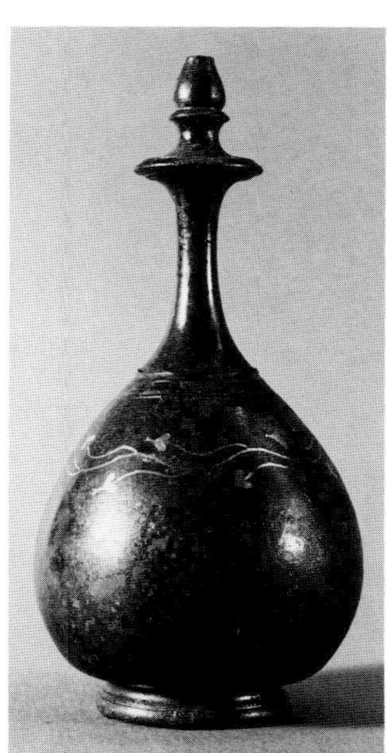

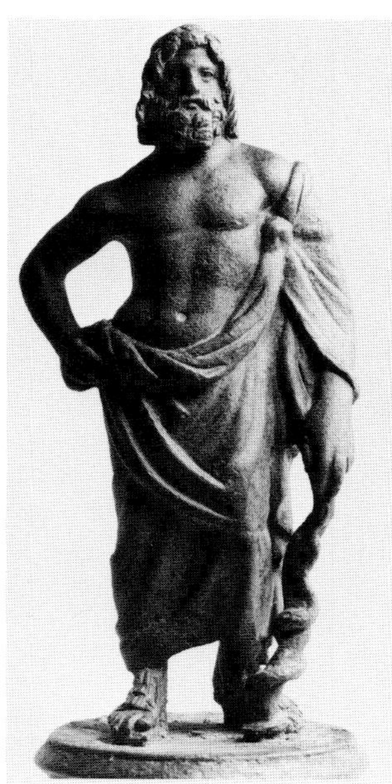

Compare *Search*, no. 111 (silver).

Published: *MFABronzes*, no. 450; A. Andriomenou, *BCH* 99 (1975) p. 571; D. von Bothmer, *Notable Acquisitions, 1982-1983, The Metropolitan Museum of Art*, p. 9.

142. Statuette of Asklepios

Roman, after a prototype by Bryaxis of about 360-350 B.C.
Purchased by Contribution 01.7484
Height 12.7 cm.

Asklepios leans on a serpent-entwined staff lodged under his left arm. His mantle is looped up over his shoulder and forearm to cushion the staff. The triangular overfold of the mantle hangs down to his left knee.

This widely-reproduced type seems to be derived from a statue at Megara by Bryaxis, who created several works in or near Athens. A statuette of Asklepios in this pose was excavated at Olynthos, destroyed in 348 B.C., and may reflect Bryaxis's statue. There are, however, certain differences in the drapery; the Olynthos figure has no overfold and the drapery does not loop over the top of the shoulder as it does here. Margarete Bieber has argued that these details reflect an early-third century version of the statue set up in the sanctuary of Asklepios at Kos. Statuetttes at Epidauros, however, have just the features found in our bronze (and in many other copies) and could well reflect the famous original at nearby Megara.

On the type, see M. Bieber, *Proceedings of the American Philosophical Society* 101, 1 (1957) p. 80ff., fig. 17ff.

Published: Morgan, *Brockton*, p. 34; *MFABronzes*, no. 96.

Jewelry in Gold and Bronze

The fourth century was one of the great ages of jewelry. In recent years, gold treasures associated with northern Greece in the Age of Alexander have captured the imagination of an enormous public and have been celebrated in major exhibitions.[1] Thessaly, Macedonia and Thrace are looked at as strongholds of this cultural development. The customs of this region were thought to have been more barbaric and more inclined to external show than those of the classical heartlands to the south. The populations of northern Greece, furthermore, participated more fully in the military campaigns of Alexander and consequently had greater opportunities to engage in plun-

1. Hoffmann/Davidson; *Thracian Treasures from Bulgaria*; *Search*

der. In addition, northern Greece was generously endowed with the raw materials for precious jewelry; the richest gold and silver mines of the Balkans were located around Mount Pangaion, which marked the division between Thrace and Macedonia.

Central Greece in general and Athens in particular seem to lie outside this development. After all, Athens formed the backbone of the resistance to Macedonian expansionism and contrasted her Greek culture to the barbaric culture of Macedon. It would be easy to translate this intellectual and political polarization into a contrast between a Classical culture of marble sculpture and painted clay vases and a "Graeco-Balkan" or "Graeco-Thracian" culture of luxurious metalwork and jewelry. This view is abetted by the scanty finds of jewelry in Athens and Attica. In the hundreds of tombs that have been excavated with scientific methods, the contrast between the riches of Macedonia and the apparent simplicity of Attica is striking.[2]

Some recent finds of jewelry in Athens, however, have shown how wrong this austere view of Athenian culture would be. In a tomb in Aiolos Street dated to the early fourth century, a fine pair of hoop earrings terminating in bull's heads was found.[3] Even more striking are several beautiful pieces excavated in a well in the Agora that had been filled in during the Hellenistic Period. Several pieces of the fourth century were recovered, including an earring with a splendidly sculpted Eros pendant, a figure-eight or "Herakles" knot from a necklace and several simple necklace beads.[4] It should be underlined that these are fine quality pieces fully in the grand manner of the Age of Alexander. It seems evident that goldwork rarely was put in Athenian tombs not because such jewelry did not exist but because of differences in funerary customs. Macedonians and Thracians might fill hidden chambers with treasure, but Athenians focussed their artistic energies on sculpted monuments placed over a grave where all could see. Such monuments would have been signposts for grave robbers had there been a regular pattern of burying treasure in the grave itself.

These few examples of Athenian goldwork make it clear that the craft flourished at a very high level there in the fourth century. One unprovenanced piece of jewelry in the Museum of Fine Arts is rather similar to these finds. A hoop earring with a gazelle-head terminal can be compared to the bull earrings from the tomb in Aiolos Street. The gazelle's head has the same solid anatomical structure that the bulls' heads have. The detail of the twisted hoops and the triangular collars are also rather similar. The more elongated proportions of the Boston piece probably reflect a somewhat later date. The subject itself, the gazelle, seems to have entered Greek art in the Age of Alexander, when goldsmiths were influenced by the art of Egypt and Persia, where these animals were familiar artistic subjects.

In Antiquity as today, gold jewelry was not within the reach of all, and much jewelry must have been made in less expensive materials. Some was certainly bronze. A bronze earring and a mould for a bronze earring have been excavated on the Pnyx in Athens in a fourth century context.[5] The two pieces from the Pnyx are exactly the same type as a bronze earring in the Museum of Fine Arts. All three have a pointed pendant suspended from a simple loop. The pendant is a rather complex geometric composition that passes from a pyramidal to a conical shape via a series of globular elements. Pointed earrings must have been a very popular adornment in the fourth century. They appear on numerous female heads on coins, like those from Histiaia (nos. 111, 112).

143. Bronze pointed earring

Greek, fourth century
Gift of E. P. Warren 90.238
Length 4 cm. Cleaned electrolytically for the exhibition.

A circular loop supported a conical/pyramidal pendant. The square upper platform is trimmed with a stamped tongue pattern. Below it are two tiers of four globules of decreasing size. Wires descending from the middle of each side lead to a wire-wrapped, conical lower section of the pendant. The terminal is a crested ball that might represent a pomegranate.

Published: *MFABronzes*, no. 255.

144. Gold earring with a gazelle's head

Greek, late fourth century
Gift of Susan M. L. Wales 14.3
2.0 by 2.6 cm.

The slightly tapering hoop is of plain gold wire twisted around a core. The gazelle-head finial was made in two halves with ears and horns added separately. Eyes were inlaid. A triangular collar with filigree and bordered with elongated tongues joins head and hoop.

For an example on the Athenian market during the 19th century, see *Antike Denkmäler, I* (Berlin 1891) p. 5, pl. 12, no. 15. For other examples of uncertain provenance, see Hoffmann/Davidson, no. 27f.; A. Herrmann in *Search*, no. 70. For a more stylized example studded with paste garnets that was excavated in a tomb of the third century on Samothrace, see E. Dusenbery, *Archaeology* 12 (1959) p. 167, fig. 5.

2. One of the major students of Greek jewelry has commented on how little we know of jewelry from Attica in the Classical period: B. Segall, *Katalog der Goldschmiede-arbeiten: Benaki Museum* (Athens 1938) p. 30.
3. *Deltion* 18 (1963), B'1, p. 34, pl. 31
4. T. L. Shear, Jr., *Hesperia* 42 (1973) p. 131f., pl. 27, f, h
5. *Hesperia, Supplement* 7, p. 102f., nos. 5, 6, fig. 46

145. 87 gold biconical beads from a necklace
Greek, fourth or third century
H. L. Pierce Fund 99.438
Length of each bead about 2.2 mm.

Compare P. Amandry, *Collection Hélène Stathatos: les bijoux antiques* (Strasbourg 1953) nos. 225-6 (Thessaly, Early Hellenistic): length of each bead: 6 mm., 12 mm.

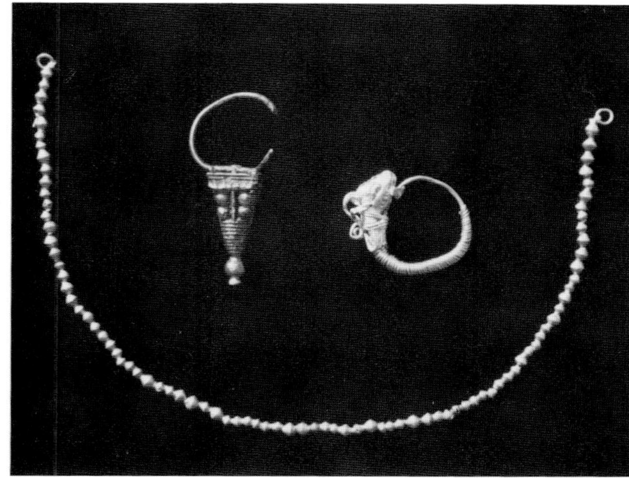

Engraved Gems and Finger Rings

In Classical Athens, the engraved gem functioned as a seal so versatile that it was an essential element in a variety of security systems. Many references by Athenian playwrights make it clear that the engraved seal or signet was used to give authenticity to written documents and also to verify the integrity of various kinds of storage systems from voting urns to household larders.[1] There are some indications that in the fifth century, the owners of seals tended to be regarded as refined and somewhat pretentious members of the upper class, but the use of seals must have rapidly become quite broadly based, since by the fourth century even very modest objects like terracotta loom weights were frequently marked with stamps that bore figurative devices.[2] Considering how common the practice of marking with stamps apparently was, it is surprising that more seals of the Classical period have not been recovered. It seems possible that many were made of perishable materials like wood. Some seals certainly were in metals like bronze, silver or gold that were often melted down and recast for other purposes.

Engraved seals did not have roles limited exclusively to the practical realm. Clearly, they must have had a certain value as a status symbol. Since their devices were frequently divinities or mythological creatures, they must have had religious or even magical significance; that is, they functioned as amulets. Seals were also considered highly esthetic objects. Seal rings in precious materials like gold or silver or with hard stone bezels were dedicated as worthy gifts to the gods. Fourth century inventories of votive offerings accumulated in the Parthenon list many seals and in some cases detail their materials.[3] The stones used in the Classical period and represented in the exhibition are rock crystal, a crystalline quartz, and various kinds of crypto-crystalline quartz: orange or red cornelian and milky or bluish chalcedony. Seals were also made of glass.[4] The artistry of the engraving was highly appreciated, and gems are among the relatively few Greek objects signed by their creators. Included in the exhibition is a fine cornelian ringstone signed by the artist Kallippos (no. 160).

Gems were engraved in many areas of the ancient world. Persian artists produced gems entirely in the style of Mesopotamia. Schools of Greek artists working in the areas of the eastern Mediterranean controlled by Persia created intaglios in a hybrid Graeco-Persian style. Gem engravers were also active in mainland Greece, in South Italy or Sicily and in the Etruscan areas of central Italy. Works by most of these various groups seem to have circulated through all parts of the ancient world, and scholars have despaired of systematically identifying the different regional Greek schools.[5] The few well-attested finds from Classical Attica illustrate the mobility of seals very well indeed. One of the finest of all East Greek gems is a portrait of a man in the Museum of Fine Arts from a tomb at Kara in Attica and signed by Dexamenos from the island of Chios, just off the coast of Asia Minor. A purely Achaemenid Persian cylinder seal of the fifth century was also found in Attica.[6] A gem in a mixed Graeco-Persian style was discovered in the Piraeus.[7] Included in the exhibition is a bronze stamp said to come from Athens that could well have been cast by an artist from either northern Greece or from the coast of Asia Minor.

Stone seals were normally mounted in rings. In the Classical period, the stones were usually made with a flat underside for the engraving and a convex upper side. The scaraboid form is derived from stamps shaped like scarab beetles. Scarabs and scaraboids alike were perforated by an

1. Richter, *Gems* I, p. 1f.
2. G. Davidson and D. Thompson, *Hesperia, Supplement* 7, pp. 65ff., 104ff.; Boardman, pp. 190, 234ff., figs. 269-273
3. Richter, *Gems* I, p. 20; Boardman, p. 235f.
4. On the materials of seals, see Boardman, p. 374ff.
5. Boardman, p. 193
6. Boardman, pl. 831, p. 351
7. Boardman, pl. 938, p. 355

axial hole so that the stone could be swivelled one way for wearing and another for stamping. In the course of the Classical period rings with fixed stone bezels (ringstones) became more numerous. From the end of the fourth century on, rings with swivelling scaraboids seem to have been entirely superseded by the ring with fixed bezel. All-metal rings with engraved stamps were also made throughout the Classical and into the Early Hellenistic period. Several bronze rings have been excavated in Athens,[8] and numerous gold and silver rings have passed through the Athenian market. In the course of the fourth century, rings evolved from light loops or bands with slender oval bezels to heavy bands with circular bezels. The larger bezels came to be set off by a groove from the narrower loop of the ring proper.

Seals seem to have circulated so freely that it would not be completely unfair to include almost any engraved gem or ring datable in the fourth century in our picture of the material culture of Athens at that time. In the hope of focussing on the creativity of mainland Greece, some groups of rings that seem to have been diffused primarily in the eastern Mediterranean or in Italy have been excluded. The nucleus of the group is made up of rings or intaglios said to have come from the Greek art market, especially the Athenian market. Stones of unknown provenance are included in cases where they present subjects that are also known from impressions of seals found in Athens. Seal impressions, it might be added, have been found on bits of terracotta and lead as well as on loom weights.

The period around 400 B.C. is particularly well represented. Two "Classical heavy rings" (Boardman type III), a group datable around the last quarter of the fifth century, have been included since both examples are rather rich and fluent late pieces. One shows a nude girl dancing in a twisting pose and in a three-quarter view. Pose, presentation and subject are all very unusual at this early date, and the ring is an outstanding illustration of the creativity of gem engravers of the time. Probably the greatest of High Classical gem engravers was Dexamenos of Chios (active about 450–425 B.C.), and his legacy of smoothly elegant outline and broad areas of empty space colored much work of the late fifth and early fourth centuries. Two animal studies present somewhat simplified reflections of his style: a Pegasos and an insect (nos. 149, 148). A pair of smoothly outlined quail against a spacious background (no. 150) also seems derived from the style of Ionian artists like Dexamenos. The severely symmetrical composition and certain technical details reveal that the Greek artist was working in the Persian Empire. It has been classified in the "Wyndham Cook Group" of Graeco-Persian gems, an example of which was found in the Piraeus.

A very fine piece in the post-Dexamenos current and acquired on the Athenian art market seems especially closely connected with ancient Athens. The gem (no. 147) shows the Athenian hero Theseus in one of his mythological labors: subduing the Krommyon Sow. Its composition, moreover, is closely related to that of the bull sacrifice on the Nike Temple parapet on the Acropolis.

The tradition of emblems in bold relief and with spacious fields continued through most of the fourth century. An elegantly elongated tripod, which evokes either the worship of Apollo or a prize in a theatrical contest, displays these compositional principles. It belongs to a small group of still lifes dating from around the middle of the century making use of a beautiful mottled jasper stone.

Engravings in bronze and glass lack something of the hard precision of works in more precious materials, but in many cases, they present sophisticated treatments of unusual themes. A glass scaraboid looks forward to Hellenistic art in a feminine toilet, probably cast in a mythological mold. With a puzzling sense of humor, a bronze ring shows a mock cult-image of Silenos wrapped in an indecent costume of a kind popular in the Athenian theatre.

The Siren, a monster that was half bird and half woman, was an occasional subject on fourth century gems. Early in the period, the Siren was a music maker of the kind that lured mariners to their doom.[9] In a later piece, the Siren becomes a sympathetic and protective creature and a mourner who accompanies souls on their journey to the next world. This conception of the creature is known above all from Attic funerary monuments. The Siren is carved in a ringstone in the somewhat wispy "Common Style" of the middle part of the century.[10]

Eros is a favorite theme of the fourth century, and typically, he is shown as a long-winged and long-legged adolescent. Artists delighted in showing love conquering all or charming all, perhaps by spirited flute playing. The paradox of love is made all the greater by contrasting an almost effeminate Eros with the spoils he has taken from the hardened soldier. The theme is handled best of all at the end of the Classical period in a wonderfully fluid and spacious treatment of victorious Eros signed by the engraver Kallippos.

One of the principal innovations of the Hellenistic period was the introduction of portraiture as a major theme. Idealized portraits of the divinized Alexander the Great are among the favorite subjects of Greek gem-cutters, and one example in a rock crystal ringstone of unusual shape might well go back to early Hellenistic

8. *Hesperia, Supplement* 7, p. 102f., nos. 3, 4, fig. 46
9. Boardman, pl. 615; Richter, *Gems* I, nos. 351, 362
10. On the Common Style, see Boardman, p. 207f.

times, perhaps the late fourth century. In its technique, it shows the dense, sculptural forms, the packed surfaces and the polish of many high-quality Hellenistic intaglios.

146. Silver ring with a dancing maenad
Greek, Kassandra Group, around 400 B.C.
Bought in Athens
Purchased by Contribution 01.8186
Length of bezel 15 mm.

The ring is a Classical Heavy Ring, type III. The maenad's Dionysiac staff (thyrsos) falls behind her as she advances in ecstatic movement. The nude girl with upraised arms is a favorite theme of a small group of rings that bridge the transition to the fourth century.

On the Kassandra Group, see Boardman, p. 222, pls. 709-712.

147. Cornelian scaraboid engraved with Theseus subduing the Krommyon Sow
Greek, early fourth century B.C.
Said to be from Greece
Francis Bartlett Fund 21.1205
Length 25 mm.

Theseus wears a traveller's hat slung back over his shoulders and withdraws a trident from the boar's neck. Boardman has included this piece in the post-Dexamenos group. The soft, rich modelling suggests that it is close in date to the representations of Herakles wrestling with the Nemean lion on gold coins of Syracuse about 390 B.C. Theseus's exploit could have been intended as an Athenian parallel to the saga of the Peloponnesian lion hunt. The composition seems inspired by the Nike sacrificing a bull on the parapet of the Nike Temple and on fourth century Attic vases like no. 22.

Published: *Lewes House,* no. 61, pl. 4; Boardman, pl. 539.

148. Rock crystal scaraboid engraved with a bee or fly
Greek, late fifth or early fourth century
Theodora Wilbour Fund in Memory of Zoë Wilbour 63.481
Length 19 mm.

Boardman has ascribed intaglios with flies both to the Eastern post-Dexamenos group and to simple Western Greek workshops of the later fifth century. This subject also appears on a seal impression and a clay token of the fourth century found in Athens.

For the seal impression, see *Hesperia, Supplement* 7, p. 106f., no. 12, fig. 48. For the token, see M. Crosby, *Agora* 10, pt. 2, C 21, p. 129, pl. 32. For other intaglios with insects, see Richter, figs. 474-479; Boardman, pls. 502, 505, 523, 581-2, 589, pp. 200, 202, 206.

Published: C. Vermeule, *BMFA* 64 (1966) p. 20, no. 2.

149. Chalcedony scaraboid engraved with Pegasos
Greek, late fifth or beginning of the fourth century B.C.
Bought in Athens
Purchased by Contribution 01.7549
Length 22 mm.

For Boardman, a summary version of the post-Dexamenos style. An even more summary Pegasos appears in a seal impression and on a bronze ring found in Athens. Both objects come from a layer of debris excavated on the Pnyx and dated 338-326 B.C.

For the seal impression and the ring, see *Hesperia, Supplement* 7, pp. 102, no. 3, 108, no. 15, figs. 46, 48. For the date of the layer, see above, no. 69.

Published: Boardman, pp. 292, 411, pl. 558.

150. Chalcedony scaraboid engraved with two quail
Graeco-Persian, late fifth or early fourth century
Purchased by Contribution 01.7564
Length 22 mm.

The high convex side (type C) of the scaraboid is characteristically Graeco-Persian. The piece is ascribed by Boardman to the Wyndham Cook Group, two examples of which have been found in the West, including one from Piraeus. The relationship to the post-Dexamenos style indicates it was carved by a Greek.

Published: Boardman, pl. 946, p. 355.

151. Bronze scaraboid engraved with a seated griffin and a horse's head
Greek, late fifth or early fourth century
Said to come from Athens
Gift of Edward Perry Warren 27.771
Length 27 mm. Mounted in a modern swivel.

For Boardman, an example of the post-Dexamenos style. He points out that the griffin motif finds an approximate parallel on coins of East Greek and North Greek mints (Teos and Abdera).

Published: *Lewes House,* no. 85, pl. 5; Boardman, pp. 202f., 292, pl. 583.

152. Bronze ring engraved with a figure of Herakles
Greek, first half of the fourth century
Bought in Athens
Purchased by Contribution 01.7531
Length of bezel 19 mm. Much of loop missing.

Herakles is loaded with attributes; he lurches forward extending his wine cup (a kantharos), he carries his weapons (club and quiver), and his left arm is wrapped in his lionskin trophy. Hard-muscled masculine divinities are common on intaglios of the fifth century. The springy pose, however, is characteristic of "Fine Style" gems of the first half of the fourth. The ring is the fourth century type VI. The elongated oval of the bezel supports a dating in the first half of the time span.

Herakles with his wine cup evokes the idea of rest and happiness after labor. To the fourth century viewer, the scene probably would have suggested the apotheosis of the hero, a major subject of contemporary vase painting.

For some comparable figures and for the ring type, see Boardman, pls. 485, 596-8, 663.

Published: *MFABronzes*, no. 288.

153. Bronze ring engraved with a figure of Silenos

Attic(?), mid to late fourth century
Bought in Athens
Purchased by Contribution 01.7532
Length of bezel 20 mm. Much of loop missing.

Silenos holds a thyrsos against his body, and he is dressed like a comic actor; he wears a short himation that muffles his hands, but he is nude from the waist down. He stands on a pile of rocks, presumably a rustic altar. The composition is a parody of archaistic images like an Athena on an intaglio in the Museum of Fine Arts. Boardman attributes the archaistic Athena to the "Fine Style" of the first half of the fourth century. It was in just that period that the ludicrous costume worn by the Silenos was popularized by terracotta statuettes of actors. The close dependency on the Attic terracottas suggests that this ring is also from a workshop located in or around Athens. The form of the ring may be a simplified version of the fourth century type VI. On the other hand, it almost seems to be a light and delicate version of Boardman's type XVII, a Ptolemaic design derived from Pharaonic types.

For the Athena, the Fine Style and type XVII, see Boardman, pp. 207, 213f., pl. 599.

Published: *MFABronzes*, no. 290.

154. Bronze ring with an eagle and palm branch

Greek, first half of the fourth century
Bought in Greece
Francis Bartlett Fund 27.748
Length of bezel 19 mm.

The bezel is set off by a groove from the loop (type VI). The oval bezel may indicate that the ring dates from well before the end of the century. Eagles looking backwards and with a variety of symbols in the field are common subjects on stamped clay tokens of the fourth century at Athens.

For the tokens, see M. Crosby, *Agora* 10, pt. 2, C 19, C 20, p. 129, pl. 32.

Published: *MFABronzes*, no. 292.

155. Greenish glass scaraboid with the head of a young man in a laurel wreath

Greek, about 410-350 B.C.
Bought in Athens
Purchased by Contribution 01.7538
Length 25 mm.

Apollo wearing a laurel wreath and with his long hair loose on his neck much in the manner of this intaglio is a major theme of coinage in the north Aegean. The heads of Apollo on the coins of the Chalcidic League are particularly similar. The subject also appears on a stamped lead token of probable Athenian provenance (no. 134).

For the coins, see Brett, nos. 577-582 (Chalcidic League); 1378-9 (Kios); 1618-21 (Abydos); 1886-90 (Miletos).

Published: Boardman, pp. 295, 416, pl. 648.

156. Greenish glass scaraboid with a nymph at her toilette

Greek, about 380-320 B.C.
Bought in Athens
Theodora Wilbour Fund in Memory of Zoë Wilbour 64.145
Length 26 mm.

A woman, wearing a chiton and swathed in a himation that covers her head and hands, is seated on a stool and views herself in a mirror. Before her stands an amphora, probably a loutrophoros carrying water for her bath. At the side grows a tree, described by Cornelius Vermeule as "resembling a feather duster." The outdoor setting suggests that the scene is not a portrayal of everyday life. The woman may be a nymph, the presiding deity of a natural feature like a cave, spring or grove.

Published: C. Vermeule, *BMFA* 64 (1966) p. 23, no. 7.

157. Gold ring engraved with the head of a youthful god or hero

Greek, about 380-350 B.C.
Theodora Wilbour Fund in Memory of Zoë Wilbour 63.252
Length of bezel 11 mm.

The girlish figure wears his hair in a cluster of tight curls in a fashion that evokes both Praxitelean taste and the corkscrew curls of Aphrodite on a figural vase in the Museum of Fine Arts.

The ring is type X, a variant of type VI. Even though the bezel is not set off from the loop by a groove, the full oval shape indicates a fairly advanced date. The head seems to be a simplified variant of the female heads of the "Iunx Group" engraved on type VI rings during the first quarter of the century.

Published: C. Vermeule, *BMFA* 64 (1966) p. 21, no. 4.

Impressions of Greek intaglios (rings and gems): types circulating in Greece and Attica.
Cats. 146, 147.
Cats. 149, 148, 150.
Cats. 151, 152, 153, 154.
Cats. 155, 158, 156.
Cats. 157, 163, 159.
Cats. 161, 160, 162.

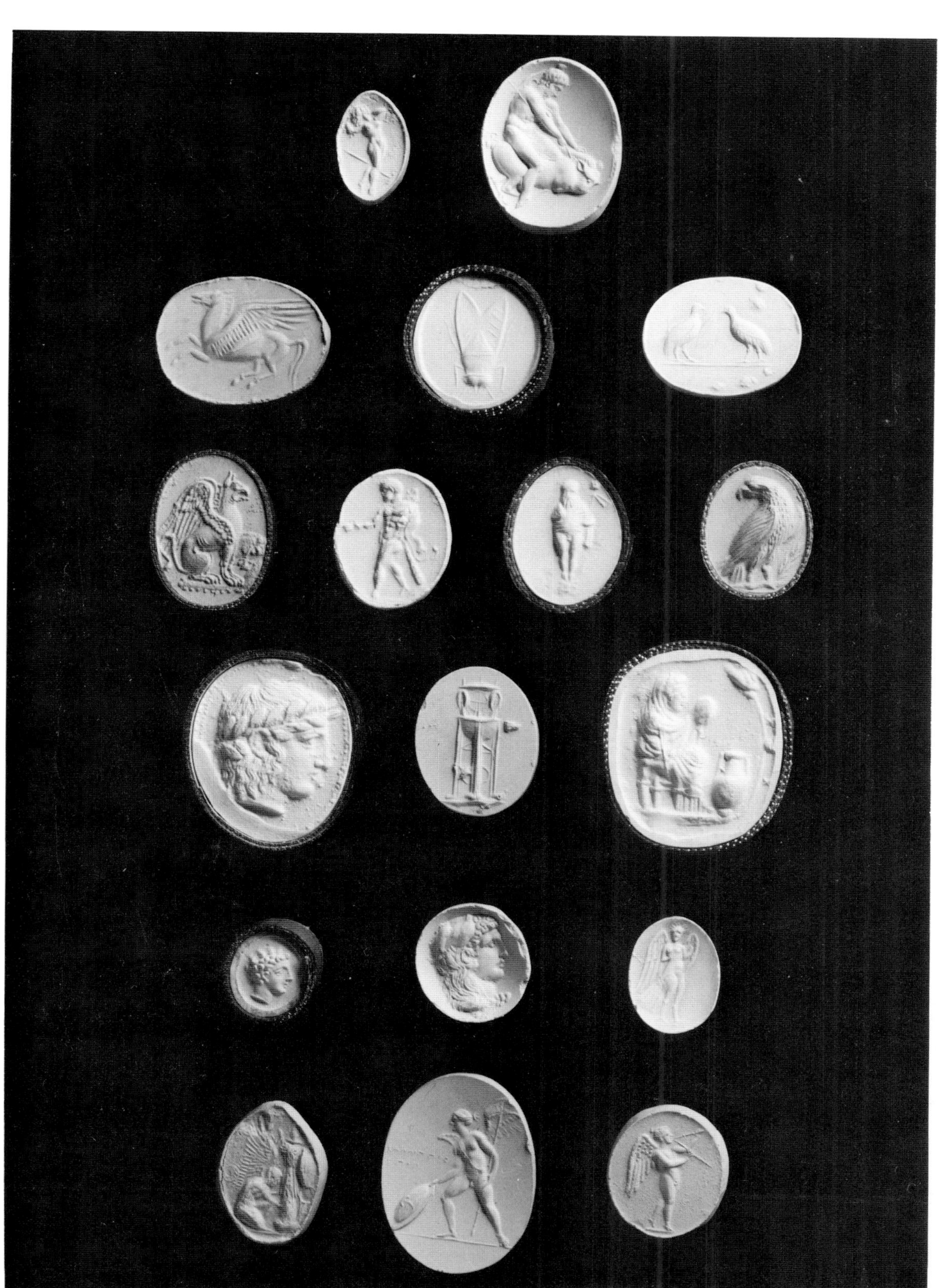

158. Mottled jasper scaraboid incised with a tripod and spiked cover

Greek, about 375-325 B.C.
Bought in Athens
Gift of Edward Perry Warren 27.769
Length 21 mm. The material is like that used by Dexamenos.

Tripods with these elongated proportions and this deep basin become popular late in the century. The tripod on a coin of Megara is quite similar (no. 101). Closest of all is the tripod with spiked cover on coins of Kassander minted between 306 and 297 B.C.

For the coin of Kassander, see *SNG*, 10, no. 116lf.

Published: *Lewes House*, no. 84, pl. 5; Boardman, p. 208, fig. 215 ("Common Style of the Fourth Century," therefore, presumably 375-325 B.C.).

159. Cornelian ringstone engraved with a mourning Siren

Greek, fourth century
Purchased by Contribution 01.7576
Length 16 mm. Thickness 4 mm. Slightly convex above.

The Siren beats her breast and tears her dishevelled hair much as on Attic funerary stelai of the fourth century (see no. 5).

160. Cornelian ringstone engraved with Eros holding a shield and spear

By Kallippos, Greek, second half of the fourth century
Francis Bartlett Fund 27.761
Length 29 mm. Thickness 2 mm.
Signed ΚΑΛΛΙΠΠΟΣ ΕΠΟΕΙ.

Eros wears a ribbon with pendants that crosses his chest like a sword-belt. The shield has a winged thunderbolt as its device. Eros presents the weapons as if for dedication at a shrine or a trophy. The action recalls the warrior on the lekythos with a bull sacrifice above (no. 22).

Marie-Louise Vollenweider has attempted to identify Kallippos with a Tarentine die-cutter (or mint official) who uses the monogram ΚΑΛ. This gem, however, seems closer in style to Boardman's group of "Latest Classical Gems," which he attributes to mainland Greece, than to Tarentine coins.

For the "Latest Classical Gems," see Boardman, p. 209f., pls. 632-641.

Published: M.-L. Vollenweider, *Genava* 12 (1964) p. 56, pl. II, 2, 4; *idem, Musée d'Art et d'Histoire de Genève, catalogue raisonné des sceaux cylindres et intailles*, I (Geneva 1967) p. 162; Boardman and Vollenweider, p. 86, under no. 299.

161. Bronze ring engraved with Eros setting up a trophy

Greek, mid fourth century
Bought in Athens
Purchased by Contribution 01.7533
Length of bezel 20 mm. Much of loop missing.

Eros kneels to work on the victory monument that consists of a post, a conical helmet, a shield, a belted tunic and probably a sword and spear. The bezel is set off from the loop by a groove that runs around the ends (Boardman type VIII).

Published: *MFABronzes*, no. 289.

162. Silver ring engraved with Eros playing a double flute

Greek, about 360-330 B.C.
Bought in Athens
Purchased by Contribution 01.8184
Length of bezel 17 mm.

Eros has his hair tied up in a topknot. The ring should perhaps be included in Boardman's "Salting Group" that largely dates from the first half of the century. The elegant and fluid style, however, approaches that of Kallippos. The ring seems to be Boardman's type VI.

On the Salting Group, see Boardman, p. 224, pls. 733-741.

163. Rock crystal ringstone engraved with a head of Alexander as Herakles

Greek, late fourth or third century
Bought in Corinth, found near Acrocorinth
Purchased by Contribution 01.7557
Length 16 mm. Thickness 8 mm. Front slightly convex, back egg-shaped.

Like Herakles, the figure wears a lion's skin over his head and back and has the paws knotted around his neck. Unlike the lumpy mythological hero, this head has smoothly youthful features. Such ideally beautiful young men with the attributes of Herakles on intaglios have frequently been regarded as later Hellenistic kings or Roman emperors. The beardless Herakles is, however, especially popular on coins in the late fourth century, and Alexander is the most likely candidate for the Heraklean young hero. Throughout his domains, Alexander was widely viewed as a kind of new Herakles. He wears a lion-scalp like a helmet on the sarcophagus of King Abdalonymos of Sidon (the "Alexander Sarcophagus"), datable before the end of the fourth century. In this gem, the features are very like those of the youthfully smooth Alexander on the late fourth century tetradrachms of Ptolemy I (nos. 125, 126). Such coins have been found in a hoard buried at Corinth, also the reported origin of this gem, in 306 B.C.

Cat. 64.

Cat. 65.

On the Alexander Sarcophagus, see Robertson, *History*, p. 481, pl. 151a; *idem*, *Shorter History*, p. 170f., fig. 235; A. Herrmann in *Search*, *Supplement*, no. 19. On the hoard at Corinth, see G. K. Jenkins, *Museum Notes* (ANS) 9 (1960) pp. 32ff.; *Inventory*, no. 85, p. 15.

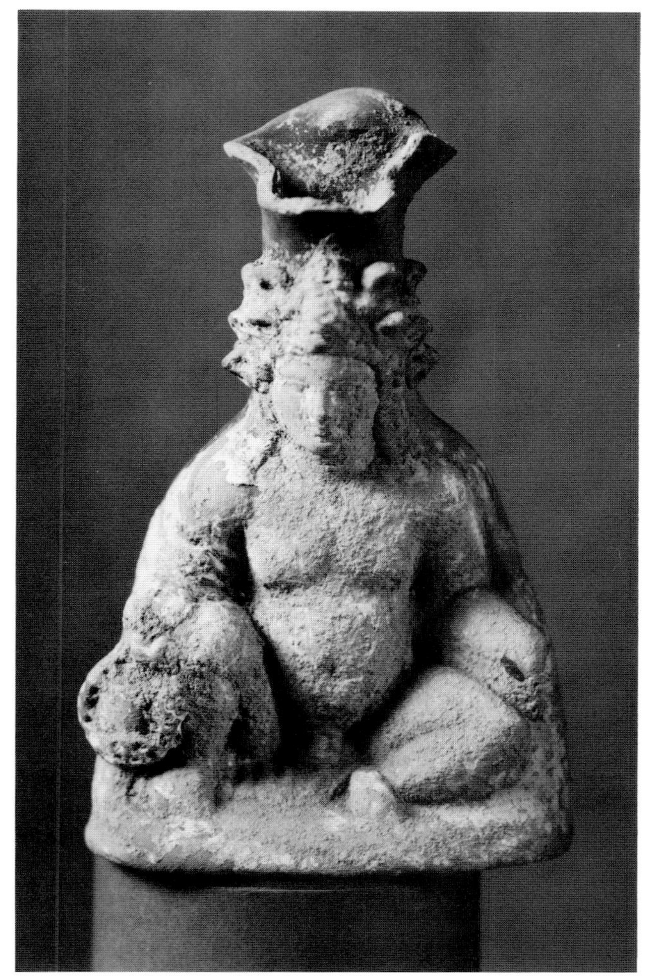

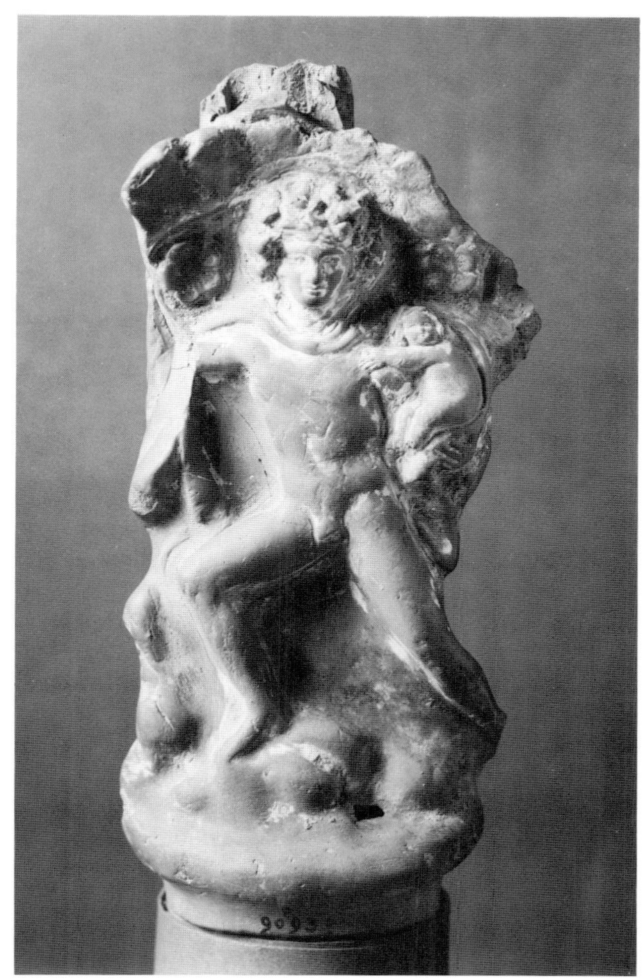

AA = *Archäologischer Anzeiger*

Agora 12 = B. Sparkes and L. Talcott, *The Athenian Agora, XII: Black and Plain Pottery of the 6th, 5th, and 4th Centuries B.C.* (Princeton 1970)

AJA = *American Journal of Archaeology*

Allentown = G. Pinney and B. Ridgway (editors), *Aspects of Ancient Greece* (Allentown Art Museum 1979)

Annual Report = *Annual Report, Museum of Fine Arts, Boston*

ArchEph = *Archaiologike Ephemeris*

AthMitt = *Athenische Mitteilungen*

BABesch = *Bulletin van de Vereeniging tot Bevordering der Kennis van de Antieke Beschaving*

BCH = *Bulletin de correspondance hellénique*

Beazley, *ABV* = J. D. Beazley, *Attic Black-figure Vase-painters* (Oxford 1956)

Beazley, *ARV* = J. D. Beazley, *Attic Red-figure Vase-painters* (Oxford 1942)

Beazley, *ARV*² = J. D. Beazley, *Attic Red-figure Vase-painters. Second Edition* (Oxford 1963)

Beazley, *Paralipomena* = J. D. Beazley, *Paralipomena: Additions to Attic Black-figure Vase-painters and to Attic Red-figure Vase-painters (Second Edition)* (Oxford 1971)

Bieber = M. Bieber, *History of the Greek and Roman Theatre* (Princeton 1961)

BMC = *A Catalogue of the Greek Coins in the British Museum*, 29 volumes (London 1873-1927)

BMFA = *Bulletin: Museum of Fine Arts, Boston*

Boardman = J. Boardman, *Greek Gems and Finger Rings: Early Bronze Age to Late Classical* (London 1970)

Boardman and Vollenweider = J. Boardman and M.-L. Vollenweider, *Catalogue of the Engraved Gems and Finger Rings in the Ashmolean Museum, I: Greek and Etruscan* (Oxford 1978)

Brett = A. Brett, *Catalogue of Greek Coins, Museum of Fine Arts, Boston* (Boston 1955, reprinted New York 1974)

BSA = *British School at Athens, Annual*

Burn and Glynn, *Beazley Addenda* = L. Burn and R. Glynn, *Beazley Addenda: Additional References to ABV, ARV² & Paralipomena* (Oxford 1982)

Comstock and Vermeule, *Sculpture* = M. Comstock and C. Vermeule, *Sculpture in Stone* (Boston 1976)

Crosby = M. Crosby, *Lead and Clay Tokens: The Athenian Agora*, X, 2 (Princeton 1964)

CVA = *Corpus Vasorum Antiquorum*

Deltion = *Archailogikon deltion*

Dohrn = T. Dohrn, *Attische Plastik vom Tode des Phidias bis zum Wirken der grossen Meister des IV. Jahrhunderts v. Chr.* (Krefeld 1957)

EAA = *Enciclopedia dell'arte antica e orientale*

Fairbanks = A. Fairbanks, *Museum of Fine Arts, Boston: Catalogue of Greek and Etruscan Vases, I (Early Vases, preceding Athenian Black-figured Ware)* (Cambridge, Mass. 1928)

Greenwell = W. Greenwell, *The Electrum Coinage of Cyzicus* (London 1887)

Hahland = W. Hahland, *Vasen um Meidias (Bilder Griechischer Vasen, 1)* (Berlin 1930)

Head = B. Head, *Historia Numorum* (Oxford 1911, reprinted New York 1983)

Hellenistic Art = J. Charbonneaux, R. Martin, F. Villard, *Hellenistic Art* (London 1973)

Higgins = R. Higgins, *Greek Terracottas* (London 1967)

Hoffmann/Davidson = H. Hoffmann and P. Davidson, *Greek Gold: Jewelry from the Age of Alexander* (Mainz 1965)

Inventory = M. Thompson, O. Mørkholm, C. Kraay, *An Inventory of Greek Coin Hoards* (New York 1973)

JdI = *Jahrbuch des Deutschen Archäologischen Instituts*

JHS = *Journal of Hellenic Studies*

Klein = A. Klein, *Child Life in Greek Art* (New York 1932)

Kleiner = F. Kleiner, *Greek and Roman Coins in the Athenian Agora* (Excavations of the Athenian Agora, Picture Book No. 15) (Princeton 1975)

Kraay = C. Kraay, *Archaic and Classical Greek Coins* (Berkeley 1976)

Kroll = J. Kroll in *Greek Numismatics and Archaeology: Essays in Honor of Margaret Thompson* (Wetteren, Belgium 1979) p. 139ff.

Lang = M. Lang, *Weights and Measures: The Athenian Agora*, X, 1 (Princeton 1964)

Lecuyer = A. Cartault, *Deuxième collection Camille Lecuyer: terres cuites antiques* (Paris 1892)

Lewes House = J. Beazley, *The Lewes House Collection of Ancient Gems* (Oxford 1920)

Loeb Coll. = J. Sieveking, *Die Terrakotten des Sammlung Loeb I* (Munich 1916)

Metzger, *Recherches* = H. Metzger, *Recherches sur l'imagerie athénienne* (Paris 1965)

Metzger, *Représentations* = H. Metzger, *Les représentations dans la céramique attique du IVe siècle* (Paris 1951)

MFABronzes = M. Comstock and C. Vermeule, *Greek, Etruscan & Roman Bronzes in the Museum of Fine Arts, Boston* (Boston 1971)

Morgan, *Brockton* = S. K. Morgan, *The Art of the Ancient Mediterranean* (Brockton 1975)

Pausanias = Pausanias, *Description of Greece* (London and New York 1918)

Richter, *Gems* I = G. Richter, *Engraved Gems of the Greeks, Etruscans and Romans, I: Engraved Gems of the Greeks and the Etruscans* (London 1968)

Ridgway, *Copies* = B. S. Ridgway, *Roman Copies of Greek Sculpture: The Problem of the Originals* (Ann Arbor 1984)

Ridgway, *Fifth Century* = B. S. Ridgway, *Fifth Century Styles in Greek Sculpture* (Princeton 1981)

Robertson, *History* = M. Robertson, *A History of Greek Art* (London 1975)

Robertson, *Shorter History* = M. Robertson, *A Shorter History of Greek Art* (Cambridge University Press 1981)

Robinson = E. Robinson, *Museum of Fine Arts, Boston, Catalogue of Greek, Etruscan and Roman Vases* (Boston and New York 1893)

Schefold, *Göttersage* = K. Schefold, *Die Göttersage in der klassischen und hellenistischen Kunst* (Munich 1981)

Schefold, *KV* = K. Schefold, *Kertscher Vasen* (Berlin-Wilmersdorf 1930)

Schefold, *UKV* = K. Schefold, *Untersuchungen zu den Kertscher Vasen* (Berlin and Leipzig 1934)

Search = N. Yalouris, M. Andronikos, K. Rhomiopoulou, A. Herrmann, C. Vermeule, *The Search for Alexander: An Exhibition* (Boston 1980)

Search, Supplement = J. Herrmann *et alii, The Search for Alexander, Supplement to the Catalogue* (Boston 1981)

SNG = *Sylloge Nummorum Graecorum: Copenhagen*, vols. 1-43 (Copenhagen 1942-1979)

Süsserott = H. K. Süsserott, *Griechische Plastik des 4. Jahrhunderts vor Christus, Untersuchungen zur Zeitbestimmung* (Frankfurt A/M 1938, reprint Rome 1968)

Travlos = J. Travlos, *Pictorial Dictionary of Ancient Athens* (London 1971)

Trumpf-Lyritzaki = M. Trumpf-Lyritzaki, *Griechische Figurenvasen des reichen Stils und der späten Klassik* (Bonn 1969)

van Hoorn, *Choes* = G. van Hoorn, *Choes and Anthesteria* (Leiden 1951)

Vermeule, *America* = C. Vermeule, *Greek and Roman Sculpture in America: Masterpieces in Public Collections in the United States and Canada* (Berkeley and Los Angeles 1981)

Vermeule, *S to S* = C. Vermeule, *Greek Art: Socrates to Sulla* (Boston 1980)

Züchner = W. Züchner, *Griechische Klappspiegel, JdI, Ergänzungsheft 14* (1942)

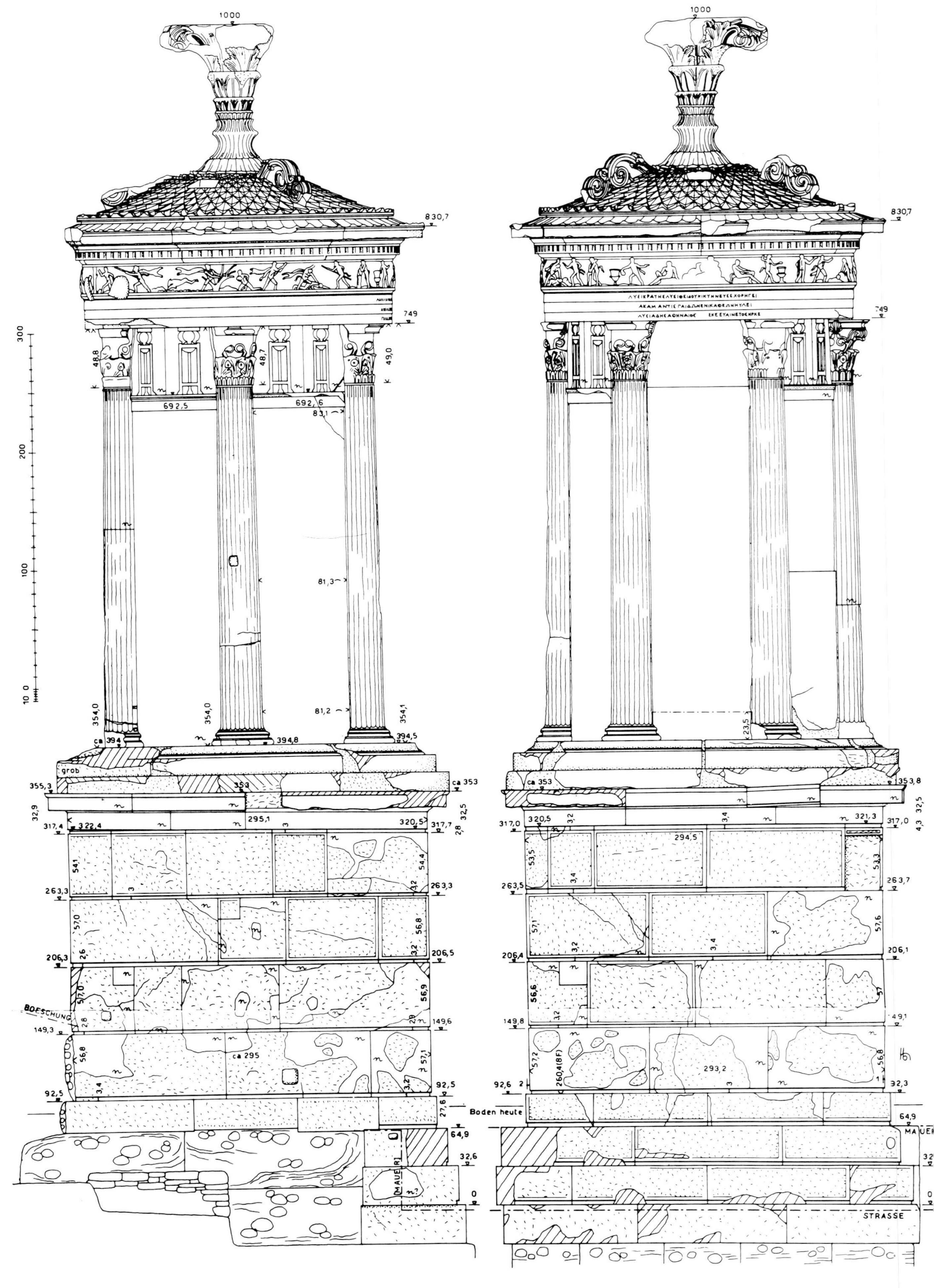

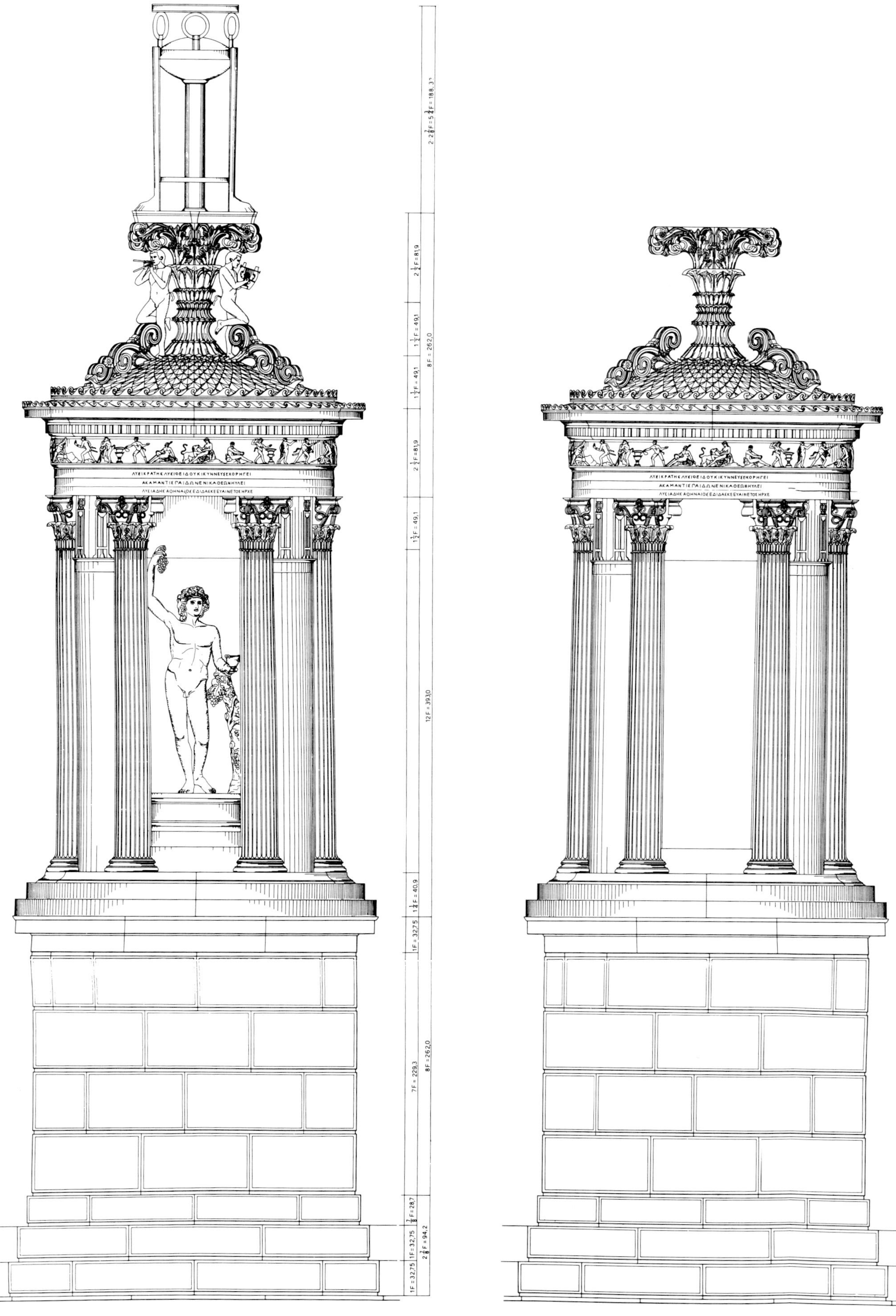